AFTERLIVES OF CONFINEMENT

ILLUMINATIONS: CULTURAL FORMATIONS OF THE AMERICAS

John Beverley and Sara Castro-Klarén, Editors

Afterlives of Confinement

Spatial Transitions in Postdictatorship Latin America

SUSANA DRAPER

UNIVERSITY OF PITTSBURGH PRESS

Published by the University of Pittsburgh Press, Pittsburgh, Pa., 15260
Manufactured in the United States of America
Printed on acid-free paper
10 9 8 7 6 5 4 3 2 1

Library of Congress Cataloging-in-Publication Data

Draper, Susana.
  Afterlives of confinement : spatial transitions in postdictatorship Latin America / Susana Draper.
    pages   cm. — (Illuminations : cultural formations of the Americas)
  Includes bibliographical references and index.
  ISBN 978-0-8229-6225-0 (paperback : acid-free paper)
    1. Southern Cone of South America—Intellectual life.   2. Southern Cone of South America—Social conditions.   3. Prisons—Remodeling for other use—Southern Cone of South America.   4. Dictatorship—Social aspects—Southern Cone of South America. 5. Democracy—Social aspects—Southern Cone of South America.   6. Consumption (Economics) —Social aspects—Southern Cone of South America.   7. Architecture and society—Southern Cone of South America.   8. Motion pictures—Social aspects—Southern Cone of South America.   9. Prisons in literature. 10. Spanish American literature—Southern Cone of South America—History and criticism.   I. Title.
  F2217.D73 2012
  980—dc23   2012030696

To my parents, Ramiro and Susana

CONTENTS

ACKNOWLEDGMENTS

This book would not have been possible without the support of many friends who gave me courage and love at moments of change and transitions. I am forever grateful to all of them. Most of the text was written under the tenure of a fellowship from the American Council of Learned Societies. Most of the research was carried out with the support of summer grants from the Program in Latin American Studies at Princeton University.

Early versions of some chapters were published in *Discourse* and the *Journal of Latin American Cultural Studies*. I thank the journals for allowing me to reprint modified versions of articles that were published by them. I would like to thank Fidel Sclavo for creating different drawings for the cover of this book; Pata Torres for kindly taking the pictures; and Jon Snyder, Patricia Draper, and Catherine Jagoe for taking care of the long process of editing and translation of different parts of the texts at different moments.

Introduction
The Afterlife of Prisons

Historical "understanding" is to be grasped, in principle, as an afterlife of that which is understood.

—Walter Benjamin, *The Arcades Project*

When thinking about transitions from dictatorship to neoliberal democracy in Argentina, Chile, and Uruguay, how do we critically analyze the transformations of time and place in cities, where the end of the dictatorships' carceral imaginaries and the beginning of a postdictatorial consumerist life of new freedoms were most clearly seen? More specifically, how does analyzing the history of the life and afterlife of the different prisons and clandestine detention centers (CDCs) that were crucial to sustaining the dictatorships contribute to the historical understanding of the "post" of postdictatorship? I explore this problematic by focusing on the transformations of key prisons and CDCs into malls, cultural-commercial centers, museums, and memorial sites. I have created an itinerary of readings that show the questionable and unstable nature of dominant assumptions about the concept and the process of transition to neoliberal freedom. Tracing other (hi)stories that demonstrate how the notion of dictatorships "ending" becomes problematic, as does the notion of democracy and freedom after them, this book explores alternative textual and visual imaginaries that reveal spatiotemporal layers in and through which the dictatorship continued (and continues) to speak.

The postdictatorship era saw the emergence of the dream of a new time that demanded an erasure of certain unsettling temporalities and the proliferation of spaces of consumption that would become host to the free market imposed upon them. The material transformations in urban spaces throughout and beyond the transition from military regimes to democracy in Southern Cone countries entailed a wave of privatization of public space. These transformations coincided with an overarching modification of the experience of temporality within these spaces. In particular, there was an emerging official demand in the early 1990s to enter a new time severed from the dictatorial past, perhaps nowhere more evident than in the decisions made regarding the impunity granted to military crimes.[1]

This book takes as its point of departure the case of Punta Carretas Prison in Montevideo, Uruguay, which was built as a model penitentiary at the beginning of the twentieth century. It functioned as a detention center for political prisoners in the late 1960s and early 1970s and was subsequently transformed into the most exclusive mall in Montevideo at the moment when decisions on the military regime's human rights violations were being made. The transformation of Punta Carretas Prison into Punta Carretas Mall represents a paradigm of postdictatorial reconfiguration of spaces of incarceration, in which prison features, systems of impunity, spatial fantasies from the Cold War, and ideals for democracy were equated to the capacity for consumption. The palimpsest created by the superimposition of the architectural models of prison and mall involved the temporal reconfiguration of a carceral space that bore significant political and semantic weight in the 1960s and 1970s. It evokes not only the imprisonment and torture of political dissidents but also the massive jailbreak in 1971 by prisoners from the Movement of National Liberation–Tupamaros (Movimiento de Liberación Nacional–Tupamaros, or MLN-T), the word's largest recorded escape of prisoners. At the time the escape was regarded as an insult to Uruguay's authoritarian regime. This architectural conversion, which won the International Council of Shopping Centers' prize, is an ideal starting point because the remodeling took place at the very moment of transition to democracy, thus making explicit the historic conjunction between freedom, democracy, the market, and the spatial management of the collective memory of the military past.

Taking the transformation of Punta Carretas as a point of departure, I analyze the afterlives of other key prisons and CDCs, examining the ways in which material spaces and temporal experiences have been reconfigured in different ways since the early 1990s. Other carceral openings that represent unique forms of superposition are the Buen Pastor Women's Prison in Córdoba, Argentina (now a cultural-commercial center) and a series of former CDCs in Buenos Aires: the Naval School of Mechanics ESMA (now a human rights memorial space), Olimpo (today a memorial site), and Automotores Orletti, run by Operation Condor (currently being transformed into a memorial site after being denounced as an underground sweatshop for undocumented Bolivian workers). The trajectories of these incarceration sites problematize the museification of memory, the naturalization of certain forms of violence, and the reformulation of the past that museification promotes. For instance, the case of the Buen Pastor prison is similar to Punta Carretas Mall (even with regard to the breakouts), but Buen Pastor's transformation was carried out a decade later as part of a process of memory marketing and museification. Like Punta Carretas and most of the penitentiaries, the Buen Pastor prison and chapel opened at the beginning of the twentieth century (in 1906) and became an important detention center for women in the 1960s and 1970s. Closed as a prison in 2004, it was made into a cultural, commercial, and recreation center as well as a historical site called the Paseo del Buen Pastor. Although the goal of the transformation was to preserve the memory of the place while adjusting it to the commercial necessities of the city, the whole complex of prison cells was demolished and replaced by commercial lots.

If Punta Carretas Mall was part of an architectonic of active amnesia paradigmatic in the early 1990s, the transformation of Buen Pastor that took place a decade later as part of a memorial boom is intriguing. The commercial function prevails to make memory a profitable operation. This prevalence became explicit when former political prisoners asked to speak at the inauguration ceremony and were told that the event was all scheduled (*sincronizado*) and that there was not much time left for the ex-prisoners to participate. This gives rise to a series of questions regarding the ways in which the open prisons redeemed by commercial and memorial functions can be read as acting out forms of imprisonment and surveillance of uncomfortable parts of the political past that are still kept under control to avoid a disruption of the scheduled time of the market. The forms of service sites (shopping malls, the hospitality industry, archives, spaces for cultural heritage) superimposed upon the prisons display cases of culturally relevant sites where property would become the stage for new official imaginaries. Within these sites the relationships established between social space and historicity are still operative today, as they were for the jail, forging a new neoliberal dominance.

In this sense, as the cultural theorist Andreas Huyssen has proposed, it is crucial to examine how "memory and forgetting *pervade real public space*, the world of objects, and the urban world we live in." These modes of constituting inhabitance are rarely lived critically or reflected upon, given that they constitute the horizon of everyday trajectories and habits. Huyssen maintains that "we need to discriminate among memory practices in order to strengthen those that counteract the tendencies in our culture to foster uncreative forgetting."[2] When addressing postdictatorial geographies, it is important to problematize the "we" that one is assuming when addressing memory practices. Who are the subjects imagined or presupposed by such practices? Where and for whom may these memory practices prove meaningful? The figures of the prison and the commercial center—specifically malls and hypermarkets—allow me to explore what is included in and excluded from the "we" that produces the fantasy of the transition, in the material sense of organizing the habitus into certain spaces (and trajectories traversing and tracing them), and likewise the specific temporalities these materializations uphold. I analyze both real prisons that were transformed during processes of redemocratization and the image of the open prison as a central trope that emerged in the literary and visual realm as dramatization and critique of the reduction of freedom to the spaces of the neoliberal market and a questioning of the subjects that qualify for such space-time of freedom.

Examining the afterlife of certain penitentiaries and former CDCs that were central to dictatorial operations also leads me to interrogate the temporal meanings and passive subjects of the temporalities implied by the category "transition." This word was central to the end of the dictatorial processes and to the beginning of a democratic imaginary of consumerism. By exploring the spatial meanings of transition, I show how the production of new spaces for consumerism and memory museification has functioned as stages for official performances of advancement to a postdictatorship society at different historical moments. The book analyzes how the temporal imaginaries of entering or transitioning toward a new time of freedom was spatially materialized or translated into built space at two different moments: one being the early 1990s, when the open prison became an architectural event that conveyed a sense of opening society to a new time of freedom of the market; the other being the years that followed the economic crises of 2001, when the open prison began to be linked to a memorialistic process centered around the appropriation and transformation of former sites of detention into spaces for memory. At this point the development of a politics of memory was opposed to the politics of amnesia of the 1990s, thus becoming a territory for exploring other forms in which the dictatorship had outlived its so-called end. So, a decade after the architectonic of transition was configured, the transformation of spaces that had been highly symbolic of state authoritarianism became a central issue within the development of a struggle for social memory and a demand for justice. The book takes the open prison as a common trope that traverses different spatiotemporal imaginaries and practices, and analyzes the ways in which the end of the dictatorship has been problematized, questioned, and figured in different signifying practices.

The figure of the open prison leads me to explore the notion of afterlife in the sense that is posed in the quotation by the philosopher Walter Benjamin at the opening of the chapter—that is, the ways in which and through which those forms of figuring the afterlife have also been transforming the understanding of the ways in which the dictatorial past had been conceived. The afterlives of confinement produce a constant process of resignification of the ways in which the past has been understood. How do the practices of resignification constantly change the ways in which the past is understood? How can an analysis of the afterlife of certain key spaces of confinement—an afterlife essential for establishing a logic of inevitability of authoritarian rule (and its pursuit of economic progress and market freedom)—help us create a different historical understanding of the idea of transition? Here, the notion of afterlife becomes crucial, because it allows us to question temporal sequences in a nonsequential and nonteleological way. The term "afterlife" acquires the sense of a mode of experiencing the echoes of a past that is lost to history but that has the potential to be heard and made legible. It is a missed possibility that keeps open the promise of that which did not / could not take place.

In "The Task of the Translator," Benjamin talks about the translatability of a text in the sense of a certain potentiality that any historical form has of outliving something.[3] In a fashion that resembles the way he speaks of quotation in "One-Way Street," Benjamin uses the image of echoing to convey the singular process of transformation that takes place in the act of reading and listening to (and thus, of reconfiguring) a text in the act of translation.[4] In my analysis of the afterlife of prisons, I observe how the processes of transformation to different forms and functions (prison to mall, CDC to museum and memorial space) can resemble the act of listening to echoes not only of that which the transformation is superseding but also of that which has been always left unheard—the zones that did not and do not qualify as recyclable or memorable themes or subjects for the current market and citizenry.

Within this context the book focuses on the ways in which confinement affects the modes of historicization (the making perceptible of the past)—a process that is continually contested by different forms of art and literature that insist on refiguring unstable and uncomfortable layers of pasts. Therefore afterlife poses an instance of dislocation of the teleological enframing of time, thus deconstructing the supposedly "common" understanding of the dominant narrative of redemocratization as an opening up and passage toward neoliberal modes of freedom (from/for consumption, choice between imported brands, deregulation of labor and the market). The issue of how to translate the past life of these former spaces of confinement into the present puts the critic in a singular situation where the very possibility of listening to the echoes of the past is problematized, for in what form and by what means can the echoes be heard? What idea of historicization does this practice of listening imply, and why is it connected to the material sense of a space that is always about to become a place?

The idea of afterlife implies a problematization of the dynamic and finite way in which past and present are signified, as with the idea that an echo is related to the voice producing it. In the texts where Benjamin analyzes this word, his "The Task of the Translator" and "Convolut N" from the *Arcades Project*, the "after" in "afterlife" emerges as a search for spectral echoes between times (echoes between past and present) and as an ongoing task of historical interpretation that works on and with the afterlife of other interpretations of history surviving the past. "Afterlife" refers to the impossibility of full translatability between times and spaces, as well as to a counterintuitive relationship between the original and the translation, since the former not only exists as a consequence of the latter but also undergoes changes according to it. This is a notion that aims at the historicity of language whereby history becomes perceptible and narratable. As stated by the cultural theorist Werner Hamacher, Benjamin's notion of historicity relies on his proposal of afterlife not only as the rescue of an alternative temporality to the prevailing one. It also relies on a way of thinking the affective structure of the political as a demand that starts to reshape a different "us" by listening to the echoes of a past within the present.[5]

This book examines the perspectives of those who built the spaces analyzed, showing how they became something different according to the forms in which their histories were imagined and rebuilt. For instance, in the case of the former Punta Carretas and Buen Pastor prisons, the different outlooks of prisoners, consumers, and architects end up reshaping sites that are problematic and incommensurable among themselves in light of their different historicizations. Benjamin refers to a way of making history perceptible at different times, how each present is opened or fissured upon the emergence of a "now time" in which a certain image becomes recognizable, understandable (legible)—a now that fissures the continuity of the illusory timeline linking past and present. Nevertheless, the way in which the image of an untimely past irrupts and links different irreducible (incommensurable) times refers to a relationship in which not only is the past told in the present but also each present makes different ways of understanding that past recognizable (legible). Thus Benjamin's quotation at the opening of the chapter refers to a notion of afterlife in which the historical emerges as an ongoing work of resignification and reinvention of what becomes understandable and recreated with respect to that which we believed to be already understood. On the verge of historicity's excess and mise en abyme lies the potentiality and promise of rethinking the dictatorship not so much as an "object" of thought but as a form of reading and criticism, since it is in historicization itself that we will find the new areas awaiting exploration. Although the present time of the postdictatorship is heir to the dictatorship, the ways in which this relationship is signified and resignified vary over the decades, thus acquiring different conceptual figures.

My use of the word "afterlife" aims to problematize the ways of understanding and resignifying the temporality of "after," which marks and becomes involved in the "post" of postdictatorship in a way that rejects the linearity of market-driven progress and adds to the complexity of approaches to dictatorship as a field of study. Although the "post" of postdictatorship is marked by the discursive and affective horizon of the idea of transition as passage, this book seeks to problematize that perspective, not only by examining the prevailing allegorization of failure that has governed the horizon of studies but also by proposing—within this theoretical horizon—the possibility of reading another temporality of the political, which the notion of failure apparently cancels. Another reading of Benjamin is thus presented here: the possibility of transforming the postdictatorial obsession with the politics of memory (which often involves selective forgetfulness of certain affects linked to politics) into a memory of politics, which the transitions marked by "post" sought to cancel through the time horizon in which they were shaped as a token of the "end" of history.

Since the early 2000s, the issue of spaces and territories associated with the memory of state authoritarianism has been one of the major focal points for resignification of dictatorships in the fields of history and the social sciences. Based on historian Pierre Nora's notion of *lieux de mémoir* and on sociologist Maurice Halbawchs's collective memory processes, Argentine sociologist Elizabeth Jelin's pioneering studies on memory works in postdictatorship situations have foregrounded the relationship between territoriality and memory, promoting the study of urban planning and monument construction processes.[6] This book can be ascribed to the field of studies on territoriality and memory. Its contribution lies in problematizing the ways in which the politics of memory have turned into a profitable business, thus bypassing the question of the frames delimiting what is acceptable and recognizable in these memories. I pose the inconvenient question of what subjects and histories are assumed by these memories, not only within the map of the postdictatorship but also within the framework of that which neither qualified nor qualifies as a memory subject, either in the past or in the present. I am posing a question about subalternity (the nonsubject in politics) in social science studies and historicization processes, which tend to neglect it as a problem concerning politics and therefore outside their sphere of interest. This book also returns to the field of early postdictatorship studies to introduce the question about prisons, historicization, and literary and artistic imagination processes that the studies of the early 1990s made possible.

Spatializing Histories: The Trope of Postdictatorship as Open Prison

The French philosopher Michel Foucault has argued that writing a history of spaces, which is simultaneously a history of different powers, could be considered "from the great strategies of geo-politics to the little tactics of the habitat, from institutional architecture of the classroom to the design of hospitals, passing via economic and political installations."[7] Such histories confront us immediately with a complex network in which structural repetitions are interwoven to constitute a particular spatial organization. The histories of repetitions urge us to think of what makes them at once possible and impossible, the subjects they involve and exclude, and the ways in which a temporalization of the recently lived past is elaborated from spatial figures (the vector of progress, the impossibility of forgetting what this vector attempts to erase, and so on). Within this context a question arises: What kind of histories and critical itineraries can be configured when one takes the prison as a problematic nucleus from which to rethink and question the histories that mark the "post" in postdictatorship? Constituting crucial instances of control, detention, and/or extermination of what the military administrations considered subversive (political dissidence), the places of imprisonment did not lose their social significance immediately after the military regimes were officially concluded. On the contrary, key sites of imprisonment continued to be important in order to mark a certain power over the past in a present in which they became refunctionalized, thus remaining the targets of certain operations in which the past and the present were (and are) joined by means of different signifying regimes.

The different forms and functions that the prisons and CDCs have acquired in their afterlives open up a still-unexplored field in which one can read different processes and zones of the past(s) that continue to be uncomfortable over the past decades. A careful analysis of the figure of the open(ed) prisons in architecture and literature leads us to reflect on the different forms and possibilities for historicizing zones of the past that have been lost and disappeared, locations that become key for performing different practices of reading and imagining those (political) pasts and their (dis)connections with the present. For instance, in the elite Punta Carretas Mall it is interesting that there are no markers of the past of the prison. However, just when it opened as a mall, a plaque commemorating the victims of the Holocaust was being unveiled around the corner. Since the early 2000s in Argentina, many well-known landmarks in Buenos Aires have been marked with the words: "A center for the torture, disappearance and extermination of political prisoners functioned in this place during the last military dictatorship."

These contrary gestures, which continued decades after political transitions to neoliberal freedom were over, make one reflect on the ways in which places and histories are composed as well as on how different literary and artistic practices insist on approaching them from different critical perspectives. I offer a contribution to the study of (post)dictatorship and memory practices by creating the first critical history and analysis of the afterlives of prisons as spaces that question the temporal framing of repressive regimes. They open up the possibility of searching for invisible processes in which the imagination of time and freedom is materialized and contested. The goal of this book is to articulate ways in which the creative and critical cultural practices of literature and film problematize the connection between democracy and freedom in the form of the open prison. I explore how these cultural practices question the restrictive geography of the open prison and posit other forms of opening connected to the task of rethinking parts of the past that remained outside of the dominant architectonic of neoliberal freedom. Exhibiting correlations between historicity and spatiality, the creative and critical works studied here point to the modes of framing performed by these spaces of new time and freedom, questioning the manner in which action, performance (in the theatrical sense), and temporality (both dominant and subaltern) are interconnected. A theory of postdictatorship spaces emerges when one examines their ways of recounting history; therefore I question the ways in which political imagination itself is the crucial node that the different spatiotemporal dramatizations attempt to redefine.

In "Postdictadura y reforma del pensamiento," a seminal article in the creation of postdictatorship cultural critique, the cultural theorist Alberto Moreiras has connected the possibility of a transformation of critical thought to an insistence on the role of historicity. Inspired by Benjamin, historicity emerges as a perspective from which to engage in a critique of persisting forms of oppression hitherto camouflaged by the dominant discourses on postdictatorial neoliberal freedom (of/from the market). Moreiras states: "In its more radical Benjaminian sense, historicity is that which the oppressed try to save and what the oppressors erase."[8] In this vein he emphasizes the difficulty of creating alternative histories that would avoid two evils: on the one hand, the trap of adopting a melancholic position that, finding no political alternatives, would end up "embracing misery" as the "only possible horizon"; and on the other, the historicist attempt to reconstruct the finite past into an epic of the left containing an atemporal, idealized figure.[9]

The postdictatorial critical project uses Benjamin's problematization of the writing of history both as its source of inspiration and as promise of the creation of a different perspective from which to consider the relation between marginal languages and temporalities. The Benjaminian inspiration was, however, progressively reduced to an exclusive focus on the figures of mourning and melancholy, which became theoretical stereotypes in any study of postdictatorship thought. In an attempt to avoid falling into either a historicist or a positivist account of the past, the possibility of articulating a sense of historicity connected to the history of oppressed struggles was reduced to the expression of a failure. Here I do not intend to argue against the relevance of mourning and melancholy to the analysis of postdictatorship literature. What I question is rather the reduction of a loss of historicity to the idea of a "truth of defeat" posed by the paradigmatic reading of Benjamin's allegory in cultural theorist Idelber Avelar's *Untimely Present*, a book that became, and still remains, a mandatory reference in the study of postdictatorial art and literature.[10]

Avelar follows Benjamin's study of allegory in *The Origin of German Tragic Drama* in order to analyze what he has called "mournful literature"— a literature that, in trying to "overcome the trauma" of the dictatorship, "remind[s] the present that it is the product of a past catastrophe."[11] To define the notion of the defeat that permeates his allegorical reading, Avelar poses an opposition between what he calls a "factual truth" and a "truth of defeat."[12] The former works as a critique of testimonial narratives valued only for their "factual truth," while the latter works as a key for "mournful literature" as allegorical configurations of defeat. Although Avelar's analysis cannot be reduced solely to this point, it limits the Benjaminian reflection on historicity to an opposition between the "factual" and the "allegorical," limiting the allegorical to the textual expression of a "truth of defeat" that runs the risk of treating the historical and historicity as two uncontaminated poles. It thus runs the risk of establishing an opposition that the allegorical in Benjamin already tried to question. Therefore, it is important to note how the reduction of allegorical readings produced an idea of historicity that was limited to the idea of the truth of defeat and that forestalled other possible approaches to configuring historicity (for example, another style of thinking of past struggles).

In a way the very notion of defeat and the narrativization that it assumes requires further analysis. What kind of temporal imaginaries does the defeat imply? What happens with the figure of mourning, reduced to the truth of defeat, when we engage other areas in which the very notion of postdictatorship (like the category of the transition itself) becomes problematic, with the continuation of the forms of exceptionality that characterized the dictatorial past (lack of rights, police abuse, and so on)? A question that still needs to be addressed within postdictatorship critique is: Who are the subjects of that specific form of narrating mourning as the truth of the defeat? What are the zones that this truth leaves aside, without meaning by this a mere either/or between factual truth and the truth of a form of defeat? These questions call for a different form of historicization, in which a rereading of Benjamin could play a crucial role, as he attempts to think about the role of awakening as a permanent form of questioning the formation and transformation of the remembrance of the past.

This book approaches the image of the open (refunctionalized) prison in different realms (literature, film, architecture) to provide a cultural history of the life of prisons and detention centers after the first legislation of impunity for military personnel was passed. The dramatization of postdictatorship as a form of open prison poses for readers the question of how and from where this seeing is made possible (visible) and what marks the differences between functions and subjects that it implies. This needs to make us think about how to trace the border that produces the differentiation (which the texts analyzed in this book dramatize in their style, composition, and word play) and how spatial indistinctions open the possibility of seeing the miracle of market freedom as a great discursive prison where the expropriation of time is also an expropriation of any possibility of thinking or imagining the relationship between emancipatory temporality and the political. The image of the open prison appears in some key authors of postdictatorship literature and film as a way of questioning a dictatorship's legacy of limits and limitations of the ability to imagine politics and reimagine a political past that had become abject for both the right and the left.

If the main problem posed in the literary texts analyzed here is how to use the open prison as a place to rethink an escape by reimagining imprisoned fragments of political pasts (citing action), then the other task that remains is to question the citability of the critical tools used throughout the 1990s. I take the writings of Benjamin that were crucial to the elaboration of postdictatorship thought in the countries of the Southern Cone in that decade—namely his last works on the *Arcades* and on Brechtian epic—and rework them to decenter what I call the paradigm of postdictatorship focalization on the figure of the defeat to open a different allegory of reading the postdictatorial for/from our times. Instead of erasing Benjamin's name and the relevance of mourning, I propose to open up and read another line of investigation within his work, one in which he reinvents politics in his attempt to rethink the writing of history and the possibility of creating other ways of imagining (quoting) political histories.

This book is a response to the great discursive void in postdictatorship studies on the relevance of the trope of the prison not only during the dictatorships but also after them—that is, in their different afterlives. The prison is a central theme in literary reflections on the narrative possibilities of a past as a political past and, above all, on the areas of political imagination that remained confined by the limits and limitations inherited from dictatorships in Southern Cone countries. I emphasize this problem in the literary works addressed throughout this book by looking at the figure of the prisons' discursive afterlife (its literary form) and by examining how the texts can be transformed in different ways for territorial readings capable of gesturing toward other relational forms between emancipatory (revolutionary) past utopias and present utopias of unlimited exploitation in the democracies of neoliberal consumerism. Here my approach takes a double form: I analyze both real prisons that were transformed during processes of redemocratization and the figure of the open prison, which emerged in the literary and visual realm as dramatization and critique of the reduction of freedom to the spaces of the neoliberal market and a questioning of the subjects who qualify for such space-time of freedom. The open prison appears in each literary analysis in a different relation with respect to what I call the "architectonic of transition" and to the different critical openings that the literary texts question by means of a spacing of that which attempts to become fixed in the process of signifying the consensus. Words become sites for the emergence of an ambivalence that seeks other ways to historicize zones where freedom never arrived, thus forcing readers to rethink the historicization of labor and emancipation against the grain of the dominant neoliberal epics constructed in postdictatorship by both the right and the left.

If the architectural quotation of the prison has become the form in which renovation attempts to relinquish its ties to the past, how is this quotation cited within the field of reading and writing? Likewise, as these renovations propose other forms of quoting the past, what alternative imaginaries do they posit regarding democracy and freedom? It is within this network of reiterability that my work attempts to encounter images I find crucial to this multiple field, opening up to real and literary spaces. By analyzing these images, I search for a method to guide this book toward alternative modes of imagining freedom canceled out by the postdictatorship notion of a restricted, exonerated democracy. The images throughout my book—not as viewed objects, but in the Benjaminian sense of a dialectical constellation of readings, heterogeneous temporalities and writings that suggest processes of awakening—are approached as instances that not only space the present within which they irrupt, but also as a mode of reinventing and writing about multiple, invisible areas of the past. Following leads from the connections between multiple temporalities and spaces, my reflection turns to the globalizing, neoliberal world to expose its limitations, driven by the need to reimagine other freedoms where space proves crucial to imagine other possible worlds and interrupt the homogenizing aims of a world that closes in upon itself.

Imprisonment within the Open: Spaces of Control and Global Freedom

Imprisonment within the "open" is the figural form that permeates the different chapters in this book, and it departs from the hypothesis of reading the idea of "opening" as a crucial trope used to stage the passage from dictatorship to freedom and redemocratization. Within the context of the transitions to postdictatorship, "opening" became the keyword that worked as a stage for different signifying processes, thus constituting a sort of foundational matrix that attempted to replace the main figure of confinement and enclosure that characterized the dictatorial society. It constituted the privileged stage within the discursive realm of neoliberalism, where transitional freedom(s) were figured as an act of opening up to the global market. One can see the word "apertura" used throughout different areas of life, such as a democratic opening (*apertura democrática*), an opening to the global market (deregulation), and an opening to a vision of the future (to stop needing eyes in the back of your head [*los ojos en la nuca*]). In spatial language this opening can be seen in the gesture of closing prisons and detention centers that played a key role during the dictatorships, and reopening them transformed and fulfilling other, key functions in the new society. This leads me to think about what kind of closure and opening this freedom of consumption involves—a freedom of consumption that was installed within the discursive paradigm of the postdictatorship era as the end of history.[13]

In one of his works on control societies as configurations of global organization emerging with the Cold War, the philosopher Gilles Deleuze has proposed a unique form of opening as the central figure within the control society hatched in metropolitan countries at the end of World War II. In turn, this paradigm acquires its most salient features in developing bodies of knowledge and spaces in the United States as part of the Cold War.[14] In his essay "What Is a Creative Act?," the control society is differentiated from disciplinary power since the idea of closure governing disciplinary spaces dovetails with the notion of an opening that involves a controlled freedom, which Deleuze locates in the spatial metaphor of a highway: "Control is not discipline. You do not confine people with a highway. But by making highways, you multiply the means of control. I am not saying this is the only aim of highways, but people can travel infinitely and 'freely' without being confined while being perfectly controlled. That is our future. Let's say that is what information is, the controlled system of the order-words used in a given society."[15]

Deleuze continues by tracing a similar idea in relation to the role of language within the new control diagram, in which words and concepts are expected to become information—that is, data that would be added to the new ideal of culture as service. I connect this double figure of space and language (the freeway and the word in the information machine) to the way in which also the memory of past atrocities (suspiciously disconnected from current ones) is progressively assembled into a marketing machine. The passage from the architectonic of amnesia of the early 1990s to the boom of memory marketing and memory politics a decade later can be seen as following this process of a controlled freedom in which cognitive processes are transformed into practices of data accumulation (of information, products, and artifacts). In Deleuze's analysis, "control" refers to a new imaginary of limited freedom in which the technique of power that worked in the spatial figure of enclosure is progressively replaced by an idea of control that works through the fantasy of an opening. This is a crucial departure for this book, as it implies a problematization of freedom that involves a form of revelation in language. Deleuze states this pretty clearly when he says that "control is information"— that is, control is the fantasy of transforming practices of imagination into mere "cultural information."

Something similar to the Deleuzian notion of unconfined yet controlled freedom is what seems to govern a global system that prescribes new functions to prisons—a system that involves new modes of confinement in which prisons are made invisible by being privatized and moved to the outskirts of cities, while new state imaginaries for the neoliberal market are developing. The architecture of the open prison is becoming a kind of global phenomenon of prison transformations that pair cultural heritage with the service industry. Even though my analysis focuses on postdictatorship experience in Southern Cone Latin American countries, similar transformations of prisons in societies in "transition" can be seen elsewhere in the world, given the worldwide change in production and consumption in which the prisons become "cool" spaces for tourism. Some examples of these characteristics are present in the Russian prison Kresty, built at the end of the nineteenth century as Europe's largest prison. It was repurposed as a "museum" while the prison was still active and slated to offer other services once prisoners could be transferred elsewhere. The complex was to become an alternative site that could provide visitor services: tourism, entertainment, shopping, and a museum.[16]

Other projects, some of which came to fruition and some of which were abandoned, include plans for the prison in Alun-alun, Bandung, Indonesia, which was transformed into a mall, or the original idea to convert Musheer-abad Central Jail, today the Gandhi Medical College, into a mall.[17] Another recent case is the Turkish prison that was monumentalized by director Oliver Stone's film *Midnight Express*, today the Four Seasons Hotel, and the Hostel Celica in Ljublkana, Slovenia, a prison turned into a youth hostel and "tourist attraction." Aside from projects that transform prisons into malls, retaining the original architecture for its double function as "cultural heritage" and a feature "of tourist interest," there exist other paradigmatic sites in the disciplinary schematic that have been turned into malls: the former Ford Assembly Plant in Milpitas, California, known as "The Great Mall"; and the project for a model public school turned CDC, Patio Olmos, which is today a mall in Argentina. The transformation of Patio Olmos was carried out by J.C. López & Associates, the company in charge of the Punta Carretas Mall conversion in Uruguay.

From the standpoint of genealogical research, these juxtaposed spaces allow us to read an architectonics of the present, for they organize certain imaginaries of the crisis that the present leaves behind (a crisis made apparently visible in the 1950s) and the material that is superimposed upon or juxtaposed to the disciplinary sites as a new series of functions around which daily life would revolve: shopping, information, tourism, and entertainment. The functions of state preservation and protection of these sites' cultural heritage suggest a kind of embalming action on the part of the state, which transforms to rescue the past as a quasi-autobiographical monument to the state for consumption by foreign tourists. The prison that no longer functions as such is then turned into a mall or a hotel, in a kind of fantasy (from which the prison itself was born) of progress as regeneration, recycling the Hegelian notion of sublation as a simultaneous preservation and negation that frames the grammar of progress. The architectural history of dreams for modernization and progress coupled with different modes of social production contrasts with architectural redemption as an erasure of violence from previous processes in the attempt to promote, once again, the idea of advances that demand that a prison from a former time be renovated. Thus architectural recycling operates as an attempt to erase the ruin and turn it into a symbol without fissures—a past that has been recycled to become a new fantasy that embodies a present capable of both remembering the past and using it to produce income.

Such predeterminability refers to a certain control over the narration of the historical past that lies not in the promotion of amnesia but rather in a sort of memory surplus that paradoxically erases the possibility of establishing a link between historicity and social transformability. Turned into a fetish par excellence in the memory market, the act of remembering involves two focal points: the impossibility of questioning either the types of subjects implied by those memories or the type of temporality implied by this obsession with the collection of memory. My hypothesis is that the afterlife of dictatorial confinement observed in the conversions of prisons (the central figure and space within authoritarian regimes) into malls, cultural memory tours, or museums involves a form of control over any alternative possibility that might change the current state of affairs. In other words, by turning any act of the past into available material, memory becomes an artifact and factum that evades the question of what type of memory citizenship is implied by the systems that govern the politics of and about memory. It also leaves out the types of historicity (and therefore of the imaginary of freedom) that are both canceled and opened by those regimes of memory (not history). Since control, in the sense proposed by Deleuze, takes opening as the central figure of its imaginary, the questions that arise in each chapter are: What is the meaning of escape when the prison becomes an open prison? What form of historicity is to be rescued when memory becomes a market-driven artifact and object as well as the central concern of certain state policies of the neoliberalized left?

Each chapter deals with a form of articulation of this problem, proposing—by means of a text, film, or particular architecture—a counterpoint between the pseudo-opening system through which the freedom of the "post" in postdictatorship is signified versus a history that disturbs and upsets the new meanings of freedom and the right to remember implied. For instance, in the two cases of prison-mall transformations, I analyze the erased figure of the escapes of political prisoners as a break point regarding that memory regimes in control societies fail to tolerate. My goal is to shift the focus from the politics of memory to the forms of memory characteristic of other ways of thinking and perceiving politics that memory regimes seek to negate or control by means of a selective opening. While the main topic of postdictatorship studies in the 1990s was the politics of forgetfulness as an almost exclusive form of remembering, maybe now the question that we can start to explore is the politics of memory and how selective forgetfulness has turned into a surplus in terms of controlled memory.

The overabundance of memory and memorials not only continues a pattern of forgetfulness (as is always the case) but also functions to control the disclosure of past events within the framework left by the dictatorship. I refer here to the fact that certain limits are imposed by the market and by both left- and right-wing policies on what is tolerable for the politics (management) of memory, thus excluding certain areas that are currently undesirable (such as social transformability; memories that exceed the framework of remembrance of the educated middle class; and remembrances of the past that repeat the limitations experienced by those policies in the past). In contrast to the fantasy of spatiotemporal adjustments without fissures, this book attempts to create an alternative textual and visual corpus that makes visible those features that were never part of the national architectonic—elements which, as an excluded outside, do not and never did count as supposedly free subjects for a modern liberal citizenry. The prison serves as the framework in which this exclusion emerges, revealing a series of questions related to what I term the "minor epic" ("minor," because it refers to what goes untold, to what has no place in the global or national imaginary). Nevertheless, to advance critical thought on globalization, it is necessary to articulate these remains, which evoke the always disturbing image of what is missing from the fantasy of progress, and to examine those imaginaries likewise excluded from the modernizing neoliberal fantasy: collective laboratories of state transformation, revolutionary projects, and other emancipatory projects.

Afterlives: Reading as Stage for Different Transitionings

The figure of the open prison proves central to my analysis because it is one way of configuring the postdictatorial world in literature, and even more so, because during the processes of transition malls represented the dream of cleanliness and hygiene formerly embodied by the prison at the beginning of the previous century (more on this later). Not only does the figure of the prison call into question how to create a different history of the past from its traces remaining in the present. It also provides an alternative dramatization (whereby the page is the stage itself) of political imaginaries captured and whitewashed by the dominant organization of the postdictatorship city of consumption. In the texts and images I analyze, "free" postdictatorial life emerges as a staged occurrence in the figure of the open prison and the doubly excluded forms of subalternity (the prisoners and those who do not qualify for market freedom).

Taking these spatial histories that express ways of imagining freedom from prisons that were the ultimate symbols of totalitarianism, I ask a series of questions: Who were (or are) the subjects imagined by the transition? Where and when does the transition begin and end? How did the dictatorship continue to be evoked through spaces in which transformations and adjustments (homogenization) of times were produced, which delineated the geography and inhabitance of a limited kind of democracy of the market? What idea of rescue and temporality does this form of cultural heritage assume? How is it spatially materialized as a form that, translated into an act of reading, suggests different ways of reading between the lines?

Space and language are two theaters for reading the gestures of unique forms of continuities and discontinuities in dictatorial sites that were made invisible in their subsequent refunctionalizations. In the world after them (the "post" in postdictatorship), they create dislocations regarding the kinds of temporalities they assume and constitute through different processes of signification. On this matter it is helpful to bear in mind cultural theorist Gayatri Spivak's now classic problematization of the notion of transition, in which she points to the necessity of transforming a language based on economic models (transition between modes of production) or modes of consciousness into a "theory of change" that can be thought of as a "theory of reading," understood as the site where an "active transaction between past and future" can take place.[18] Inspired by this possibility, my analysis takes the afterlives of prisons as spaces from which to think of other modes of reading and thinking about the relations between past and present forms of violence, modes that question the dominant fantasy narratives of the transition (whether in literature, the museum, or consumerism).

I point toward the necessary possibility of imagining them from the unlivable zones in which and through which the dictatorship continued calling out to a certain layer of the population, particularly to those who would consider the equation of "more consumerism equals more freedom and more democracy" to be a prison itself. The temporal crossroads created by narratives on the prison furthermore involves suspending the exceptional character of this specific recent transition (to a neoliberal postdictatorship market and freedom), to question not only the repetition of systems of exceptional violence throughout the century, but also the past promises that remain open (that have not been fulfilled), which the Chilean philosopher Pablo Oyarzún has called in his reading of Benjamin the "truncated past."[19]

As the Chilean critical theorist Nelly Richard has argued in her introduction to *Pensar en / la postdictadura*, on a discursive level, transition assumed the logic of the market as something inevitable that was naturalized in language as a stage for a naturalized temporal imaginary in a line that went from less to more.[20] Thus the transition was embodied in a formula that posited an equivalence between more freedom = more consumption = more market = more democracy. Challenging this discursive framework, the philosopher Willy Thayer has proposed reading the transition as being the dictatorship itself, which in the case of Chile involves the economic process in which the dictatorship was a worldwide laboratory for neoliberalism— the stage chosen by the Chicago Boys to experiment with deregulation and freedom of the market (an economic framework that continues to be its matrix).[21] On the other hand, following Argentine political scientist Guillermo O'Donnell's analysis of the uses of the word "transition" in the case of Argentina, the Uruguayan historian Aldo Marchesi proposes questioning the ideological imaginary one assumes by naming the transition, arguing that perhaps it is time to stop speaking of transitions, since the word evokes a language of inevitability and an erasure of a series of political discourses that remain silenced by the effects of the dictatorship in the present.[22]

Many texts have pointed to the histories and political imagination closed by the transition in its aim to homogenize times to the same clock. Nevertheless, I believe it is important to explore further the word "transition," in the performative sense of signifying processes that materialize a kind of temporal imaginary and narrativization of politics, as well as the languages that the imaginary of transition needed to exclude from its discourse time and time again (its "constitutive constraints"—that is, its conditions of possibility *and* impossibility).[23] This would lead us to ask what happens to the word "transition" if one looks at it from the figure of the open prison, which is stressed in the literary texts I analyze as a reiteration of processes of containment and control. The idea of the transition can be approached as a process that has been consolidated over time by different systems of repetition. Here architecture plays an essential role in the creation of systems of repetition that consolidate circuits of meaning and further processes of resignification. A critical approach to the afterlife of the architectural spaces that served to contain political dissidence during the dictatorship can open up a different approach to the zones that continue to disturb the teleological narratives of the transition as a passage to an unquestioned freedom of the market. I take the figure of "repetition," which is crucial for the creation of certain habits in architectural works, but use it to examine how repetition constitutes certain norms while also exposing us to a spacing that deconstitutes and transforms naturalized spatiotemporal conceptions.[24]

What I am suggesting is that in the linear temporal imaginary of the transition, what remains imprisoned is a truncated past that had been centered on the word "transition" but in different ways related to the idea of the transformability of society as envisaged by the leftist movements of the 1970s, right before the coup. That is, if one brackets off the period of the dictatorship and focuses on a textual zone in which the word "transition" becomes a zone of indifferentiation, of a mixture of languages in which, while still prisoners of the economic imaginary (the passage to another mode of production, a socialist one), one can hear certain possible echoes of a political imaginary of truncated social change that was never allowed to take place and is therefore irrecuperable. Among these imaginaries, linked by a moment of intense political imagination (which was full, obviously, of problems and limitations), there is something untranslatable left over when we stop taking the word "transition" as an inevitable event imprisoned in the neoliberal universe and open it up to the act of reading.

I am interested in analyzing how the open prison that the market establishes in its architectural recycling can be read as an invisible metaphor of the limitation of the language of political imagination. It is odd that there are almost no critical works that place the word "transition" in the sphere of an imaginary that does not refer to neoliberalism. In this sense the word may be taken as a way of limiting in the inclusion of zones of the past where language becomes the site of thought and imagination. The literary works I turn to— *La fuga de Punta Carretas* by Fernández Huidobro, *Mano de obra* by Diamela Eltit, and *Nocturno de Chile* by Roberto Bolaño—all point in different ways to a certain emptying of the constellation-world of what did *not* happen, the truncated notion of social change as a way of incorporating the yet-to-be-imagined formation of an idea of transformability of politics as an experience that connects the historical with a perception of space and time.

This leads to a difficult negotiation, since I am not talking about idealizing a truncated past (transforming it into a big Epic) nor about denying and erasing it as being indistinguishable and identical to the neoliberal appropriation of the term, as a changeover to the shopping world. It is as if it were an element of the unnameable transition (the dual power of the MLN-Tupamaros in Uruguay in the late 1970s, the laboratory of Popular Unity in Chile in the early 1970s) that is suggested at a textual level as an empty quote, emptied by neoliberal architecture that the texts construct as a prison, but an open prison, a controlled prison, like Deleuze's freeway. This allows us to begin talking critically and creatively about zones or layers in which the word "transition" can be spaced out, relaxing the fixity of meaning imposed on it by the economy (unchangeable) or by the logic of defeat that governed post-dictatorship studies throughout the 1990s.

Prison-Malls
Architectures of Utopic Regeneration

When writing a spatial history of transitions to postdictatorship societies in Latin America, the word "opening" seems to offer a good starting point, as it traverses different discourses, habits, and languages, crystallizing the mood of the times. The notion of opening acts as a foundational matrix that implicitly highlights how the previous social dynamic was characterized by the idea of enclosure, evoking an image of a society imprisoned in a past from which it needed to flee. In the dominant languages of politics and mass media, opening (*apertura*) became a kind of order-word organizing a system of equivalences through which the passage to the "post" of postdictatorship was expressed. One can see it in different slogans of the times, such as opening up to democracy (*apertura democrática*), opening up to the global market (deregulation), and opening up to a vision of the future as opposed to dwelling on the past (*vivir con los ojos en la nuca*). In spatial language this opening can be seen in the closing of prisons and detention centers that played a key role during the dictatorships. Reopening them transformed and fulfilled other key functions in the new society.

At the same time, a decade after the dictatorships ended, critical and literary language started to thematize the keyword "postdictatorship" as an open prison, tracing a question that sounds simple but that requires a work of imaginative experimentation: How is the free postdictatorship society built around the image of an open prison? If the prison, as a space of confinement for that which disturbs or threatens a society, is the most crucial space during a totalitarian regime, then the act of figuring the society of postdictatorship freedom as an open prison suggests that society is still imprisoned in systems of control that were established in former authoritarian regimes, but in a more subtle, less obvious form. In this sense the open prison can be interpreted in relation to the working hypothesis used by many sociologists that the most recent Southern Cone dictatorships were transformative and founding moments that were not limited (as in the past) to mere reaction or counterrevolution but constituted projects of social transformation that created matrices for the future to come.[1] Therefore, instead of thinking of postdictatorships as coming after dictatorships, in a linear fashion, the figure of the open prison allows us to think of the many ways in which dictatorial processes framed the social and political life of the decades that followed as a form of afterlife of habits that had become naturalized and invisibilized.

Importing Prison Architecture: The Carceral Utopia as an Ideal of Regeneration and Adjustment

Two spaces were crucial in signaling the life and afterlife of the dictatorships: prisons and malls. My goal is to theorize the crucial space of confinement in the dictatorships, and the crucial site that was imported during and after the transitions, as spaces of the future and of commercial success. Both refer to an architecture linked to imaginaries of security and control, to patterns that define the geographies of freedom and democracy and the subjects included and excluded from them. Even though malls emerged as the dream-images of democratic freedom of consumption, they also functioned as spaces that expressed habits of social control that were imposed and naturalized during the dictatorships. One can detect a continuation of certain habits of self-imposed surveillance in the most publicized and popular malls: the sense of safety while walking about freely. Chilean sociologist Tomás Moulian has emphasized that in postdictatorship Chile, malls became a kind of utopia featuring several elements of the legacy of the military dictatorships—ideal spaces in which there was freedom of movement within a highly surveilled site, a peculiar fantasy that embodied the neoliberal sense of democracy in the form of an open prison. For this reason a critical montage that reads both spaces simultaneously allows us to see the problematic kernel of postdictatorship in the multiple temporalities they embody—a social diagram that is still imprisoned in the legacy of the dictatorship.

The case of the transformation of Punta Carretas Prison in Montevideo, Uruguay, into Punta Carretas Mall allows us to visualize a broader process in the history of confinement, the dreams of progress and social regeneration. Punta Carretas Prison was the most important detention center for male political prisoners in the late 1960s and early 1970s, and it was transformed into the most exclusive mall in Montevideo at the very moment in the transition to democracy when decisions were being made on human rights violations under military rule. The transformation of Punta Carretas offers a paradigm for postdictatorial reconfiguration processes that involve carceral features, systems of impunity, spatial fantasies from the Cold War, and ideals for democracy equated to the capacity for consumption. As the Uruguayan cultural critic Hugo Achugar has stated, the history of Punta Carretas's conversion must be considered in tandem with the referendum and the subsequent plebiscite for the Law of Caducity of the Punitive Claim of the State, in which 51 percent of the population voted to pardon military personnel for their human rights violations during the decade of terror.[2]

The opening of Punta Carretas Mall in 1994 was thus part of a larger process in which history seems to have been configured as a kind of prison that must be transformed in order to envision the country of the future—that is, the country of consumer services. The juxtaposition of the prison and the mall in Punta Carretas works as a metaphor for a peculiar form of transition from the carceral past to the consumerist present that upholds the paradoxical freedom of the mall. In this sense the two diagrams overlap to become a kind of mute monument that expresses a desire to reconfigure and dominate history by selecting and homogenizing multiple temporalities contained within its space. The fact that this architectural conversion from a prison to an upscale mall occurred at the same time as the referendum and plebiscite that brought investigations on past military crimes to a halt allows one to read an architectonics of the transition in the form of the prison-mall.

The emblematic correspondence of these two events reveals the way in which the transition's fantasy of homogenizing temporalities allowed this space to become a culturally essential stage for advertising the new possibilities in neoliberal life. After the decision voted in the plebiscite, the new prison-mall became both the paradoxical monument to forgetting and the prized example of the new regime's discourse, transactions, and measures. As the cultural theorist Brett Levinson has stated: "By wickedly granting amnesty to criminals the Uruguayan government was not asking victims to overlook past crimes, but to overlook the incalculable nature of those crimes."[3] Juxtaposing across history works to show how the incalculability of past crimes is subsumed under the logic of measurement whereby the past is not just forgotten but is homogenized within the market logic of equivalences and measures. Following this logic, the prison-mall embodies an architecture that encodes the decisions and assumptions of the transition, understood as the passage from multiple temporalities that once inhabited the site to the homogenization of the new present that retrospectively seeks to control this past—invisibilizing it without erasing it.

Interrupting a linear form of reading history, the afterlife of the prison invites exploration of the disguised mechanisms of control that permeate society in the notion of democracy opening up possibilities for consumption. It also asks us to look at the zones of confusion in which the differences between the literal and the figurative aspects of these spaces have become indistinguishable. (From where, and when, can we distinguish prison and mall once we get rid of the obvious gaze of common sense?) Here the possibility of interrupting our own act of reading signals the necessity of thinking about the differential coimplication of the spaces of prison and mall, the market and the confinement it produces, thus opening up a space from which to read the figure of the transition and to visualize what it attempted to invisibilize: the confusion of past and present. In this sense "afterlife of confinement" refers to the echoes that pose a question about the dictatorships' legacy of transformation for a future that the dominant discourses of transition pose as being totally dissociated from the past. On the notion of the break between past and present, I superpose the figure of the coimplication of different pasts and presents, so that we read the architecture in its ambiguity, opening up a space of indefinition in which other signifying acts can emerge. For instance, the celebration of the "end of history" as the end of utopias of leftist transformation of society was signaled by the mega-utopian spaces of the prison-malls, designed for a dream society of pure and absolute market(ing)—the utopia of the end of all utopias.

As the art historian Valerie Fraser has proposed in *Building the New World*, architectural imports to Latin America played a crucial role throughout the region's history in creating imaginaries for progress and modernization. By creating stages for the performance of the dominant temporal ideology, architecture allows us to see transitional moments in history from the perspective of modes of social production, particularly from the spatial materialization of utopian myths within a given era's social diagrams. The architecture imported to Latin America plays a fundamental role in materializing certain utopian myths of progress that reconfigure a specific geography through repetition, movements, and systems of inclusion and exclusion. Thus the different waves of imported architectures allow one to perceive spatialized processes without which the dominant ideological system of an era could not function (even in times of crisis or decline). Could the myth that deviant individuals might be corrected or redeemed, the guiding notion of penitentiary reform, have been developed at the beginning of the twentieth century without a specific prison architecture? Could the myth of unlimited, secure consumption that grounded the imaginary of neoliberal progress and freedom at the end of the century have been consolidated without importing the mall?

These spaces provide complex materializations of social diagrams (production and consumption) that function as key spaces for creating a temporal imaginary—that is, as theaters capable of architecturally staging certain modes of inhabitance in time (the time of modern progress in the case of the prison, posthistorical time in the case of the malls). In this sense they allow us to read an architectural organization that attempts to impose an ideal synchronization of temporalities by structuring spaces and trajectories within a delimited framework for the city. The urban landscape operates metonymically (but no less problematically) as a locus that embodies a broader field of activity on a national stage. The cultural theorist Jens Andermann has proposed reading the appropriation of urban spaces within the construction of national imaginaries as the configuration of a state optics through which "the ritual performances of showing and seeing in the public arena were not merely illustrations of a fully written-out historical script. On the contrary, they were the stage productions of national history's myths of origin, pointing us to the state's theatrical dimensions as 'display, regard, and drama,' which, as [the anthropologist] Clifford Geertz has argued, have become overshadowed in modern political theory by the State's exclusive identification with governance and dominion."[4]

The idea of the stage is crucial, for it involves the possibility of viewing these sites as laboratories and established ways of seeing and thinking about action (for the relationship architecture bears to the geography of repeatable movement). In this sense, prisons worked throughout the twentieth century in Latin America as stages upon which different notions of legal progress and social whitening were tested. Without assuming a homogeneous process, which would be blind to the various types of prison reform that took place in many Latin American countries from the mid-nineteenth century on, it is nevertheless true that the importation of prison architecture played a crucial role in fantasies for modernization. Even though one cannot speak of a precise date marking the birth of the modern prison in Latin America, it was certainly already under way at the beginning of the nineteenth century; the early decades of the twentieth century saw the rise of a penitentiary model that embodied one of the dreams of spatial materialization for progress, a utopia of a regenerative state capable of containing and correcting deviance.[5]

According to French philosopher Michel Foucault's argument for the case of prisons in France and the vast amount of bibliography on the positivist ideals governing the regenerative process in Latin American penitentiary systems, the prison synthesizes, architecturally, the ideal of correction and orthopedics for deviant persons (produced as subjects excluded from what the diagram attempts to correct in them). In their introduction to *The Birth of the Penitentiary in Latin America*, coauthors Ricardo Salvatore and Carlos Aguirre state that the importation of prison reform shows the "formation of hegemonic visions of the State" in which the prison was seen as a powerful symbol of modernity that put the law to work.[6] Adjusting deviant bodies to the temporal homogenization spatialized by prison architecture involves the notion of homogenizing heterogeneous times and spaces to one clock alone, for these multiple (and motley) times and spaces are perceived to be unproductive by the modernizing state in its creation of an ideal, productive temporality.[7] Prisons propose a space of correction (orthopedics) set within a wider context of synchronizing society as a body, of adjusting the body's time to a system of social production.

The material form of the prison becomes the physical expression of how the prison sentence affects the whole of society, spatializing a form of temporal adjustment where, ideally, synchronizing the time of transgression competes against the time of measures governing society. Thus the prison mentality that imagined the regenerative penitentiary system expresses a logic of general equivalence that attempts to adjust the patchwork time of crime with the ideal time of social reproduction, in conjunction with the deprivation of freedom and a legal apparatus in which justice is made equal by an ideal of measure (the measure of the equalizing nature of the prison sentence, of the right to liberty, of the sense of deprived freedom). Within this scheme the prison then turns into a spatialization-materialization of a common system of measurement involved in repayment to society, and of exclusion-inclusion, when the deviant individual (excluded now from the system of rights) is included in society—through his or her very exclusion—with respect to a common space of social circulation (one is included as excluded as long as he or she is being repaired). Within this framework the prison materializes a presupposition of payment in time as part of one's obligation to belong to society (a community of rights) from the spatialization of a determinate time in which the deviant individual's time is adjusted to a social time through punishment.[8]

However, the increasing use of the figure of the prison without sentencing in postdictatorship society at the end of the century, points to the end of the regenerative utopian ideal, a symptom of the time of repayment to society becoming eternal. It is important to explore this spatiotemporal transformation, as it coincides with the role the malls started to play as new figures of synchronization and limited communal regeneration, now envisaged as an inclusion in good citizenry through consumption. Thus in the new function of the prison transformed into center of consumption, we see a functional paradox that reveals the dream of postdictatorship society: the regenerated prisoner, now converted in a consumer and ideal citizen, surveilled in the mall, and the lost criminal who cannot be regenerated and who is confined in the eternal form of imprisonment (without sentence) that was inherited from the dictatorship. The questions that therefore arise are: What was the role of prisons during the dictatorships? Do the dictatorships cancel the utopian function of the prison as a site of regeneration?[9] Can one approach the mall as the new architecture that replaces (transforms) the carceral ideal of the past, proposing a new myth of progress and renovation (cleanliness), now in a system of equivalences that is centered on consumption?

Recycling Regeneration: Converting Foundational Prisons to the Services Paradigm

Even though the crisis of the carceral system runs throughout the twentieth century, in the late 1960s and 1970s the penitentiary system underwent a fundamental transformation due to the various dictatorial processes. During this period, which began with the states of exception enacted before the coups were made official in Argentina and Uruguay and the spectacular coup on September 11, 1973, in Chile, mass incarceration for political dissidents was widespread for a significant time. The form in which the extended disappearance of political prisoners was gradually naturalized (disappearance as absence from a penal and judicial apparatus that made detention legal) marks a system of violence that far surpassed the dictatorships. Here many questions emerge regarding the temporality of the transitions from dictatorial processes: When does the dictatorship begin and end? For whom are these dates adjusted? Questions also include how the processes left their authoritarian mark on subsequent legislative systems (for example, trials without a sentence became naturalized over time, an alarming development established during military rule).[10] In the three countries analyzed in this book (Argentina, Chile, and Uruguay), an unprecedented crisis unfolded in the penitentiary system during the military dictatorships, a crisis that would govern carceral life thereafter, configuring a system of exclusion of rights as its norm. Perhaps the fact that these countries saw the most extensive forms of dictatorship (in terms of length of time) and the most intensely violent perfection of kidnappings and punishment methods (torture) makes the figure of the prison occupy a fundamental place within the carceral diagram.

The debates that compose *Seminario internacional sobre la impunidad y sus efectos en los procesos democráticos* (International seminar on impunity and its effects on the democratic processes) highlight a relationship between the impunity granted to the military, the process of naturalizing unconstitutional forms of incarceration in postdictatorial carceral systems, and a naturalization of the discursive equation between democratization and elections.[11] As the pacifist Adolfo Pérez Esquivel has stated, a form of equivalence was naturalized in postdictatorship countries that "are said to be democratic because they call for elections," reducing the meaning of democracy to an electoral cycle without targeting how impunity violates the law and human, civil, and constitutional rights.[12] The state of emergency that reformulated carceral experience through national security measures effectively spelled the end of the corrective-regenerative ideal that had been in crisis since the beginning of the military regimes. This can be observed in the dictatorships' proposal for carceral experience, which involved eliminating or repressing the visibility of deviance in different ways (disappearances, shootings, inciting madness, and so on) rather than humanitarian regeneration (the normative, modernizing fiction that gave rise to the modern prison at the beginning of the century). The development of a clandestine system of detention centers to accompany the penal system and the multiple measures legislating what had only been states of exception until then (practiced but not legally naturalized—such as the systematic practice of torture, legal limbos, and so on that were applied during the final dictatorships) introduce another kind of social diagram, one that still prevails today and has its matrix in the decades of military states.[13]

After the so-called *reaperturas democráticas* (restorations of democracy) in the postdictatorial era in the Southern Cone, the prison would once again become the center of attention, now within a different system of functions that involved abandoning the regenerative ideal (orthopedics) in favor of disposability, as seen in the legal limbos for incarcerated populations and the progressive privatization of the penal system. This moment marks a fundamental shift from the notion of orthopedics (as correction for production), which was fundamental to the modernizing programs at the beginning of the twentieth century, to the new ideal of disposability seen in attempts to privatize the prisons and likewise to the notion of compulsive consumerism that made the work of repairing objects almost obsolete.[14]

Thus the carceral transformation that takes place in Southern Cone societies during the twentieth century's final dictatorships can be read as a limit in which the prisons employed another kind of confinement and treatment of detainees, marking a peak at the end to the liberal paradigm. The beginning of another form of carceral organization may be traced to the official consolidation of military dictatorships in the 1970s, which produced the most explicit case of naturalized authoritarianism. Many of these forms of authoritarianism continued to operate in carceral life in the society that came after them, delimiting a restricted type of democracy divided between consumers (as a mode of citizenship) and prisoners (the criminalization of poverty). The carceral crisis was accompanied by a crisis in humanitarian ideals for punishment, causing a repositioning of the theoretical role of human rights in the late twentieth century, a debate that continues today.

It seems symptomatic that the many prisons opened in the late nineteenth and early twentieth century as fundamental strongholds of a carceral network within the modern state's architectonics were subsequently closed down for their inability to contain their prisoners successfully. These foundational prisons were largely converted to different uses, leaving behind the project of regenerating criminals as a relic of the kind of state that now superimposed other functions onto these structures. Buildings that were once model prisons but became troublesome ruins in recent decades include Cárcel de Miguelete in Uruguay (1890), Lecumberri in Mexico City (1900), Cárcel (Asilo) del Buen Pastor in Córdoba, Argentina (1902), Punta Carretas in Uruguay (opened in 1910), and Carandiru in Sao Paulo, Brazil (1920). Each of these was recycled into something different: Miguelete an art center, Lecumberri a national archive, Buen Pastor a cultural-commercial center, Punta Carretas became a mall, and Carandiru was demolished and replaced with a "memory park." The need to bring closure to these sites and recycle their architecture at the end of the twentieth century marked the end of the model of regeneration in the carceral diagram and its replacement with another form of confinement. A peculiar process of recycling modern architectural sites began at the end of the twentieth century, superposing newly imported service diagrams (consumerism, tourism, museification as an industry) onto hypersymbolic structures within the modern state's architectonics of progress.

This opens up a series of questions concerning other forms of naturalizing violence and restructuring state-market relations (the future of the prison-mall, the prison-archive, the prison-hotel, the prison-museum of memory), for the shift in ideological systems from modes of regeneration to modes of consumption is crucial to understanding the dominant idea of a transition as the installation of a new temporal imaginary for postdictatorial times. Conceived as an importation of a series of solutions and programs of political-economic development at the moment of neoliberalization, the paradigm of the prison as a model for a determinate geography of freedom and productivity in the service of whitewashing and hygiene has as its counterpart the imported concept of the mall. The ideals of cleanliness, hygiene, and order that once characterized the model of regeneration accompanying architecture in modernizing processes at the beginning of the twentieth century are embodied in another architectural import, which staged a kind of freedom by and for consumption: the mall. The architectonics of transition involved developing a new myth of progress, now embodied in the idea of the present time as a posthistorical time. The space that would stage the new sense of temporality for endless consumption would be the mall—one that was associated with the notion of closing history and opening up the market to the globe.

The importation of this architectonic form (as both an architecture and a systemic foundation) as part of the configuration of the postdictatorial world of freedom shows the spatial repercussions of the novel language of temporal development. A new progress was imagined, one that defined democracy as a mode of importing progress and freedom but that constructed redemocratization as choice within a consumerist framework (the possibility of accessing a greater variety of merchandise) requiring privatization of space (seen in the widespread privatization in Argentina and Uruguay of services that once belonged to state-owned companies). The fact that the mall, as part of a fresh kind of social and urban organization, was imported en masse to the Latin American Southern Cone precisely when these countries were ushered into the postdictatorship era reveals a different kind of architectonics that echoes the impulse once seen in the penitentiary's importation to Latin America at the beginning of the century. I read the unique way in which the mall was imported as a way of redramatizing and restaging a new kind of national-global imaginary that brought with it the dream of a novel temporal adjustment to progress, capable of homogenizing a contentious field of histories and times impossible to subsume within the neoliberal utopia.

The importation of the mall came to embody the ideal of a kind of temporality that framed an "end of history" as the end of earlier emancipatory and transformative ideals. As spatialized imaginaries of unlimited consumption, representing the myth of national renewal in a new metonymic equivalence with society as a whole, the malls highlight the reduction of democracy during the transitions to a mere call for national elections and consumerist freedom of choice.[15] On this map it is essential to analyze the genealogy of a utopian component in the mall, which confronts us with a key stage for developing notions of temporality and historicity that, until today, are found to be at odds in different ways when articulating the past and present in urban terrain. The program of malling had its roots in the military dictatorships and constituted an importation of architectural forms central to the creation of a democratic imaginary of abundant supply in the United States as a counterbalance to the USSR during the Cold War.

The new societies of the postdictatorship era needed to replace the imaginary formed by more than a decade of civic-military rule, and they appropriated (imported) the utopian dream of freedom of consumption to symbolize their success and arrival at peace (in an imaginary of reconciliation)—the end of the previous history of emancipatory struggles. Just as prisons had imported a regenerative ideal, now malls also played a role in importing a dream that supplemented various notions of the "end." The malls organized a system of inclusion and exclusion that would be questioned with the rise of different financial crises in 2000, when for many this dream turned into a nightmare. I am interested in examining the war imaginary that permeates the invention of the mall as a social utopia because this imaginary is usually erased or invisibilized. In the interval between the proliferation of malls in the North and their importation and adaptation in the South, dictatorships transformed the social, political, and economic apparatus into which the mall would be inserted. The mall inserts itself in a militarized society that has naturalized military intervention as a form of solving social conflicts.

Building the Cold War Utopia of Democracy: The Malling of America

As most of the bibliography on malls states, they were born in the midst of war and soon became a powerful symbol of what democracy in the free (that is, noncommunist) world might look like. The creation, development, and perfection of the mall can be read as a powerful instance of how market-based ideas of freedom and democracy were staged in the space of the here and now. Undoubtedly, presentism was a crucial component in the importation of the mall concept at the moment of transition in postdictatorship countries, for malls bear their own history—an ideal of happiness and abundance tied to a feeling of security. It is impossible to talk about their invention and improvement without paying attention to the essential role they played within Cold War logic as well as within the imaginary of nuclear threats. Their inventor, Victor Gruen, envisaged malls as a solution to urban problems that could also be readily converted into nuclear shelters or triage sites in the event of a nuclear attack.[16] As he put it: "Shopping centers have the further advantage in that they can be built without government money and in that they serve the dual purpose of being useful in case of a war emergency, as well as for our peace economy."[17]

Although the military aspect of the mall has yet to be explored in greater detail, the historian Jeffrey Hardwick mentions it as part of the idealism in the mall's invention but remarks that it was a civil defense failure. Based on Gruen's documents, the geographer Timothy Mennel has traced the double fantasy that constituted the mall as both the site for magical consumption in an administered haven and the peaceful shelter where communities would be protected in the event of a foreign attack. "Defense concerns thus played a central role in the physical makeup of Gruen's projects," Mennel wrote, and the marriage between economy and patriotism was essential for the "vision of shopping center self-sufficiency."[18] By analyzing these secondary elements within the mall imaginary, we can trace how a link was forged between freedom, security, and surveillance in the obsessive attempt to assert absolute control over contingencies or random encounters. In this sense, architectural designs for malls expressed visions of protection, patriotism, and consumption in the utopia of a receptacle that contained an absolute inside—that is, one without an outside, either in a spatial or a temporal sense.[19] We cannot underestimate the power of this metaphor essential to the process of malling in the United States and the rest of the world. Protection, immunity from violence, and security are the features that justified the implantation of malls throughout the world. It is the task of literature and criticism to point to the aporias of this dream.

The process of creating and perfecting the mall serves as an example from which to read the main functions of a new social diagram. Mennel summarizes this point in his comprehensive analysis of Gruen's invention: "In the post–World War II era, as social progressivism vanished from America under the onslaught of prosperous consumerism and ideology-driven fear, the site of a social utopia shifted to a form that embodied both the ideals of capitalist community and the control necessary to achieve rationalized order in a time marked by equally powerful technological innovations and fears of those very innovations: the shopping mall."[20] As Mennel underlines, the mall was to embody a social utopia in which the ideal of freedom would result from consumer choice in a hypersurveilled, highly controlled space, thus conflating freedom with gratifications designed and imposed on agents from the outside. The process that the writer William Severini Kowinski has called "the malling of America" gives us a framework from which to approach different elements essential for studying diagrams of control and the consolidation of neoliberal democracies.[21]

The main functions of the mall were derived from the closed environment through which Gruen solved the problem of shopping in the cold weather of Minnesota. Temperature controls would become associated with the whole imaginary of the mall as the site for endless consumption, as if the end of contingency (rain, snow, cold, and so on) were also the end of the passing of time. The solution proposed by closing the roof and creating "an eternal spring" with air-conditioning and heat in Minnesota became a model applied to places with highly volatile weather throughout the country. Gradually, the controlled climate generated further modes of security as the mall became a kind of nonplace in which the time of the day and the seasons were suspended in a paradise of the eternal present, a present spent eternally consuming, where people could shop without having to think about the outside—the weather, street violence, beggars, and so on. There exists an ideal to erase the finite temporality of bodies and clocks through a space capable of paradoxically embodying something outside contingency, an eternal dream where there is no weather, no hot or cold, no snow, and one can forget about the time outside in the streets.

The utopian component of the mall, where people could meet and feel free while being protected, became naturalized in the United States in the 1960s, when cities were undergoing a series of crises and political upheavals. Interestingly enough, the mall proposed by Gruen forged an ideal for democracy and urban life, serving as a third space contesting the perceived totalitarianism of Soviet Russia and the dangers of technology and machinery. Gruen's project entailed creating an indeterminate site in which civic and commercial spheres could converge in one protected walkway.[22] He imagined synthesizing ordered space where people could walk around freely but do so *protected*—that is, without being exposed to danger in the street (what he called "protected pedestrian areas"). Thus in the mall there is room for chance encounters but always within a controlled and secure field. Enclosure is the mode that makes it possible to secure control over the world outside (temperatures, climate) and the inside (security, vigilance); this space reorganizes an imaginary civil practice and citizenry by conflating the civil and commercial world (purchasing power and structures for civil services, general hospitals, and so on).[23]

The original function of the mall as offering a kind of security involves or presumes a form of thought on freedom, which at its core provides the possibility of feeling safe, with the guarantee of not having to run into poverty or robbery. What is reiterated by the concept of the mall as a democratic imaginary in (nuclear) war, and what allowed malls to flourish during the most intense moments of urban violence, is the idea of a freedom in which every encounter that takes place can be reduced to the horizon and parameters of what is permissible. The mall therefore provides us with a democratic ideal expressed in spatial terms, a form of containment whereby freedom is secured through vigilance (protection)—that is, paradoxically, as a form of open prison. The mall offers a freedom that is contained and controlled; freedom can take place in this space, within a horizon of surveilled possibilities without risk (again, a feature that would be fundamental to the postdictatorial city).

A free citizenry calls for a discreet surveillance system like that formerly used in the prison system, therefore the cynicism with which the prison-mall structures were received in postdictatorship societies. Chance is a given, but within a mall it is controlled. The mall offers a world of possibilities within what is the only possibility for its world. What remains concealed is a kind of interaction that makes it a danger for an unsurveilled outside, the dark (in contrast to its well-lit space) and gray reality (poverty) beyond its walls—all adjectives used in the United States to describe Soviet communism, which served as a dialectic countermodel to establish the idealized mall as a democratic form in the "free" world. In a certain sense the mall provides us with an ideal of freedom of consumption ruled by a supreme principle—that of being able to choose everything in it, except the possibility of *not* choosing this configuration of choice.

Real estate developer James Rouse, whom author Ira Zepp has called "the mahatma of the malls," perfected controlling the shoppers' affective mall experience by creating an atmosphere that induced emotive care, fantasy, and nostalgia.[24] Inspired by Disneyland, Rouse's dream was to create the fantasy of a space in which people could have everything previously sited in the community—churches, shops, coffee shops, restaurants, medical doctors, and so on—while feeling security in a controlled space (temperature, parking, security patrols, cameras, mood music, and so on). The dream is also seen in the mall's designed temporality: an idealized eternity, in the sense that a fantasy of an absolute present (presence) within the interior of a space operates to obliterate the subjective sense of the exterior. Most of the existing bibliography dealing with the mall's transformation of urban experience refers to the mall as the ideal of a self-contained bubble that parodies a city that does not need an outside world. Thus it embodies the site of the "end of history," becoming the model toward which the rest of the world needed to move. As Zepp states, Rouse visualized the mall as the realization of a perfect ideal of

American democracy, a place where everyone could go, have fun, and be together; it was figured as the site for perfection, the paradise of consumption.[25]

This idea that renders democracy and freedom in spatial terms from, by, and for consumption was crucial to the importation of the mall to Southern Cone countries (as well as to the subsequent process of malling) and to the role these sites played during key moments of transition. It is easy to understand the novelty appeal of malls for part of the population, particularly when a new discourse on democratic freedom rooted in consumer choices was being forged. This discourse urged subjects to leave the dark past behind (not to look back, *no vivir con los ojos en la nuca*) and to create a more progressive present: it is possible to argue that what was being imported with this urban utopia of democratic consumption was the ideal opposition to a stereotyped imaginary of communism as a world without purchasing options or variety. At the same time, the temporality of the malling phenomenon in Southern Cone countries is important, given that it arises amid the formulation of an end to the Cold War era as a worldwide threat (the fall of the Berlin Wall, the end of the dictatorships, and the end of "subversive" activities) so that malls came to fill a certain void. The end of the utopia arises from importing this idealized form within a posthistorical time. Indeed, one may read the proliferation of these sites as a form of living monumentalization (or museification) of the world proclaimed to be at the end of history, staging the image of an arrested time in which the present of the mall was the measure of all time, its future made present.

If this notion sounds rather elementary today, it is pertinent to analyze the genesis of how these ideas spatialized into a point, then turned into the most novel architectural spaces for these centers. The peculiarity of the mall at this moment of redemocratization as democratic and consumer choice was its way of marking the present through protecting society regarding the notion of its potential transformation. Nevertheless, the kind of democracy and implicit civic ideal in the concept of the mall employed a similar language to the dictatorships in Latin America. For example, the mall's "protected pedestrian walkway" echoes the idea of "protected democracy" in the legacy of Pinochet's rule, as both imply a trajectory of already traced possibilities, whether in legislation or in passing through space with a kind of freedom. This is the difference based on closure that imposes control on disciplinary societies that the philosopher Gilles Deleuze described in his spatial idea of social control as a highway where there is freedom unlike that of the prison, but where the possibilities of movement are already determined beforehand. What this new naturalization of controlled freedom presupposes is exclusion: the mall as a democratic dream excludes from its ideal a great part of the population unqualified for citizenship. Furthermore, for the consumer to experience freedom, the malling model requires a significantly high area of determinability, for like the dictatorships it proposes its horizon as the only one that makes the market possible. In other words, the mall operates to protect the feeling of freedom from having to witness poverty, other social classes, crime, and robbery, so the malls become powerful sites that naturalized the criminalization of poverty. The great importance these sites achieved after the end of the dictatorships worked toward an architectonics of the neoliberal state, which aimed at achieving a symbolic closed totality.

This is one of the cornerstones of the postdictatorship era, synonymous with its newfound freedoms; malling constituted one of the pillars of transitional architectonics in order to refound the time of progress in the new temporality of consumption by negating all historical temporality as subject to transformation. In the constant, controlled temperature of the mall (a crucial point for its success in providing both security and a predictable context), its utopian time is ahistorical and unchanging: an eternalized present of consumption. Temporality and politics are divorced from the present in this dream, which attempts to replace the notion of citizens' rights with the idea of passive subjects who use services. As the malls began to offer hints of a populist discourse for the market (sites that are pleasant to be in, as spaces for all), the question of the kind of citizen implied by this dream for an entire country was kept entirely at bay (submerged), as was the notion of democracy: the transparent assimilation of citizenship and consumption, rights and transactions.

Urban Whitewashing and Synchronization: Importing the Cold War Utopia

There are strong parallels between the key figures Victor Gruen and James Rouse, who found their guidelines for spatial articulation in a kind of democracy developed in the United States in the Cold War era, and the controversial figure of Argentinean architect Juan Carlos López. If we take López's brand name as our guide, we can see how the mall underwent a peculiar transformation when he imported it. What is striking in the majority of malls created by his company, Juan Carlos López & Associates, is the firm's habit of positing new architectural structures and forms for sites that were once heavily symbolic of the modern state's projects—a prison in the case of Punta Carretas, a school in the case of Patio Olmos, a railway agency in Galerías Pacífico, an auction house in Patio Bullrich. The company is internationally renowned, having won many awards for its designs from the International Council of Shopping Centers. The first design award was given in 1990 to Patio Bullrich Mall, one of the first two malls in Buenos Aires, opened in 1988. The second was given to Alto Palermo Mall in 1992, and the third to Galerías Pacífico, another juxtaposition of the mall's structure to a very old building that had various uses. The next two awards were given in the same year to Punta Carretas Mall in Montevideo (the prison-mall) and Patio Olmos Mall in Córdoba (the school-mall) in 1996.

The López projects open up a manner of reading the malling process as a kind of spatial translation or resignification of expressive structures from an expired time. What has been called the architecture of "great works by the state" (seen today as remains) is now resignified by the private work of architects according to the plans of developers. The new commercial function resignifies the place, now as a consumer site, but leaving the traces of the past in the materiality of the building (the structure on which the new forms are superposed). The peak of recycling occurred during the 1990s, an instant of urban resignification that adjusts and homogenizes different temporalities, placing the architect as metaphorically both entrepreneur and collector. On the one hand, the architect recycles and renews sites, resignifying and revaluing them according to the novel process of capital accumulation. On the other hand, he or she preserves the architecture of the past as a sign of a different time. This resembles the dynamic of a collector, for whom objects become sites to be integrated in a series that gives them a new meaning, while they keep their singularity as unique figures in the series, pointing to another temporality. There are two dynamics in this dialectic of urban renewal: one is the signaling of progress as a dialectic that moves forward and that removes the ruins of the past (the logic of modernization as superation). The other, less visible and more complex dynamic, emerges in another reading of this process in which the trace of the past that is camouflaged as progress emerges in an arresting ambiguity. For example, in the case of the refunctionalization of Punta Carretas as mall, the reopening of the most important prison built for the dictatorship established a past time that was refunctionalized on the city's outskirts.

I now turn to the transformation of the temporal imaginary that is carried out by commercial architecture. The work of this sector, as seen in firms like Juan Carlos López & Associates, involves starting with the cultural gesture of historical preservation and adding economic value to it, given that the buildings they work with are assessed at a higher market value for their historical worth.[26] The logic of preservation is subsumed by an economic logic whose aim is to generate a memorialist capital gain, by initiating the task of municipal regeneration. Here, within the trajectory of development in commercial architecture, a point of discussion arises among architects regarding the increasingly widespread practice of replacing state projects with the schizophrenic plans produced by developers. According to articles published in architectural magazines like *Arquitectura Sur, Elarqa*, and *Suma* in the early 1990s, commercial architecture may be questioned as a substitute for what had once been the twentieth-century monumental architecture of developing public works to bolster and celebrate the modern state (as architecture that turned into a symbol of power to be expressed).

These works were part of a state performance that did not predate them, but through which they served to express public will, forever fissured and chaotic, like the entire history of modernizing development traced in twentieth-century Latin American cities. In the 1990s nearly all organization of urban space moved toward a language that became difficult to understand, for the syntax governing this group of works outside the logic of safe investment, control, and earnings could not be grasped by architectural critique. This is one of the points at which the neoliberal city began to redefine what was once staged in terms of the public but that now remains limited to the practice of private consumerism.[27] In his writings from 1993 the architect Ruben García Miranda expresses the fear that design competitions would gradually disappear, transformed into bids where "compensation sought will never be more *direct*, more *linear*: money." He associates this new logic to a novel manner of thinking about cities: "Enterprises driven by their interests that lean towards a kind of autism, 'urban simulacrums' as A. Sato and F. Liernur have called them, 'internal fictions of an orderly, clean, and functioning city made to size. The most notorious cloistering in the jail-mall substitution, where one can perceive to what point isolation and the need for control prevail."[28] The malls' cloistering or desire to provide controlled, safe forms that substitute the streets, began to be associated with political scientist Francis Fukuyama's theory of the end of history.[29] Architects saw a symmetry between the postdictatorial ethos as the framework for a fantasy of the end of history (as the end of historicity) and the proliferation of malls as a present dispossessed of both the potential for transformation and of any exterior world outside of them. Reflections on architecture during these years locate malls as the site of a radical transformation of the urban ideal, questioning the connection between urban space and the idea of a civic center now guided toward an aggressive policy of privatization and exclusion.[30]

It seems curious that the role of development is only maintained in this architectural imaginary now that investment and speculation come as part of the so-called private initiatives staged by the neoliberal state. We move from project development promoted by the state to the word *developers* in Spanish, which was incorporated as a foreign loan-word in the same way as the *mall* in the 1990s (known also as *shoppings* in the Southern Cone). This untranslatability would also prove characteristic of the importation of malls to Latin America, a process that originates in the United States Cold War context. In my reading, this untranslatability may be read architecturally—that is, in the very form of juxtapositions and layerings proliferating during the postdictatorship era as substitutes for progress within a neoliberal ideal of permanent transition toward a better future. Above all else, the question that guides my analysis in the following section is how to approach Punta Carretas Prison within the city's most upscale mall: when reading this architectural ideal to measure out and adjust temporalities, in what ways do these untranslatable elements open up other layers in their own history?

In reference to López's peculiar form of malling design carried out in only a few years, the urban historian Adrián Gorelik has asserted that the architect was the "author of the real city." He states: "In an infinite number of reports, and above all *in his own words,* the builder of the real city, Juan Carlos López, describes and celebrates an urban world—this new exported product called the Argentinean 'mall'—made of irreconcilable fragments in which precariousness and insecurity are proportionate to the concealed demand for new forms of consumption offered by his *malls*."[31] Juan Carlos López & Associates are crucial to approaching the malling phenomenon in Argentina and beyond, since Gorelik speaks of this import as an "Argentineanized" phenomenon, later exported to the rest of Latin America. In a certain way, the malling phenomenon developed by López generates the need to construct a specialized self-knowledge that the public university did not supply at the time he undertook these conversion projects. As López stated, the architect's studio became a kind of mini-university where knowledge on his own malling style was imparted. On the one hand, the figure of this architect as author of the novel concept for the malled city materializes a series of contradictions that characterize the neomodernizing project of an imaginary for the neoliberal city (as an imaginary of a nonproject or nonuniqueness). However, there are very few studies on López's work in the field of cultural critique, an absence that may have to do with the cynicism with which his architectural career came to be viewed. López was an important figure in the social, militant architecture in the 1970s and later transformed into a crucial figure in the privatization of urban space and the development of private commercial space in the early 1990s.

This shift through different utopian projects—from the revolutionary public sphere to the architectural avant-garde in idealist neoliberal urbanism—is intriguing. I propose to sketch out schematically one part of the malling imaginary as a central figure in a new life and new era. Malls, according to López, filled a void, which he supplemented in his excessive designs with their borderline kitsch aesthetic. He says that the mall ideal arises as a supplement that attempts to compensate for a lack:

> The "mall" appears as a system that tends to replace a lost or inexistent urban rationality, that tends to "make the city" where it literally does not exist for its novelty or incompleteness. After this initial supplement for an inexistent urbanism, I believe the "mall" as a concept offers more than urban life, more than the traditional conditions for streets, public squares, etc. For this reason, the "mall" is probably the urban innovation, the architectural typology, which most radically contributes to the formation of the modern, contemporary city. The "mall" as an idea comes from replacing and completing what the modern utopia cannot for its true inability to "make the city." The "mall" is likewise a great productive revolution. In the United States, it is the second leading rubric in commercial invoices, overall; there are some 35,000 of them, and they employ more than 10 million people.[32]

At the same time, I wish to highlight the problematic justifications offered by the architect, particularly on the malls' centrality to a new way of imagining a communitarian utopia when redefining the public, which his project viewed as spaces of social exchange. An extensive quote from an interview with the architect explains this idea:

> -If it's true, as I believe, that the idea of the mall is seen as an improvement in urban quality, it should surpass its apparent reduction to a commercial center, towards a much broader notion, which is what I call "centers of social exchange" in a course I will begin to teach next year at the FAU [Facultad de Arquitectura y Urbanismo] in Buenos Aires.
> -Would it be a different idea than that of a "consumer center"?
> -Yes. Although the dominant center is consumption, given that its rent is what constitutes the capital disbursement to finance it, today a "mall" offers more than pure or direct alternatives of consumption. It's a kind of walkway that's not necessarily linked to the obligation to buy. . . . With the difference that these centers offer something else, like regulated access, climate control, a specific program of leisure activities, the very spectacle of a kind of much more qualified commercial design, security, the possibility of leaving your car in one place, etc. . . . This has to do with imagining new programs for future uses of the city, programs in which public financing, which has almost disappeared, is replaced, but not their public uses. There would probably be many new alternatives to urban-architectural programs. . . . In a certain sense, architectural freedom only works after having guaranteed the basic question for a solid commercial activity.[33]

The firm's experiments stand out, as López states, for dealing with architectural transformations that involve recycling. In a certain way the figure (not necessarily the person himself) of Juan Carlos López as an architectural brand that began to fascinate developers can be read as a history of transformation of the connection between architecture and historical experience. López knew how to play his cards at this moment, fantasized as the end of a history, by filling the void of dreams with a kind of exuberant theater. The malls come to function as supplements to the ruins of the past, which the new neoliberal configuration came to repair (recycle) in excess. Its malls continue to impress the public for their kitsch aesthetic, excessive ornamentation, and theatrical play between features that occupied a central role in developing its architectural imaginary. The work of malling arises in this context as an acceptance of the culmination of a series of emancipatory experiences and the need to install a form of diversion in this socially projected architectural void. The architect perceived malls as new utopian spaces of social exchange that would resignify the experience of traversing public space.[34]

Staging History Spatially: Malls and the Architectonics of the "End of (Cold War) History"

Even though nearly all the critical writings on the involvement of malls in the urban fabric posits them as playing a key role in defining diagrammatic functions for the new society of consumption, it is highly uncommon for architects to problematize the former city, now transformed. Nor do architects mention the interim period of more than a decade of military state rule, in which urban experience had begun to transform imperceptibly due to the self-imposed control of its citizens. Even if the mall produced and exploited the idea of consumerist space as its foundation, it is only seldom emphasized in certain circles of cultural critique that the mall's proposed diagram (which, of course, fails time and time again) is associated with everyday habits of control and security that have their roots in the dictatorship. In the case of the mall, the idea of the open prison I analyze on different levels (architecture, literature, critical theory) was realized in the literal sense of the security cameras, which the Chilean sociologist Tomás Moulian sees as "the guarantee of always being watched by a Big Eye," promoting a sense of security from the increasing levels of criminality that followed the devastated economy left by the military regimes, further accentuated by the financial restructuring of the state in the postdictatorship era.[35] As self-contained bubbles that attempted to homogenize (make calculable and measurable) a series of unbalanced temporalities under the model of a surveilled freedom corresponding to the moment of transition, the malls operated as spatial markers of a triumphal new time and freedom that were transforming the carceral network. Their proliferation at the inception of the postdictatorial era was therefore symptomatic.[36]

Reading the discussions on malling in architecture magazines with some hindsight, it is noticeable how they associate malls, the end of dictatorship, and the end of history; however, the irony is that malls came to be seen as the fantasy of a classless place where everybody was equal under the aegis of consuming commodities. Both Beatriz Sarlo and Tomás Moulian have emphasized the paradoxical ascription of democratic equality to malls and their role in configuring neoliberal cities in Latin America through an imaginary classless spatiality. It is as though the end of political utopianism (understood within the history of political emancipation) was replaced by an uncritical and apolitical consumerist utopianism in which freedom was constituted by an unquestioned purchasing power, whereas the issue of who had this freedom and why (in relation to the decades of military rule) went unquestioned. The propagation of malls as sites that materialize the promise of freedom and progress can therefore be read as staging the new posthistorical imaginary. In this imaginary, as cultural theorist Gareth Williams has stated: "The social field reproduces itself through unambiguous icons that are designed to fabricate images of common immanence between the global marketplace and all individuals, collectives, traditions, nations, pasts, presents, and futures."[37] If this common immanence goes unquestioned as part of its very constitution, then one way of problematizing it would be to approach and analyze the form in which the contradictions of posthistorical freedom and the market are enacted.

The Chilean philosopher and translator Pablo Oyarzún has proposed an insightful approach to prevailing narratives on the end of history in the postdictatorial realm. In his introduction to translated fragments of Walter Benjamin's *Arcades Project*, particularly the "Convolut N," Oyarzún proposes a critique of how a relationship to the past is established within the context of the end of history, defined as "a general tonality that permeates the discourses in which there is an attempt to measure the relation of our present with history itself. . . . It does not signify, obviously, that nothing else can happen. It means that *all that can happen could be administered*, and, moreover (and this is the administrative postulate par excellence), that it is *administrable beforehand*."[38] This fantasy of the end—what I call the administrative utopia linked to the form of the mall as the spatial embodiment of state architectonics of transition—is based on an equation defined by Oyarzún as the attempt to measure the present (the realm of current phenomena) with history itself. Architects and cultural critics grew to associate the administrative utopia—understood as the ideal of measuring the whole of time and the equivalence between the whole of history and the present, presumably from the neoliberal market (as its endpoint)—with the architectural form of the mall.

Following what Oyarzún called in the early 1990s the tonality of the predominant discourse, I propose to read malls as spaces that functioned as stages for a utopian conversion and adjustment (synchronization) of contentious temporalities into an ideally dehistoricized form of the present of the market, made present within the mall's space. The ideal of conversion that characterized the penitentiary model now acquires a different tone and register. Like the prison, the mall adjusts disjointed temporal forms into the homogeneous time of the same clock, but now in tandem with the ideal of separating the present from all forms of historicity capable of transforming this present. In other words, the posthistorical imaginary envisions a frozen present with no form exterior to, or other than, its own. In this sense, time is divorced from its potential to produce substantive change, for politics becomes an administrative ideal that is detached from transformative ideologies. Thereby the malls not only became the embodiment of the dream of the end of history (a dream I problematize in my analysis of literary texts by examining the role of awakening as a political imagination for other temporalities) but also of the dream of conversion into the new (administration) of time. The key issue to tackle here is how this relation between architecture and discourse constructs the architectonics for a dominant sense of transition to a new present for consumption as well as how the materialization of the ideology of the end of history in these spaces resignified temporal experiences.

Architects' vision of malls as spaces for the end of history made me curious about how certain temporal experiences are materialized in or excluded from dominant architectonics that trace modes of inhabiting a world, a time, or a site. The mall's architectural form and the discursive architectonics of the end of history operate as a stage for the tensions of the transition. Malls are a space of negotiation, a crossroads between different types of pasts (predictatorial histories in relation to revolutionary struggles, dictatorial histories, and prison histories for the recently freed population); the present unsettled by an inability to historicize this past as a past; and the future as a projected site in which differences must hypothetically be united so as not to "miss the train" of history. Within this framework the revolutionary and military past remained equals (following the structure of the Cold War on a narrative level) as two evils from which the society of consumption attempted to distance itself in its very creation, opening up to a new chapter of history.[39]

The mall was, at that moment, a way of imagining the future, the final destination onto which the end of history and the imaginary for a future were projected. As is the case in carceral utopianism, however, total adjustment and synchronization proves impossible. To see how the malls sutured disjointed temporalities belonging to their recent history, I propose analyzing those malls that were not built from the ground up but rather reconstructed. That is, their new structure as a mall was superimposed upon former sites that had once functioned as the very foundation for the disciplinary diagram.[40] In their completed state, a kind of intermediary diagram is created through temporal juxtaposition; the process of malling becomes, literally, a sort of malling of history that stages the tensions between past layers, as though they existed in the architectural unconscious, so to speak. Within this architectural transformation, some of the original structural (past) features were preserved as ornamental elements in the mall, designed to fit the needs of a present that manifests itself as posthistorical, existing in the pure presentism of eternal transactions. For, according to the architects, if the present is to achieve a new time of progress, different layers of the past must be shaped and subsumed (homogenized, domesticated) under the new architectural form and function of the mall, the site for the new measure of social life par excellence.

Punta Carretas's transformation into a mall synthesizes this expressive continuity in which two utopian ideals of containment and vigilance—two historical moments—overlap. The analysis of the architectural transformation of an imaginary that materialized in prisons, which survive today as service-oriented centers, allows me to describe a spatial history of transition. Creating this history from a critical view of its architectonics entails a process that proposes "to make visible or material the ideological systems that structure social spaces."[41] Meanwhile, such analysis also opens up a dual task: if Punta Carretas's renovation shows a staging of a certain spatiotemporal discourse of the transition, the task of criticism is to open up different ways of thinking about history and about how the past has sedimented within the spatial structures of our present. Punta Carretas Mall stands as an exemplary transformation (both architecturally and functionally speaking) for the series of spatiotemporal relations it establishes with the world in which this transformation took place, a singular diagram where prison and mall overlap (prison-mall).

The palimpsest created by the superimposition of these architectonic diagrams creates a temporal reconfiguration of a carceral space of great semantic importance in the 1960s and 1970s, not only as a detention and torture center but also because of the prisoners' collective escape from it—the largest recorded prison break in the world, regarded at the time as an insult to the authoritarian regime. The site's transformation exposes a certain irony, for the deprivation of freedom of the prison was transformed into an area for a secure (protected), more up-to-date freedom achieved by the postdictatorial system: consumption. The crisis of the penal system leading to Punta Carretas's close in 1986 and its reassigned function are interwoven with the history of another prison that was built exclusively for the dictatorship's ends, which would reopen as a system in the regular prison for common prisoners when Punta Carretas was finally closed.

The adjustment of prison to mall in Punta Carretas involves a spatialization of the end of history in the sense that Oyarzún proposes, a transformation of the present that attempted to measure it against history. This idea was expressed, literally, in the words of President Luis Alberto Lacalle at the opening ceremony for the first Disco Hypermarket inside Punta Carretas Mall, in 1994: "This is how Uruguay will be in the year 2000."[42] These words, pronounced onsite from the peculiar form of prison-mall embodied by Punta Carretas, mark the triumphalism of the first half of the 1990s, when consumer society was posed as capable of cleansing the murky waters of dictatorial rule, but they also express an interesting synecdoche. A hypermarket within a mall, grafted onto a model prison, was the part that in 2000 would express a whole (the country). In the prison-mall the national imaginary acquired its new delimitation of the visible and invisible, tracing the mall as the future *made* present, and as a place that (for a good portion of the population) continued to be seen as a prison.

Earlier, when analyzing commercial architecture, I mentioned that there were at least two ways of reading the prison renovations: one is shown by the dialectics of progression in which the past is sublated in a Hegelian fashion—that is, both canceled and preserved. The mall resignified the prison by opening the imaginary of confinement to include the function of consumption, while retaining the dream of security once represented by the prisons as spaces of containment and correction. The way of reading the malls is less clear and it involves looking at the different temporal layers of the architecture of juxtaposition, suspending the ideas of adjustment and/or homogenization to see how certain elements of the prison could talk to another history of the present—the dream of contention and imprisonment of the secured present imposed by the mall on other temporalities. A reading of Punta Carretas through the history of its past and transformation can facilitate another poetic in which the literary afterlife of the prison narrates the collective space of the prisoners. There are two structural reminders in the building of the history of the tunnel out of the mall and the life and escape of the prisoners:

the doors and the clock. The elements of the prison that were preserved in the mall are the doors (*aperturas*) and the time-marker (an old stopped clock at the entrance). Reading these elements, one can create a space in the mall's dream of enclosure by thinking of how to create another poetic of freedom in a different time-zone in which past and present still look like a prison.

Punta Carretas: Prison and Mall

The Punta Carretas Penitentiary opened its cells in 1910 as an integral part of the "group of monumental buildings with which the State endeavored to represent itself."[43] Under the charge of architect Domingo Sanguinetti, the penitentiary embodied a kind of model architecture in Latin America; it was a faithful imitation of Fresnes Prison in France (opened in 1898), a living monument to the Uruguayan state's modernizing plans.[44] As the cultural critic Victoria Ruétalo has argued, Punta Carretas "served as a model for all of Latin America. The vanguard institution was praised for its architectural wonder, which incorporated many aspects from its French archetype, Fresnes, a modern prison system based on the telephone-pole layout."[45] As a model form of penitentiary, Punta Carretas embodied the crucial elements of the modernizing project in its ideal to rehabilitate individuals, which the Uruguayan historian José Pedro Barrán designated as a diagram for an "orthopedics of the pitied"—that is, it abandoned the idea of irreformability embodied in the death penalty in favor of potentially humanitarian punishments capable of converting and domesticating those who were once deemed unruly.

The opening of Punta Carretas in 1905 must be considered in the context of the closing of the Correctional Jail on Miguelete Street (built in 1889) and the abolition of the death penalty (1907), which marked the beginning of another powerful (disciplinary) technique. However, alternative histories of the site mark points of irruption that fissured the ideal of humanitarian punishment. In the early 1930s Punta Carretas was an important center for political prisoners belonging to an international anarchist network that had immigrated to Montevideo from Argentina, Italy, Paraguay, and Spain, often through clandestine operations. The 1931 prison break caused a sensation in the press because it involved a tunnel dug from outside the prison to free Catalan anarchist political prisoners. Miguel Angel Roscigna, of Italian and Argentinean descent, who was one of the most important anarchist figures (and the most wanted in Argentina) active on an international level, carried out a plan to construct a tunnel to the penitentiary from a neighboring house to free his detained comrades. The tunnel extended from "Carbonería 'El buen trato'" run by Gino Gatti, another Italian anarchist seeking refuge in

Montevideo, to the bathrooms at Punta Carretas. The escape was a success, and a photograph of the tunnel was published in the newspapers. Shortly afterward, the fugitives were arrested again, and even Roscigna was captured, as seen by the letters written to his wife and daughter from Punta Carretas.[46] After completing his sentence at Punta Carretas, Roscigna was arrested by Argentina's Federal Police at the doors of the penitentiary and moved to another jail, where the police vowed to kill him. According to family narratives, the detainee was supposedly transferred to different underground detention centers until he finally disappeared in the River Plate, anticipating the fate of thirty thousand disappeared men and women in the most recent military dictatorship in Argentina.

At the end of the 1960s and early 1970s, Punta Carretas was the most important detention center for the country's political prisoners and likewise the site of a record-setting prison break in 1971. In that year 110 prisoners (106 of them Tupamaro political prisoners) left the prison nearly empty, fleeing through a tunnel excavated from within the prison. When excavating their escape tunnel, the prisoners crossed paths with the tunnel that had been excavated by anarchist prisoners some forty years earlier in the break that had been directed by Roscigna in 1931. This encounter forged a unique historical crossroads in the underground layers of the prison, constituting an entirely unknown occurrence until after the military dictatorship ended, since the fugitives had died, disappeared, or had been incarcerated once again. After another minor escape in 1972, the political prisoners held in Punta Carretas were moved en masse to the new military jail project Libertad Penitentiary, which was also an architectural palimpsest of sorts.[47]

After these events, Punta Carretas would be used exclusively to house common prisoners, and Libertad dedicated to confining male political prisoners. The crossing between escape tunnels from political prisoners in the 1930s and 1970s is echoed in another crossroads in official state architectonics. The beginning of the penitentiary crisis in the 1930s produced the blueprints for Libertad as an imported model "rural penal colony" copied from those in fascist Italy, and its unfinished structure became the most important men's jail during the last military dictatorship at another moment of crisis for the penitentiary system. When Punta Carretas was finally closed, it was slated for demolition because it was located in an area with rising property value, but the decision was annulled because of the prison's architectural value. Punta Carretas was transformed into a national site of cultural heritage, a reminder of the (ruinous) monumental fantasy that had helped configure the modern state. Nevertheless, as Ruétalo analyzes, the property was too costly for the state to maintain, since it had inherited an unparalleled fiscal deficit from the dictatorship. Even if the state wanted to conserve Punta Carretas's historical and cultural value, it lacked the economic means to do so, which led to an open bid to reassign a function to the property to rescue and preserve its value as a prison but with a lucrative use.

The bid was won by a project to transform the prison into a model mall financed by a corporation. Its investors included the former minister of interior affairs during the transition (Antonio Marchesano), who was the legal partner to a crucial figure (Julio M. Sanguinetti) in negotiating the transition to democracy with military leaders, thereby becoming the next president during the transitional government. All of this negotiation took place behind the scenes, while national attention was focused on the debate about impunity for military personnel, which was eventually instituted after the 1989 plebiscite. Marked by the rhythm of a campaign that debated how to grapple with crimes against humanity under the dictatorship, the transformation of Punta Carretas Mall was silently being decided in backstage dealings that would allow its new life to be made visible once the decision to grant amnesty to the military had provided the country with erasure and a fresh start.

After his first visit to the architectural site of the Punta Carretas prison, architect López remarked: "I was shocked when I entered the place (prison) for the first time . . . and . . . I saw this three-story building with all the floors leading to a central plaza, and I said to myself: This looks like a mall, a mall of prisoners. And I grasped a very special idea there that I could never forget."[48] The irony here shouldn't be lost: one of the most important specialists on malls in Latin America saw in a prison the very structure of the mall as though it were already part of the architectural form in the prison. Beyond the commentary, we know next to nothing about what the mall customers thought of its past. It is interesting to note that the only comments available are from foreign tourists recommending it because they find the fact that it was a former prison appealing. No protests from former prisoners have taken place in a form other than writing.

The architectural conversion of the site involved transformative work in which different layers of the past architecture had to be shaped and subsumed (homogenized, domesticated) under the mall's new architectural form and function as a site for the new measure of social life. Speaking about the selective demolition and preservation of its features, architect Estela Porada stated: "We tried to preserve the spirit of the prison, but in a way in which this 'preservation' would not be an obstacle to developing its new function."[49] Porada's comment in the context of the site's architectural needs can also be read in relation to the conversion that took place architectonically over time, connecting the turbulent past of the prison to the present of the mall. This quotation makes one wonder what the word "obstacle" would signify in the context of such a highly emotional transformation for the many people who were incarcerated on-site, had close ties with people imprisoned there, or were seen there for the last time before they disappeared. This remark about preserving the spirit of the place without turning it into an obstacle to development shows the relationship established between series of pasts and presents in the prison-mall, appealing to a critical reading that can be perceived in the transformation of those areas that could be an obstacle for the function of consumption. What kind of connection is established between the past quoted by the mall as its spirit? And in what way is this quotation an obstacle, or not, for its new function?

A key word here can be found in the word "spirit," which operates in this site to denote an unsettled form in which the past can be preserved as a memory, in an implicit counterpoint to burying the possibility of the irruption of specters of the past that the former space, as a material ruin, would provoke. Different from the spirit, the specter of the prison would refer to an unpredictability of the apparition or unpredictable return (*revenant*) of the prison's layers that could interrupt or disturb the mall's new function. In other words, the architecture firm's desire to maintain the prison in spirit (in a merely immaterial form) appears to be tied to leaving the prison behind in architectural form without bringing forth the painful, past specters of this site. The prison's past turns into a preservationist form that plays with the present on a site that, architecturally, produces an erasure of the connection between political history and economic policy in which these spaces actively participate and operate as centers of inclusion or exclusion. Implicit in this spirit is the inscription of those who are qualified subjects for consumption, presumed to be a minority segment of the population capable of consuming in this space without citing the prison to be something more than simply a decorative ornament. The architectural theorist Anthony Vidler has expressed a similar tendency in contemporary architecture:

> The apparently irreconcilable demands for the absolute negation of the past and full "restoration" of the past here meet in their inevitable reliance on a language of architectural forms that seem, on the surface at least, to echo already used-up motifs *en abime*. Deployed in this way, the uncanny might regain a political connotation as the very condition of contemporary haunting; what in the sixties was so overtly a presence in theory and practice, a presence that largely denied the formal in architecture in favor of social practice, utopian or material, is now, in the nineties, apparently suppressed by an ostensibly nihilistic and self-gratifying formalism. But the political, I would argue, cannot be so easily eliminated from cultural

practice, and it is precisely the point at which it re-erupts within the very formal techniques of its repression that it takes on the characteristics of the uncanny.[50]

This condenses the essential problem of the transition in architectural terms. How might the architects propose building a mall within the architecture of this (symbolic) prison without either erasing the past structure (as was mostly done decades later in the Paseo del Buen Pastor in Córdoba) or leaving the prison so very present that consumers would simply prefer to go to another mall? The question, which is a question of art and technique or of how to deal with the relationships between space and memory, leads me to consider the status of the historical, and the relationships and syntheses at stake in the mall's success as a paradoxical denial of the past that salvages it. The central idea is that what is maintained is already transformed, determined by its denial. Therefore, denial can be read in the case of Punta Carretas as delicately eliminating a certain experience of historicity from the remodeled prison structure, which exposed raw divisions of power and social class—a disavowal of politics implied by the fact that the mall's spirit already assumes the triumphant perspective of history's victorious agents, those who count as subjects for the shopping transaction. To accomplish this shift to a new site by means of selective erasure, the mall was promoted on television and throughout the city with the slogan: "In Punta Carretas Mall . . . you'll fall in love."[51]

This love, which can be read both as the demand for reconciliation and its encountered other half in the form of a commodity, was based on the need to forget the concealed, tortured bodies of political and common prisoners who were imprisoned in this site not so long ago.[52] In this sense, within the architecture of the new absolute present, the past remained suspended as a quotation, a reference without contents, left as a kind of domesticated prisoner being held as a trophy and a threat. At the same time, the mall's layering suggests another possibility regarding the final part of Vidler's quote, taking us back to López's first uncanny impression: the paradox sustained by the fact that the very space of newfound freedom is the structural equivalent of a new *open* prison. In a repetition that suggests Freud's notion of the *unheimliche* (the uncanny), one looks at the mall, and it resembles the prison that was built as an inauguration of the disciplinary diagram. Read critically, this overlapping not only exposes the shift between different social diagrams and the functions they imply but also questions what is to be understood by "historical" within the new system's paradigmatic façade of global sites: Sheraton Hotels, McDonald's, Blockbuster Video—all enclosed within the bars of a former prison.[53]

The dream of this very peculiar communal form of mall came to work upon the multiple temporalities haunting the place, performing a homogenization that camouflaged the figure of finitude and death, as though the mall now constituted a successful aesthetic surgery upon a nonunified body. Malls became monuments to express the silent contradictions grounding the dream of a posthistorical time, contradictions that still unsettled each mall's past within the total environment of consumption, thereby staging the transformation of the exhaustion of time and history into an object of consumption.[54] Coauthors Fabián Giménez and Alejandro Villagrán expressed this idea at the moment of the malling boom in Montevideo: "The mall is the facelift of the city. . . . A nonplace indifferent to traditions and customs of the city, an abrupt arrest of social temporality. At the mall time comes to a stop . . . the end of history is materialized in these spatiotemporal capsules . . . the realized utopia of neoliberalism! The secret of eternal youth . . . No one gets old, no one dies, stores do not close for mourning, death dies amid the system of objects. . . . The malls become metaphysical objects that are immune to criticism."[55]

The authors emphasize the connection between the mall and its disavowed historical times, as though these spatial capsules had come to stage the dreams of a posthistorical (postfinite) life that leave no room for death.[56] However, a critical analysis of this process will inevitably lead us to the tensions that these sites were concealing as they were created, a moment when dealing with past deaths and disappearances was highly relevant. Here, one can think of cultural theorist Fredric Jameson's proposal of a critical potential of irony in architecture in terms of a way of negating certain actions and systems while seemingly repeating them—the minimal gesture as the "almost imperceptible point" where "replication turns around into negation." In his view "a minimal gesture" is what allows one "to replicate the city fabric, to reproduce its logic, and yet maintain a minimal distance that is called irony and allows you to dissociate yourself ever so slightly."[57]

Reading the Destabilizing Temporalities in the Prison-Mall (What Remains)

How might one read the tensions in the work of the mall-prison between the allegorical meaning of the space as the pinnacle and end of modernizing state projects and the new temporal system governed by consumerism and private users (and companies) of the neoliberal state? The question that arises in the case of Punta Carretas Mall is how irony can create a critical reaction to this site. After all, this irony characteristic of the transformation was made explicit in López's own surprise when visiting the site (the idea of juxtaposing the mall and the prison's original structure). How can one take the mall's citation of the prison, which seems to condense the twentieth century within it, and in turn explore what commercial architecture does *not* achieve? An analysis of the site is rarely undertaken, but the functional and architectural success of the work raise the question of how to approach architecture characterized as preservationist, which is seen as problematic by a large part of postdictatorial literature.

When discussing the transformation of Punta Carretas, architects speak about a dialogue between the past and present, but they never address those areas in which this dialogue gets out of hand. What are the untranslatable or fissured areas in this fantasy of translating the past, packaged purely in terms of earnings? Looking at the transformed prison, one can see that the new architecture's ruinous character seeps through in several remainders of the past: the façade, the two gateway doors at the entrance and inside the interned site, and the gateway through which prisoners were led to their cells. The basic structure of the prison's entrance has remained in the form of bars, the inspection area (today a McDonald's), the façade of the former prison with its old clock and inscription that reads "Administración" (figure 1.1 and 1.2), and the enormous door at the entrance of the cellblocks inside (figure 1.3). Today the basic structure of walkways leading to the main interior patio and the former cells contain shops, food courts, and entertainment complexes. Intriguingly, the doors are the feature that the architects chose to preserve and touch up, creating a series of jarring departures from the mall's ambience. It is as though this passageway between times constituted a transformation that does not fit within the mall framework. The disproportion of the entrance to the cellblocks inside, in relationship to the play area, is now as a central feature of the mall's architecture, surrounded by a peripheral catwalk of the cellblock. Disproportion seems to be one of the forms in which the prison-mall's transformation left a series of questions open on where to allow the prison to begin and end in this past, and where the mall begins and ends in this selective present of the market. It is as though between the spirit of the prison (left undisturbed) and the specter of the prison (as what cannot be dominated or calculated), disproportion appears as a referent to the dead and to the incalculable, impossible erasure of them from this architectural project, rooted in the temporal homogenization of Punta Carretas Mall.

The contrast between the façade with its stopped clock suggesting that time is no longer in motion, the vast door at the prison's entrance, and the mall's interior suggest a reading of the kind of operation established within the carceral form. The tension between inside and outside created by the mall (its side facing the street) is replicated within it. The door to the cellblocks creates a kind of tension with its interior structure; in the middle of this organized totality, we stumble across an enormous gate that does not lead

Figure 1.1. Façade of the former prison with its old clock.

Figure 1.2. "Administración."

Figure 1.3. Entrance of the cellblocks.

visitors to anywhere in particular. This oversized door forms a kind of architectural punctum that is also a reference to the cellblock door, urging one to think about what this door opens onto or closes, what occurs in this passageway that now stands as a silent, extravagant, unbalanced quotation. Where are the cells located? To where does this door lead? The door remains as a reminder, a mute quotation or node from which to visualize excess—a lack of proportion between juxtaposed forms. This monumental remain where the cellblock begins is perhaps the only possible moment of defamiliarization in the new mall because it cannot be readily assimilated (a reminder, an orthopedic member that does not fit within the mall, although it proves essential to its structure), or at least not for those who were prisoners there.[58] This unassimilated feature allows us to read not only this site's past as the history of producing-excluding-regenerating poverty, the law, crime, and politics in the twentieth century, but to question what sense this cellblock door makes in a prison that is now a mall—even in the world of schizophrenic fragments overhauled by the postdictatorial city and its architecture—what Gorelik has called a series patchwork without a dialogue.[59]

Considering the architects' tedious task of selecting and discarding the prison's original features, it seems curious that they chose to leave the doors as the only past referents that would remain nearly unchanged. This point reveals a critical tension that requires a (non-Hegelian) dialectic: (1) the play between all doors as openings and closings; (2) the way in which the remaining doors are restored to their original color, a form of the prison in contrast to colorful fantasy world inside, which powerfully imitates the neoliberal city in miniature and brings it from the "outside in," in a constant dialectic between paleness and color, between entrance and interior turned inside out; and finally (3) the door as a site that confronts visitors with the uncanny element of the prison-mall transformation, which can be read even on an official level as the need to glorify the neoliberal present's compensatory fantasy with its cornucopia of merchandise (an interior of colors, games, shops, lights, the ideal climate cleansed of death).

Likewise, on another critical level, one may read the dialectic tension that problematizes López's essential argument for the architectural play between times, postulated as a play between image and architecture. He states: "It's important to motorize sensations, to work on the user's memory. . . . All of this forms part of the problem of the image in these projects, of how to create stages that guarantee an emotive, memorable impact."[60] Here architecture and image are associated with the user's memory from an image that is theatrically laid out like a stage set. The image here proves highly curious because its size is so disproportionate, raising the question of what determines this memory's contents for the "user" who knows little to nothing about the prison.

The remains of the disguised prison and its fetishized form in the novel structure of a new, colorful mall reveal the impossibility of communication between its parts or series (past-present). At the same time, the fantasy of integrating the prison into the mall shows the neopopulism of the market and the move toward marketing the past. The possibility of connecting this series, of thinking about and questioning modes of citing what can be established, is upheld by cultural and art criticism where literary space offers ways of writing from residue. The question becomes how to read these prison remains without treating them as translatable into the market's drive for more goods and without leaving them empty as a purely evocative sign. In this sense, the idea of taking remains to propose a critical regionalism that ties together architecture and discursivity allows us to think of these residues of the past that cannot be incorporated into the mall. The unassimilable nature of these residues suggests the untranslatability of an idiom that forever posits a peculiar detention in passing between languages, appealing to a kind of relationship between the unique and the universal, which cannot be traced in a transparent way.

Read as idioms, the door, the clock, and the façade require readers to face areas that resist being translated easily (because of their disproportion), while stressing their peculiar role in marking time (the clock) and in opened and closed areas (passages). These elements that cannot be adjusted to their intended use will prove central when analyzing the literary afterlife of Punta Carretas in escape narratives: the problem of misadjusted (or disjointed) temporalities and the question of freedom, explored through what is excluded from the prose in the free world of the mall. The escape narratives suggest ways of thinking about what does not belong to the narrative of freedom embodied by the mall (superimposed upon the prison), which leads me to propose a different way of reading the territory within the architecture of the text itself, from its cracks, foldings, and spaces—in short, they pose a different way of measuring time, one related to the question of flight and the material conditions for another form of freedom.

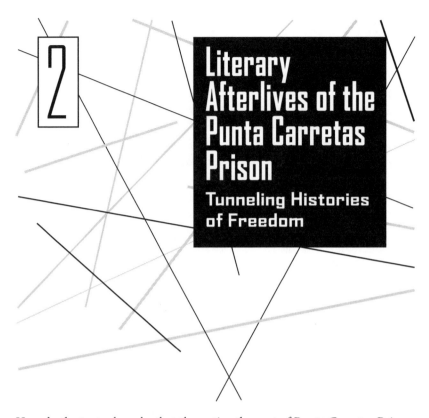

2

Literary Afterlives of the Punta Carretas Prison

Tunneling Histories of Freedom

How do the textual works that thematize the past of Punta Carretas Prison contribute to an understanding of the afterlife of confinement? Moreover, how do they differ from the architectural and critical work on the mall that was analyzed in the previous chapter? It should be noted that the majority of writings on Punta Carretas tend to focus on the site's past as a prison, and on recreating the political prisoners' massive prison break in September 1971, when 111 prisoners (106 of them political prisoners from the Movimiento de Liberación Nacional–Tupamaros [MLN-T]) fled Punta Carretas through a tunnel excavated from inside the prison's walls. Setting a Guinness World Record as one of the largest prison breaks in history, the 1971 escape was one of MLN-T's most disturbing collective actions for the military authorities, since the prisoners showed considerable audacity in building their exit tunnel within the prison walls. The escape was in part a response to the authorities' refusal to negotiate over MLN-T's request for political prisoners to be freed and for an end to the torture and mistreatment of inmates.

Within this context the form of their escape embodied a kind of response in which prisoners found a different means of freedom. The first escape plan from Punta Carretas consisted of a tunnel built from outside, using the city's drainpipe infrastructure. But this attempt failed when a storm flooded the route, dragging the prisoners' tools and plans above ground, where navy officials policing the river discovered them. Even though the discovery was made in the midst of an already forceful wave of military repression, it triggered an even stronger crackdown on civilians, resulting in massive detentions and home arrests throughout the country. There were repercussions in the Punta Carretas prison as well. Political prisoners there were punished for a month, and they responded with a hunger strike that, according to Eleuterio Fernández Huidobro, a former political prisoner and one of the MLN-T's founding members, fueled their ever-growing obsession with escape. They came up with a new plan: to dig holes between the prison cells, creating an interconnected passageway toward the tunnel. Then a final plan was devised in which prisoners themselves excavated a tunnel from within the walls, threatened by a looming deadline for the transfer of detainees to other new detention centers under construction, Isla de Flores and the grim Libertad Penitentiary, which opened in 1972 after a second, albeit minor, escape of MLN-T prisoners from Punta Carretas.

After news of the escape became public, the authorities prohibited journalists from taking pictures of the underground tunnel, thus leaving the prisoners' work forever invisible. This decision can be read as part of a wider process of concealing and silencing the massive escape, a process that would persist until the first narratives of the event began to surface more than a decade later in the mid-1980s. The only existing images of the tunneling are those found in the literature written by the survivors—that is, in a textual afterlife that figures confinement as a tension between the perception of the escape and the possibilities of literary imagination. How does the narrative figuration of this erased episode in the history of political resistance within the prison relate to the possibilities of escaping from a present whose most important utopia is a prison-mall of prisoners-consumers—a present in which free consumers are confined in the mall?

Moving away from the original architecture of confinement, the texts that thematize the collective escape point to the possibility of figuring other temporal images that open the place up to other signifying processes. By doing so, they spatially situate the dominant dreams of cleanliness and social regeneration embodied in the prison and the mall, building other histories of freedom that relate to subalternized histories that had been systematically erased throughout the century. The prison-mall's architectural objective of becoming a symbol of plenitude that might embody the promise of democratic freedom through and for consumption becomes interrupted and critically supplemented by a literary-testimonial field that situates Punta Carretas's new architectural form in textual space. When former prison architecture enters the textual realm from the perspective of political prisoners, we notice a spatial configuration that problematizes the excluded areas of political struggles, past and present, made invisible through the naturalization of a signifying chain in which containment and freedom are tied to the logic of progress and productivity.

The textual afterlife of Punta Carretas constitutes an attempt at writing that points to the conditions of production and reproduction of certain invisible spatiotemporal borders between prison and outside, dictatorship and postdictatorship—a problem crystallized in the image of the open prison suggested by the mall. Literary texts featuring Punta Carretas pose another way of thinking of confinement that denaturalizes the political economy of the mall's borders and subjects—that is, the invisible system of inclusion and exclusion in the surveilled freedom of the market. Can a former political prisoner see the mall as the new dream of postdictatorship freedom? Can a consumer see the former prison in the practice of going shopping? These are questions that literary texts on Punta Carretas problematize by playing with the construction of place and the assumptions made when the words "freedom" and "opening"—central to the transition—are used.

Taking this into account, the narratives of the prison escape prompt us to think of another geography of freedom that can be read in critical tension with the architectural remainders of the prison and the logic of the transition that was analyzed earlier. The figure of the escape tunnels brings to the fore a shift and aperture that differ from the transition's notions of opening. Two possible readings of the afterlife emerge. The first is the obvious mismatch between the dream prison and the forms of resistance that took place from within, the dreams of emancipation that were confined, historically, to a realm of invisibility. In this reading, the remainders of the prison in the mall (all of which are apertures, openings, doors, entrances) are resignified from other angles that privilege the memory of the prisoner and that resist the restrictive democracy offered by the mall. The second reading opens up a temporal imaginary that undermines the transition's idea of opening prisons as signifying freedom by introducing another sense of space-time in both past and present. This is another way of perceiving and reading the prison and the mall that thematizes the failure of the prison to successfully contain prisoners who escaped. By questioning the sense of an "end of history" that the mall was to embody, the escape erodes the architectonic of the transition by introducing another way of signifying this space of neoliberal success.

The afterlife of confinement in the textual inscription of the escape relates historical understanding and the temporalities in which those processes of understanding take place. "Afterlife," following the philosopher Walter Benjamin, refers to the survival of historical understanding within a practice of interpretation that constantly resignifies itself in nonlinear and unpredictable ways. The afterlife of the prison in the mall referred to an ideal of adjustment of time and surveillance that erased historicity in the dream of its end. The textual afterlife of the escape creates another angle of vision through which the notion of the end of history is problematized in other temporal sequences as the writing of the past of one prison (the prison in the early 1970s) is immediately followed by other prisons and times. However, the connection among fragments becomes problematic as the histories of the escape remain episodic and fragmented and therefore without the linearity of a beginning and end of action. Confinement emerges as an eternal hell as well as a space in which the notion of opening acquires a different (finite) meaning. The recurrence of attempts to escape marked the failure of the dream of dissidents' conversion into normalized individuals while also pointing to the failure of reaching a point of absolute escape in the sense of finding a fixed and final sense of emancipated state of freedom.

I use the notion of afterlife to show how prisoners' narratives of confinement and escape question dominant narratives of freedom in the past and the present of the place (the prison and the mall), but now in a textual form, as a problem that concerns the very practice of writing and reading temporalities that exceed the confines of dominant historicization. We approach a textual afterlife of the Punta Carretas prison in terms of a transmission and communicability of subaltern temporalities that remained outside the prose of History—that is, of the possibilities of imagining and re-creating episodic and fragmentary forms of a past that had been lost from any register. Such attempt of re-creation of subaltern temporalities from the prisoner's gaze cannot assume the same sense of place that the notion of containment in the prison and the mall has for the architects and consumers, opening the question of a different relationship between time and place that resists the notion of a homogeneous space and time.

This also affects the very textual space as the afterlife of the prison enters into the gaze of the oppressed (the prisoner) as a problem of language, as the image of the tunneling implies the act of writing a different account of history and place that can only take place *in language*. This account moves in an attempt to escape from the dominant narratives, opening a zone of non-equivalence between the past and present of the place. Here one sees a form of excavation within language that implies the ability of making critical constellations from within but opposed to the confinement and imprisonment as affecting the prison-mall (confinement to freedom of the market is opposed to the figure of the escape). To the dominant image of postdictatorship as a society that opens itself to the free (deregularized) market (in Punta Carretas Mall, the opening of a former prison), the textual afterlife of the place that focuses on the escapes brings another fictionalization of an opposite form of opening from within the prison: the tunneling that spaces the building materials and reflects on them from a place that escapes the surveilling gaze of the prison and the mall. From here, it is perhaps in writing that the early 1990s can counterpose a fragmentary resistance to the closure of the dreams of emancipation with a dual strategy that can work only in a figural sense.

Keeping in mind the relevant return to memory for the 1971 escape within a field that textually rebuilds Punta Carretas's past, one of my first questions is: What problematic constellation does the figure of the collective escape entail if we conceive of it in the context of postdicatorial life where Punta Carretas Mall operates as an emblematic form of the present as an open prison? The question refers to the context of the late 1980s and early 1990s, in which the transformation of the prison and the first writings on its past by political prisoners were produced. This raises a question concerning the idea of escape when the prison is open and turned into the basis upon which another space and form of containment is produced. Approaching postdictatorship society as an open prison critically juxtaposed to the figure of collective escape suggests an interesting image of the present as mall (an expressive architectonics of the freedom of the neoliberal market) and the space of a representational return to remembering, re-creating, or reinventing a violent past that was once again being made invisible (selectively white-washed) for this triumphal work of political architecture.

Writings on Punta Carretas

El abuso, La fuga de Punta Carretas, and *La comisión aspirina* provide narrative accounts of the mass escape in 1971.[1] The first of them, *El abuso,* was hardly distributed, perhaps because of political tensions still surrounding the memory of the MLN-T's actions (the last remaining political prisoners had been freed from Libertad the year before under the Amnesty Act of March 1985). *El abuso* offers a testimony by Brazilian citizen, Antonio Bandera Lima, who had crossed the border into Uruguay to work on the sugarcane harvest. There he came into contact with a group led by then Tupamaro founder and leader Raúl Sendic of the Artigas sugarworkers' union (Unión de Trabajadores Azucareros de Artigas, or UTAA), which would subsequently form part of the MLN-T.[2] While he was a political prisoner in Punta Carretas, Bandera helped excavate the tunnel used for the first mass escape in 1971, and would seek exile in Sweden after the coup, where he would provide several testimonies of his experience. Drawing from newspapers at the time, *El abuso* describes the entire excavation process in detail, stressing repeatedly the prisoners' ability to organize and mobilize within the prison. Bandera's surprise at how 111 people could plan an escape without any of the other (common) prisoners revealing this information—emphasizing the solidarity of the prisoners' networks and the arduous work of words—seems to suggest a certain communality in which prison life figured as a kind of social experiment for what an alternative society could achieve.

The author of *La fuga de Punta Carretas*, Eleuterio Fernández Huidobro, was a boxer and worked in a bank until he became one of the founders of the MLN-T. After the mass escape from Punta Carretas, he was captured again and became one of the nine male political prisoners who were taken hostage by the military dictatorship. Huidobro became a writer after his experience in prison, emerging as one the most prolific writers on this episode in the MLN-T. *La fuga* was published in 1990 and constitutes the most widely circulated narrative on the escape, reissued four times (1991, 1993, 1998, and 2005).[3] The text is located at a crossroads between literary narrative, testimony, and historical recreation, narrating in great detail the process of planning the escape. Its narrative style reflects the codename for the prison break (*abuso,* or "abuse"); the book was aimed at a mass market and includes plans, drawings, and quotations from other writings. This text narrates the mass escape in the greatest detail, particularly within the context of other successful escapes from the women's prison and various other failed attempts.[4] The most widely read and most extensive narrative (nearly four hundred pages), *La fuga de Punta Carretas* was written and published at the very moment when Punta Carretas closed, the Libertad prison had reopened, military impunity was granted by popular vote, and the future plans to open a mall in the former prison were made public. This fact is stated at the outset of the book, turning it into a kind of first textual response to the prison's close and news of the site's future transformation into a mall.

The final narrative on the escape, *La comisión aspirina*, was published in 2007, compelling us to consider how important the event continues to be in rewriting history, as each decade brings with it a new way of questioning the prison break. Written by researcher and journalist Samuel Blixen, *La comisión aspirina* takes its title from the prisoners' committee assigned to planning the escape. This is the first publication to include the prison's history after the escape of 1971, when some former prisoners who had fled were again imprisoned in this site to form part of the last minor prison break from Punta Carretas by the MLN (known as *El gallo* in 1972). The asymmetry between planning the massive project for the first prison break of 111 detainees and the arduous but less epic escape of 1972 reflects some of the progressive decline in organization among the prisoners and rising tensions at a moment when repression had escalated to unimaginable levels.[5]

Blixen's text can be read as part of a history of the MLN that was impossible to write a decade before, in that the qualitative and quantitative inequalities between both escape attempts lay bare an image of the rise and fall of the MLN's Marxist concept of dual power and the beginning of an internal change within the MLN that mirrored the growing militarization of both society and the movement. While Huidobro's writing investigates what would become a poetics of escape at the most critical moment of the transition (the triumph of military impunity, the reopening of Libertad Penitentiary, the neoliberalization of the Frente Amplio), Blixen's text deromanticizes the MLN while appealing to a political contextualization of escape in the MLN's ideology. In this sense, both texts are relevant to the present moment of massive growth of the Movimiento de Participación Popular (MPP), which today holds a parliamentary majority. Nevertheless, Blixen's text was perhaps unimaginable in 1989, when the MLN was still repudiated by the left and the right, and when the theories of dual power of the 1960s and early 1970s had yet to be reexamined. At that moment, the two narratives on the escape by former political prisoners insist on writing about an area of the site's past that remained dually invisible in the figure of the prison-mall: its escape tunnels.

Even if these histories do not cause shock or commotion in the present, for even President José Mujica was among the political prisoners who played a key role in planning the escape, representations of it were still creating some trouble at the time when these narratives were written. They brought back a part of the past that did not refer to political prisoners as depoliticized victims, but insisted on referring to a politics that still constituted a repudiated part of the past at a moment of national reconciliation. Undoubtedly, the question here is to analyze how the representations of the escape evoked another history that had been strategically displaced from the struggle for human rights during the transition (when prisoners were inscribed as human beings, never as militants)—that of the political prisoners who successfully dug a tunnel through an emblematic site synonymous with paralysis and confinement (the prison).[6] In turn, this precluded history stands as a representation of a collective search for freedom. For re-creating the great escape provoked a noteworthy interruption within two fields: in the imaginary of the transition, which was rooted in constructing a national historical prose that justified the country's necessary neoliberalization, and in the prose of the political left and the MLN throughout this process of transformation.[7] Representations of the escapes involved a trial of strength between an everyday prose that conformed to the common sense of the transition as a consumerist ideal, and other narratives that discussed this key space in pre-dictatorship history in which the prison's present was undermined by the escape.

The escape also signaled the peak of the MLN-T's actions and the beginning of its decline. Due in part to the increasing wave of militarization within the movement in reaction to the ultraviolent measures of the repressive state, the big escape can be read as the instant in which the structure of the MLN-T was at its most successful before its decline (it was almost entirely dismantled a year later). Punta Carretas prison plays a relevant role within this history because the MLN-T's founders were imprisoned in it, and the direction and mission of the movement began to change under other leaders working from the outside. The big escape was the peak of the idea of dual power that MLN-T founding member Jorge Zabalza and Samuel Blixen have associated with debates that took place in prison.[8] According to them, dual power proved key to the development of the MLN-T organization until 1972. In historian Clara Aldrighi's interview, Zabalza explains that it was a way of constructing an alternative society, by creating parallel, more equitable institutions than those run by the state.

After the escape the militarization of both the authoritarian state and the MLN involved abandoning the dual power strategy and turning to military confrontation. The big escape from Punta Carretas was the last action in which politics was configured as an experiment of thinking about another escape, one related to dual power as a strategy for engineering an escape *from within* current society. After that, the MLN's policy was increasingly determined by the military state and therefore reduced to resembling the politics it was supposedly confronting. So, taking the big escape as the main focus of the history of Punta Carretas, the last big prison before Libertad's reopening allows us to explore the revelation and figuration of a truncated part of the history of the MLN, an idea of politics as the tunneling of another society, and of freedom as a process of collective tunneling. However, it proves telling that neither Huidobro's *La fuga de Punta Carretas* nor Bandera's *El abuso*— the first two narratives on the escape—use the expression "dual power" even when they are talking about the escape process within the prison that involved collective action that would have been impossible without dual power (coordination on materials, tools, plans, and so on between the inside and outside of the prison).

On another level, it can be said that dual power emerges through the description of life in prison, as a form of exercising and continuing the idea but now from the realm of writing, as if the dual power strategy was expressed and transformed (translated) onto the stage of writing, as a tunneling that takes place in the realm of the figural. In its connection to *trans-latio* and therefore as a form of rearranging the processes of signification, the afterlife of confinement in this chapter concerns the writing of subterranean, subaltern histories. An analysis of the textual afterlives of the prison turned into a mall poses a parallel task of interpretation, as the form of a dual (counter) power that imagines a society with different elements and materials than the existing ones, an act of tunneling that takes place, now, within the realm of historicization, dramatizing the complexity of constituting and inserting subaltern histories (temporalities and affects lost for History) within the space of writing.

Using the prison-mall as the place that came to signify and embody the dream of the end of history in the early 1990s, I suggest that the textual afterlife of the confinement written by former prisoners problematizes the historicization of Punta Carretas, raising other notions and imageries of freedom. When thematized in written form, dual power involves figuring out how to construct a parallel (fragmentary) history of Punta Carretas that interrupts the myth of progress of capital with the image of a conflict between the progress as a dream (the dominant version) or a nightmare from which the tunneling attempts to wake up. However, such re-creation of history can only take place in figural language, as the very content of the narration, its place, has remained underground. This complicates the practice of writing and the notion of confinement, as the prisoners attempt to insert a series of stories and images formerly confined to an invisible zone into the historical and literary realm. In this sense the analysis of the most important narration of the escape, *La fuga*, dramatizes discontinuity and interruption, as if the figure of the tunnel itself constituted a dialectical image in which subaltern temporalities could be expressed as a montage of episodic tunnelings to freedom, all trapped, like the text itself, in the confines of capital accumulation.

Huidobro's Escape Narrative

The fact that there is no existing analysis that takes writings on the escape seriously highlights an omission by critics that continues to the present day. The task I propose to delineate here is how these writings on key enclosed spaces for those who were imprisoned or silenced can turn into places from which we as readers can rethink the reconfiguration of postdictatorship sensibility. In the narratives of Punta Carretas as a prison, I am interested in exploring the possibility of reading heterogeneous spaces and times as different proposals for re-creating emancipatory and revolutionary histories, in the peculiar theatricality of books that make us think of what kind of escape can take place in the tunnel created between the practice of writing and reading. While the architecture of the transition and its global pretensions attempted to configure a homogenization and adjustment of times, with its history narrated spatially and discursively from the present in such a way that all citizens could inhabit the same page with a simple erasure and fresh start, the complex and heterogeneous narrative representations that shed light on the escape offer an intriguing commentary on what this new space and time excluded from its margins.

Huidobro's *La fuga* is the narrative that most emphasizes a crucial figure for my analysis: the moment in 1971 when prisoners excavating their escape tunnel ran into another tunnel dug by anarchists who had attempted a similar operation from the same prison in 1931. Even though all three narratives mention this discovery, Huidobro's writing emphasizes this moment the most. The image of the crossing of escape plans is reiterated throughout the work, creating a kind of poetics of encounter, an underground museum, a peculiar language in the history of the oppressed. Unbeknownst to the prisoners, their accidental encounter constructs an invisible crossroads of history. Excluded from narrative history and its hegemonic spaces of distributed visibility, this crossing of invisible escape routes from two significant political moments (the 1930s and 1970s) can only be told now, in *La fuga* (1990) as a textual space whose breakthrough awaits to be read. The author's repetition of this crossroads creates a layering of erased temporalities, which are tied to the repetition of different cycles and forms of violence. The poetics of encounter leads us to grapple with the complexity of the text's composition—its use of heterogeneous materials (plans, maps, and quotes) to configure the underground museum, evoking a multiplicity of affects and memories that resist becoming homogenized or subsumed by the site's whitewashing as a symbol of the new post-transition era.

The cultural theorist Jens Andermann has proposed reading the museum in Latin American history as a "theater of sovereignty" that demonstrates the link between the state and the accumulation of capital, tracing an optical game and temporal experience that loads the field of historicization proposed by state narratives.[9] If all museums entail some act of capture, a question worth asking about these underground histories is: Can we differentiate between the capture produced by the state narrative and this underground museum traced by the escape? The escape story involves (hi)storicizing parts of the past that were not easily accepted by right or left, parts of history that were like outcasts (imprisoned) in the realm of historical narration (anarchists in the 1930s, Tupamaros in the 1970s). This leads to a consideration of different forms of historicity that involve spatial, temporal, and optical configurations of what remained outside the prose of the state's history. Can they constitute a sub-optics or micro-optics that by inscribing what was left out from language and visibility might open up a different mode of narrating that does not reproduce the state's logic of inevitable progress as the accumulation of capital?

This line of inquiry might call into question the representations of transitional architecture that were central to the market and the museum: catalogs, citability, display, series. I am concerned with areas or tropes where the museum creates a spatial text in *La fuga* and how they are differentiated from the hegemonic state model that made it invisible. To what extent does it avoid repeating the gesture that had denied it a place in history? How might memories of an erased past (open promises) be articulated without reducing them to the reiterative mania for monumentalizing the past that characterizes the architecture of the transition, which took Punta Carretas Mall as one of its first experiments in historical recycling and earning capital gains from consumption in the cultural heritage/tourist site/mall? How might this strategy avoid falling into a mere glorification of the past that ends up turning the site into a museum, thereby seizing control of it in the same way the mall's architecture appropriated and controlled (whitewashed) the past? My reading of Huidobro's text emphasizes how the writing of the escape tends to dramatize and repeat the notion of flight as a process of distancing from the model of an unchangeable present that Punta Carretas Mall performs as prison while simultaneously reinserting formerly unrepresented histories. Narrative style itself becomes a form of reflection on the past it attempts to re-create. The peculiarity of Huidobro's narrative (and therefore my interest in choosing this text for my analysis) lies in the role played by its quotation of other escapes at other historical moments of totalitarianism, thus making the narration of this particular escape one that extends to other spatiotemporal zones that emerge in this textual site for the first time. In this light the analysis of the narrative staging (configuration-literarization) of the escape turns into an added search for ways of expressing and dramatizing the kind of spacing this representation constituted two decades later.

It allows readers to approach the text with a question that turns the historical act of constructing the escape route into a problem for the narrative itself as a performance of another kind of escape—one that now draws from language and architecture, the museum and prison, in the omitted, invisible, or illegible areas of history. Huidobro's key narrative on the escape bears with it all of time in a field that confuses the act of reading space, modes of learning to read architecture (a necessary matter for the prisoners' survival), and modes of reading histories that are created with an almost mad, encyclopedic zeal. At the crux of this interwoven texture lies a peculiar museum rendered invisible by successive waves of repression throughout the twentieth century, a museum that could only irrupt as a figurative image within the unique space of writing. Thus the underground museum of lost histories recreated by the text is one that cannot be seen but read in figural form.

La fuga begins by invoking a direct reference to the time in which it was written. The introduction refers to the figure of an empty prison, a void that uncannily repeats the transfer of political prisoners that had taken place in 1972, when Libertad prison was opened, indirectly synthesizing the process of "re-" democratization to problematize this "re-" in reference to reading return and repetition: "As we write this book, the Penitentiary is empty, about to transform—by demolition—into one of this country's most valuable areas."[10] Later, the author states: "For prisoners, the wall is the end of the world. That is where the horizon and the world available to them ends."[11] These are two temporal markers that configure the text's introduction: Punta Carretas as an empty prison that will be reassigned a new function, and the image of a wall that lends itself to different interpretations when reading. The wall is a membrane that separates the free world from the prison and a conceptualization of history in the moment of writing this text, when the Berlin Wall fell, triggering a fantasy for the end of history that had marked the free world and its other in the pantomime of communism since the Cold War. It is not by chance that the narrative begins with the word-space of the wall, given that it refers to a spatial figure connoting the border that separates the prison from the world happening outside, while it likewise alludes to a temporal imaginary for a unified world at that time in the image of a universal consumer society without alternatives.

The wall and the penitentiary's evacuation situate the narrative temporality in the first two chapters of *La fuga* as a counterpoint between past and present. The first chapter refers to the late 1960s, telling the story of the narrator's own confinement in the penitentiary. The second chapter refers to the present in which the text is narrated (1989). The time that triggers this new narrative on the escape is marked not only by Punta Carretas's close and conversion and the capitalization of the Punta Carretas neighborhood, but also by the event that goes unnamed in the text, which nevertheless proves fundamental—the reopening of Libertad Penitentiary, accompanied by the popular vote approving military impunity.[12] "Libertad" is a subtext that plays off echoes of two temporal series: the narrative past, which mentions the rumors circulating among prisoners of a high-security prison being built to which all political prisoners would be transferred (which did occur in 1972), and the present, where the emptiness or void of Punta Carretas refers to the various transfers of inmates that caused Libertad Penitentiary to reopen as a regular prison.

A brief history of the different temporal and spatial layers that compose Libertad will give the reader a better idea of the relevance of the figure of an "empty" Punta Carretas at the beginning of Huidobro's text. Libertad Penitentiary was a carceral dream dating back to 1934. It was the project of police chief Juan Carlos Gómez who, under the supervision of the General Direction of Penal Institutes, mapped out his initial idea to create an "Agricultural Industry Penal Colony," later called a "Labor Education Colony." This plan attempted to implement a new type of jail capable of resolving the alleged overcrowding in city prisons.[13] It involved a project for a prison-city that would be comprised of a Penitentiary Colony, a Corrections School for Misfits, and a Criminal Mental Ward.[14] As lawyer Gonzalo Fernández has asserted, the project was modeled on detention centers in fascist Italy, as well as on prison reformer John Howard's ideas on correctional labor (the workhouse). Two main principles emphasized by Fernández are the isolation of the city-prison from the community (to make it *invisible*) and the creation of a colonial system with forced labor that made the plan "a true penal concentration camp."[15] The carceral utopia constructed a micro-city of the prison, a "prison city" in which, as the Uruguayan critic Alfredo Alzugarat has explained, there was room for:

> correction schools for misfits and a Criminal Mental Ward . . . correction or solitary confinement cells, a central observation tower with searchlights and sirens, watchtowers on the periphery, a special guard corp, or its alternative, an outfit of Army commanders, specially trained police dogs, an electric fence around its perimeter, landing strips and special piping to pump tear gas into different areas. It would also have a hospital, a gym, its own morgue and an endless number of additional constructions in what could become a true "prison city" or, as Dr. Gonzalo D. Fernández prefers to call it, a *stalag* denying any humanitarian aim and only missing the crematorium ovens.[16]

The military dictatorship would later reactivate this notion of a penal colony conceived as a substitute for the real city in a concentration-camp dream.

Construction began on the "Agricultural Industry Penal Colony" (later Libertad Penitentiary) in 1937 in the Department of San José, but the project was temporarily suspended a number of times. As Fernández explains, the penal colony was conceived as part of the politics of the Gabriel Terra dictatorship (1933–1938), to serve "the needs for repression through a new Penal

Code—approved behind closed doors in 1934 and inspired by the Musso-lini's fascist code in 1931—a text that still remains in place today. Or rather, it was multiplied by decreeing deportations, incarcerations of political oppo-nents, some highly publicized extrajudicial executions, attempting to apply a response unleashed by democratic forces."[17] As construction efforts recom-menced in 1940, 1942, and 1957, the project created a school (the only part that was ever fully operational) and three stories of a cellblock. These constituted the foundations upon which military personnel in the 1970s took up the proj-ect to build a maximum-security prison used exclusively for political prison-ers. Superimposed upon this dream of a concentration camp in the 1930s was thus the dream of building a dictatorial prison in the 1970s. According to two former political prisoners, Walter Phillipps-Treby and Jorge Tiscornia: "For the dynamics of the building's construction, which took some thirty-seven years to complete from beginning to end, you could see the traces from dif-ferent eras of construction in its finishing, maybe ruled with lines from as-signing different resources to different building sites. In many details you could also see their haste to finish it, around 1972, when the country had al-ready lived through several years of crisis."[18]

Once again, the relationship between the 1930s, the 1970s, and the 1980s, which would also be essential in the history of Punta Carretas, brings up a map of uncanny repetitions and quotations, since we are faced with different moments of crisis in the ability to contain deviance (dissidence) in the proj-ects of constitutional reform that allowed the police-military apparatus to act on the prisoners with impunity. All of this was visible at once in the build-ings that these prison projects created in their successes and failures.[19] The Terra dictatorship's dream in ruins was shown by "embryonic buildings," the "stumps of an extravagant prison utopia condemned to remain incom-plete," upon which another sweeping dream for control was superimposed in the 1970s.[20] In this dream the military personnel hastily concluded its con-struction with a new municipal plan that took the already built structure and completed its architecture to found a new military dictatorship. Inscribed with the motto "Aquí se viene a cumplir" (Here, one comes to serve), Liber-tad opened its new structure in September 1972 with five floors of cellblocks (five hundred cells of 3.6 by 2.4 meters and 3 meters high), holding male po-litical prisoners, a majority of them relocated from Punta Carretas. Although this plan was inherited from the 1930s, the prison's lack of contact with the floor, because of ninety-six elevated pillars separating the ground and prison floor, suggests an intent to forestall the creation of escape tunnels, stemming from Punta Carretas's failure as a model prison after the successful escape of its political prisoners.[21] In Libertad the escape attempt, or the possibility of one, would have to take on other forms, since the prison from its outset had been constructed intentionally to disorient prisoners and drive them mad.

The few texts addressing the prisoners' experience in Libertad stress the disorientation induced by the prison's structure. Carlos Liscano, a political prisoner who became a writer in jail, remembers that he never could understand its layout. This point was later confirmed as part of the military's plan. Phillipps-Treby and Tiscornia remember that two years before the end of the dictatorship (May 28, 1982), the prison authorities distributed a detailed description of how the site was organized to the prisoners, a majority of whom had lived there for more than a decade. It began with the prison's location ("The establishment is located fifty-three kilometers from Montevideo") and ended with a report and map classifying the imprisoned population according to their spatial location: "The most dangerous inmates (murderers—ideologues—leaders on a core executive level—column heads—inmates strongly prone to violence) are housed on the Second Floor of the Cellblock."[22]

Undoubtedly, this report on classified space, the conditions for detention and the human material housed in each part of the prison constituted a kind of synthesis of the multiple modes in which language and architecture operated in Libertad Penitentiary.[23] In this sense, the impossibility of locating one's coordinates on the site was a constitutive part of a long-term strategy for disorienting the imprisoned population.[24] Together with the women's prison Punta Rieles, also in the process of being reopened, Libertad was one of the architectural spaces most tied to the Uruguayan civic-military dictatorship. When the last of the dictatorship's prisoners were freed (granted amnesty) in March 1985, the prison remained marked by its closure, involving a kind of culmination to the dictatorial process.[25] Libertad was vacated as a "symbol of horror from the dictatorship, as a reminder, which was open to the press to testify to the community the level of dungeons used to hide political prisoners. At that time, no one imagined any other destiny than to let it rot in the sun."[26]

It came as a surprise that the decision to shut down Punta Carretas Prison in the democratic era was accompanied by the idea of reopening Libertad—that is, that the inaugural moment of redemocratization reiterated a series of crucial acts taken at the beginning of the official dictatorship. Just as in 1972, the prisoners were moved en masse from Punta Carretas to Libertad, which despite its design for the dictatorship's ends (conceived as a plan to destroy its political prisoners), now became a jail for common prisoners. This created a new palimpsest in which the fascist dream of the 1930s and the military dream of the 1970s overlapped and were fully naturalized in the democratic era. Along these lines, Gonzalo Fernández reads the reopening process as an instance that marked the "democratic recycling of Libertad" as "civil refounding of the Penitentiary" whereby "if the military government rescues the Libertad Penitentiary project from long-forgotten shelves, the democratic government will institutionalize it."[27] Suddenly Libertad was full once again, now with common prisoners. The increase of criminalized poverty combined with a peculiar palimpsest of authoritarian dreams from dictatorships and their unique afterlife in democracy, to map out an architectonics of impunity; this impunity would be confirmed in two plebiscites on the Law of Caducity of the Punitive Claim of the State (in the years 1987 and 2009).[28]

The repetition of these acts in the late 1980s—that is, at the beginning of the so-called post-transition (postrestoration of democracy)—traces an architectonics of impunity that a report by the Uruguayan Service of Peace and Justice (SERPAJ) described as unimaginable: "With the restoration of democracy, it was almost unthinkable that it (Libertad) would come back to life. Nevertheless, in 1986 there was an uprising in Punta Carretas Prison, which served as an argument to relocate all prisoners from this establishment to Libertad Penitentiary. In the blink of an eye, almost without noticing, the Penitentiary came back to life."[29] Reestablishing in democracy a site that represented systematic torture, a site name *Libertad* ("freedom") was an event closely tied to Punta Carretas, the symbolic site of resistance against authoritarianism in the prisoners' escape attempts. This circumstance urges us in turn to reconsider the fabric of the transitional process as continuity between dictatorship and democracy for their systems of control and punishment of bodies. Libertad's reopening as a prison and the prison as a mall entail a certain uncanniness that defined an entire political, affective, and historical circuit among socially meaningful spaces in direct connection with the dictatorial past.

In this context the figure of escape in *La fuga* acquires the form of a question, particularly with regard to seeking another kind of freedom through writing. Taking architectural space as its point of departure, it opens up an issue that was crucial to the process of democratization (as a transaction) on other levels: How is freedom connected to the experience of different buried (irrecoverable) temporalities that the text attempts to recreate? Repetitions arise visibly as naturalized processes in the spatial, temporal, and narrative underground as spaces for escape whose narratives remain outside the syntax and prose of national history as unprocessed remains belonging to a marginal horizon. The first level of repetition between Punta Carretas Prison-Mall and Libertad Penitentiary duplicates itself—by the text's reiteration of collective escape attempts in which the 1971 tunnel accidentally bored into the one from 1931—in a dialectic tension with another kind of historical repetition that took place in the prison's underground foundations. What repeats itself is the very attempt at escaping. If the visible grammar was the circuit of the two prisons, the text composing the underground foundations of space and history brought with them a circuit that shares in common the collective escape in different, heterogeneous times. Signaling a present danger, the narrative of escape creates a space in this present through a peculiar image of freedom as a (collective) process that must be worked at (tunneling/writing); the space created by drilling the tunnels brought with it a counter-effect, a way of seeing the world above ground as a new prison and wall for free men.

Reading and Writing (Hi)stories, within the Walls

The narrator of Huidobro's text *La fuga de Punta Carretas* was not a writer before he was imprisoned. The case is one of many in which decades spent in prison end up producing a writer. This point seems relevant, since writing and the prison arise in the textual fabric as coimplicated elements, establishing relationships between written words and the surrounding architectural space to which we generally do not give much consideration. In the process of becoming a writer through his experience in prison, the author and his writing are affected by a peculiar perception of space and time, which becomes dislocated because of confinement (the time of the prison sentence, the daily routine, the endless waiting). The prisoner's deprivation of free movement in space (restrained by regulations, limitations) affects the mode in which his words are penned, transforming them into a place unto themselves in the radical limitation of experiences and subject materials.[30]

In this sense, words operate as a strange kind of theater that enacts the author's resistance to his confinement through the use of his imagination. The lack of material objects and novelty begin to affect his use of language; he develops an entirely different relationship to objects when so few resources are available to him. Texts written from prison tend to emphasize this point of opening up to language and constructing it as a site that supplements prison writing and is simultaneously coimplicated within it. That a majority of prisoners express some interest in writing while in prison (whether by memory or on paper) reveals a need to invent worlds in order to survive the brutal reduction of routine experience in confinement. Even the possibility of reimagining (recalling) and inventing these worlds in prison constitutes an act of freedom in its attempt to supplement the monotony and determinism of the prison sentence, which over time makes life seem like mechanical repetition without novelty, time without freedom.[31]

The complex relations that spatiality, temporality, and language acquire within the prison words (worlds) are crucial to Huidobro's narrative on the escape. Decades later, his writing attempts to express how this prison had systematically remained outside historical narratives. From 1910 to 1986 there are no existing narratives from the incarcerated population that address the political past of Uruguay's most important prison, which fuels the need to tell this history in Huidobro's own monumental work. Nevertheless, its insertion into historical narrative constitutes a problem, given that his writing addresses a vast underground layer of subaltern histories that were lost or made invisible by the textual architectonics of hegemonic prose. The relevance of the first narratives on the 1971 escape, penned by Bandera and Huidobro (even though Bandera's text has hardly been in circulation until today), converge at a critical point for what would become a growing interest in writing and imagining prison life, not only under dictatorship but throughout the century. The crucial encounter with the tunnel dug by anarchists, hidden below the prison floor since 1931, fostered growing interest in an area of history that had always remained outside History. These narratives urge us to reflect on the relationships between language, confinement, temporality, and the peculiar kind of space and action implied in the escape as a literary figuration and in the reinventive process of narrating the past.

The chapter titled "El Muro" (The wall) begins by differentiating modes of reading incarcerated space from two specific perspectives and languages—that of the architect and that of the prisoner: "It is impossible for me to describe the prison without *emotion*. One thing is the science of the architect and another one, that of the prisoner. *Let's try to enter the stones through the flesh*."[32] The text begins to configure this examination of the site's terrain, reconstructed from the prisoner's memory, as a descriptive tour taken by the former prisoners. In it, they travel through the prison's interiors, reproducing oral legends from the history of escape attempts. The oral tradition maintained inside the prison is now reproduced in counterpoint in which each spatial element contains a particular legend. Nevertheless, as we readers are told these different stories by common prisoners (those responsible for keeping the oral tradition alive within this space), a textual distortion arises when the narrative reaches the anarchists' escape attempt in 1931 and the recreation of the oral tradition is abruptly supplanted by a quotation from printed media.

This creates a series of changes not only concerning the aforementioned differentiation between the science of the architect (posed as a language of stones) and the gaze of the prisoners (reading the territory in which their lives take place in flesh), but also regarding a now internal differentiation within the prison population. The leap that takes place in the description of the territory as seen and told by prisoners opens up a gap between the escapes of so-called common prisoners and the political ones. This difference, that retroactively produces a turn of the narration toward itself, poses a shift from myth or legend (the oral tradition within the walls) to the authority of the printed word (the voice that comes from the newspaper). At this point, the narrator clarifies that the anarchist prison break was the site's most important legend. Yet instead of continuing with a free indirect discourse, the history communicated by former prisoners produces an abrupt rupture in the narrative sequence with the insertion, without prior warning, of an extensive quotation from an article from the conservative weekly newspaper *Búsqueda*, published in Montevideo in 1989.[33]

The article describes in detail the very little information known about the anarchists' escape attempt. What seems strange, aside from describing the anarchist tunnel, is the fact that the newspaper article included information on the 1971 escape attempt narrated by *La fuga*. This temporal loop not only destabilizes the sequential narrative of this history—an order established at the outset of the narrator's description of prison space in oral histories—but it also destabilizes linear chronology. Suddenly we jump from 1970 to 1989, the moment when the escape that the book attempts to describe is narrated, but from another voice. This prolepsis arising together with the first appearance of the anarchist tunnel is an interesting narrative gesture, given that it creates the first in a series of many interruptions arising within the text each time the anarchist tunnel is mentioned. It is significant that each time the narrator brings the 1931 tunnel into the story, the narrative sequence is temporally and discursively disrupted: when the anarchist tunnel appears, the reasoning of the prose is interrupted and a quote appears, referring readers to yet another text. It is as though the arrival of this other time (1931 in the time of 1971, which is narrated in 1989) simultaneously produces a disruption in narrative style, where together with the suspended temporal sequence, the stylistic echo of other voices and texts emerges.[34] The first interruption mentioning the previous escape attempt is introduced as a press quote from 1989; the second interruption introduces a quotation from Bandera Lima that, when describing the encounter between two escape routes, quotes yet another text left by the diggers themselves in the crossroads between both tunnels. It is as though this encounter in material space emerges within the very fabric of textuality as an insistent mixture of times frequently reiterated by the text. It does so by using quotation as a strategy of interruption that suspends the narrative in a scene, opening up a montage between times and textual voices as a stage for different narratives.

The fifth chapter of the book, "Los anarquistas" (The anarchists), is devoted entirely to the prisoners' discovery of the 1931 tunnel. However, the first part of the narrative focuses on describing the nervous tension felt by prisoners at the moment they make their discovery. At this point they had excavated more than seventeen-and-a-half meters of the tunnel, stirring anxieties that their plan might fail, although it seemed their efforts might prove successful. After expressing the tensions pervading prison life, and their fear of reaching a dead end when they encountered a stone while digging, the narrator begins to talk about another concept of freedom provoked by a peculiar scene. The prisoners who were on guard from their cells (while the rest were digging the tunnel underground) witnessed the release of a very old prisoner in the middle of the night, a man who had served a sentence of forty-five years: "It was during one of those nights, or rather in the early morning of Friday the 27th, that while we were on guard, we could see from the cells closest to the main entrance a silent and nevertheless great event in prison life: the freeing of Enano after completing his long sentence. . . . The slow elapse of a long time, but also the absolute, routine tranquility of the prison, remained shaped in that tremendous scene. El Enano, dressed up and smiling, was leaving after forty-five years there. . . . In silence."[35]

This silent exit, which would resonate pages later with another kind of exit from the contemporary prison to this prisoner's own life (the anarchist escape), creates a time parallel with ways of reading (viewing) architecture (for the architect and the prisoner). As a reader, one immediately senses that this scene appears out of context. It turns out, however, that this seemingly dislocated reference serves as a preamble to finding the anarchist tunnel because the released elderly man had been incarcerated in the prison when the legendary anarchists made their escape attempt. Temporally speaking, the narrative suggests different layers of time that have in common the idea of escape, emerging in double time—prison and civilian time—a time that is always being split, spatialized, encoded within the prisoner's sentence. In the first sentence of the quotation, we find two kinds of temporalities: an excessive or immeasurable time (which refers to the affect connected to a time that is not measured by historical prose) and another, measurable time (the time of the clock and calendar).

The latter is undefined in relation to chronological measurement and the former is quantifiable: "during one of those nights." The "slow elapse of a long time" would seem to involve a time tied to an affect that cannot be measured by clocks. And yet precision arises with the narrator's mention of a calendar date (Friday the 27), which is duplicated in the prison routine (repetition), suggesting a precise, calculable notion of time. This duplication between times and spaces proposed by a form of measurable geometry (clock, blueprint) and what remains incommensurable to this quantification (affect) operate as a prolepsis of narrative framing that will be crucial to encountering the unforeseen crossing between tunnels.

From the opaque figure of the elderly prisoner being released from prison in the upper visible level, the readers are taken to the following day's events in the underground, when a problem emerges while excavating the tunnel: "The drill kept going by itself to the earth, taking two hands with it toward a cable that seemed to have no end. Toward a unique void. . . . The fear for the unknown had reached the tunnel . . . the drill kept crumbling big blocks of earth behind, where there began to emerge an empty darkness, sand, a void."[36] This void that emerges, unforeseen by the so-called Engineer when he planned and measured the tunnel, provokes panic in the prisoners, since they immediately believe they have found a high voltage cable that could foil their escape. However, the designated Engineer goes down to the tunnel and discovers that they have crossed a tunnel excavated forty years earlier by anarchists for their 1931 escape. The tunnel remained intact because authorities simply sealed the entrance and exit with concrete, filling the tunnel with sand that had since shifted and settled. At this moment the narrative acquires an intensified affective tone associated with having encountered a kind of message from the past.

The prisoners interpreted this find as a gesture of support arriving at a moment of anguish and tension provoked by the fear that their work had been in vain. Every day closer to their escape, there was a heightened fear of failure. The narrative comments:

> We had found the anarchist tunnel! It was a formidable coincidence! It was unforeseen. . . . The mysterious pipes that had frightened us so much were nothing other than ventilation ducts very similar to our own, and the electric wires used for lighting by those deeply felt, distant and yet close comrades forty years ago. . . . *We had made a historic find. We were in a museum. And we couldn't tell the world.* When we finally cleared away the sand from that warm tunnel, we could see in its archways and neat walls, the traces, *still fresh*, of their tools. *They seemed to speak.* To convey a *fraternal* message to those who could have been their *grandsons*: "we too, brothers, we too." . . . We could count on those walls polished by the work of time, the solidarity and patience of the anarchists' blows, one by one. . . . *The eternal struggle for freedom, the same fight, the valiant headstrong language of the oppressed from yesterday and today, were crossing by the force of destiny*, below the concrete floors, at the exit of a prison. *Without knowing it, we had built a corner of history.* They escaped down that path. We would escape down this other path. . . . We had advanced twenty me-

ters and seventy centimeters in our tunnel, but it could be said that we were thrown back to a "time" coordinate in 1931.[37]

This plays with two temporalities and spaces referring to an underground terrain that remains outside the prose of History (as the narrative of a dominant history of freedom) and that subsists (insists) on a new time, now in the form of a memory in a text written nearly twenty years after the encounter (during a time of other forms of imprisonment). We can see that the former duality of space and time (architecture, clock) becomes part of a chain of correlations that configure a spectral museum.

The text passes from the incalculable and unforeseen elements in the escape plan to traces of the past that turn into a peculiar form of speech, to which the narrator refers as a kind of spectral voice speaking from the traces on these damp walls. This textual moment offers a unique way of reading space from the prisoners' gaze, producing a kind of tunnel within the tunnel (or escape within the escape plan) is produced, translated textually as a form of listening. The marks left on the stone in this space turn into voices since "they seemed to speak" ("*parecían hablar*"), linking spatiality and temporality. By saying "to speak" instead of assuming the form of a written text, the narrative seems to create a spectral form within this very space, as if the tunnel were a ghost configured as past voices that say something in a curious language established between the living and the dead. Their ability to convey a message transforms this passing utterance (an empty message that the narrator endows with meaning) into an overstated "we" that immediately connotes the fraternity ("brothers") and a family genealogy constructed in this underground space (grandfather-grandchildren).

This family genealogy immediately bears a kind of legacy transformed discursively into the notion of an underground museum of searches for freedom. This associative leap posits a question regarding what kind of museum could possibly be a tunnel—or what kind of museum could possibly be the act of excavating a tunnel. After all, the text proposes an image of a museum that refers to creating a passageway rather than to providing an area of contemplation of a fixed, ordered display or series of collections that create histories. Nevertheless, this encounter between tunnels occurs in passing and involves a construction we could associate, in architectural terms, with scaffolding. For a time during the tunnel's construction, the remains of the former tunnel, which the authorities did not eliminate entirely, served as necessary scaffolding for the prisoners to continue digging, a passageway that opens up to a kind of architecture and a curious museum that resists museification as embalming.

The Underground Corner of History

An escape tunnel is a passageway or temporary construction in that it can never be appropriated as housing, and yet it proves essential to the act of escaping. On a conceptual level the tunnel in *La fuga* involves a deterritorialization that is reterritorialized in the narrative by a connection to other processes of deterritorialization that figuratively create a museum in textual space. But instead of provoking an embalmed perception of what it displays, this image of the museum generates a question concerning escape—a line of flight that connects to other histories. In this sense it is not underground, but in the book itself where this peculiar collection of histories is constructed, raising the question of how one can imagine a museum of histories of the oppressed, a museum of subaltern histories. More than a museum, it appears as a process, a passage, a point of encounter that will only ever be visible in the form of a text that reaches its readers two decades after the prisoners' find. At the moment in which the image of this crossing (museum) takes place within the textual space of *La fuga* as a multiplicity, the narrative urges us to rethink modes of grappling with this peculiar form of museum that would be crucial, decades later, to redefining urban spaces for memory and political historicization in the literary field.

It is from and within this narrative, which invents an underground genealogy for this impossible, anachronous conversation between prisoners in two times, that the text is disturbed by an irreducible element. Every mention of the encounter between tunnels makes the text go mad, so to speak, by introducing other voices that reiterate, as a question, the figure of this underground corner of history. Similarly, inscribing the encounter in language appeals to a nondiscursive space-time that the narrator must construct with that which remains outside the historical narrative in both 1971 and 1989 (remains of other languages that supplement the impossible, irrecoverable remains of tunnels below the prison-mall). In this way the museum, impossible to see, is configured as a lingua franca for what would remain outside spoken language, transforming the text itself into a site in which the figure of the museum irrupts from language, which can only ever be read and seen within textual figuration. In other words, only in the 1989 text is this language able to appear as a language, and the invisible, underground site in which the encounter was produced is now the very book we read—as though this collapse between disparate temporalities (discovering 1931 in 1971) led to the need to repeat this encounter in 1989 as a gesture of escape within textuality in which the image is fixed, curiously interrupting the main thrust of the narrative sequence.

What this living museum of specters provokes by interpellating the narrator and the reader is a vision of the prison of a present in which the fraternal genealogy (which clearly connotes an emancipatory-revolutionary tradition) was in crisis. By introducing the notion of fraternity, the text continues to inscribe itself within the limitations of that same tradition: brothers, fraternity, genealogy—all components of a political concept in which the figure of a nonassimilable or dissimilar other (the sister? the common prisoner?) is excluded from the map of history. This points toward the part of the tunnel, in my reading, that the tunnel could not yet penetrate from a political standpoint that remains inscribed within the ontology of an unquestioned patriarch. If the spectral museum provokes an interpellation of the narrator and reader, to question who constitute the prisoners in the mall's present, one would need to note the kind of genealogy limiting this crossroads, a traditional male genealogy between brothers in the language of fraternity.

The questions that remain with respect to these escapes urge us to examine the ties that arise repeatedly in this spectral body of work to a figure that does not reach the text: the possibility for another genealogy, where *sister* could interrupt the continuity emerging when the discontinuous is turned into language in the fraternal museum. This does not entail bringing a sister into the picture as an essence to counteract the fraternity expressed in the tunnel, but it opens up our practice of reading to the question of what would be the dissymmetric parts of the tunnel that those tunnels had not yet excavated due to a political ideology still inscribed within the ontology of an unquestioned patriarchy. At the same time, if one keeps the idea of tunneling as scaffolding rather than a more permanent structure, one can also see this moment of building a tradition and genealogy textually as precarious and transient as well. This fraternity that reinscribes a familial system of hierarchies and lineages (in the world of the so-called oppressed of yesterday *and* today—the 1970s and the 1990s) can also be seen as the desire for a democracy that could tunnel toward other forms of politics. This is, of course, my own way of reading this singular underground terrain as a mode of tunneling the world of fraternity with the one that it has systematically left out (the nonfraternal other of the brotherhood).

In order to avoid a dichotomization that would now put the sister as a similar other that is omitted, I am interested in the interruptions that emerge within this interruption in the text and the traces of an insistence on certain nonassimilable parts of history that create a textual tunneling to the present of a state of unfreedom that asks, figuratively, for other forms of tunneling. Going back to the long quote from *La fuga* (cited earlier in this chapter), we can say that the tunnel created from the book is what creates a fraternal language, which seems to operate in reconstructing these histories as a bridge (tunnel) between the tunnels excavated by different oppressed generations. As a tunnel, it is an improper language in which freedom is not an obtainable property but a process that the text itself replicates when digging the tunnel. As architectural theorist Mark Wigley states regarding the figure of the house, if what we need to see by reading architecture is not the literal figure, but the discursive effect of this figure with respect to tradition, here we can say that this reading possesses a certain unique performativity. It allows us to see a connection between the art of making minor architecture (building the tunnel) and that of translating the tunnel into the language of an underground history omitted from the prose of dominant history.

Thus this work on the tunnel as an underground exit for the prison appears, in the book published in 1990, as a work of tunneling that no longer operates in the prison architecture itself but in the discursive architectonics of a historical prose whose freedom did not include those subjects who inhabited it on a discursive level, in the underground of visibility. This would be the mode in which the corner of history enters into History for the first time. Nevertheless, this act of inscription entails a struggle within a discursive territory, for it must avoid having the (textual, discursive) reterritorialization of residual elements from the history of escape (deterritorializations) fall into the dominant logic that embalms (or confines, like the prison) these struggles as part of the past. How can the text avoid reiterating this history of escape in the form of a museum for finished (embalmed) histories, to which the text responds at the moment of its publication, at the impossible end of revolutionary histories (that the book itself enacts by introducing the figure of the escape)?

The tunnel represents another side of Enlightenment ideals implied by the prison model—freedom's other, invisible dark side, as Foucault mentions, or its invisible double negative. The museum of specters in 1989 (the time when the text was written) undoubtedly refers to 1971 as a specter that returns in the form of a reminder and a remainder: an appeal to justice that was newly delegated and erased with the triumph of impunity (military immunity for crimes against humanity) granted on a constitutional level, which went hand in hand with the reopening of Libertad Penitentiary and the spatial and architectural conversion of Punta Carretas into a mall. Arising in the struggle for freedom that the tunnel represents, we therefore arrive at the property of these expropriated features, constituted by not being (expropriation) in history's narrative or in the space of the visible as livable. As an act of inscription that problematizes the possibility of reading that which cannot be seen within the prose of an architectural freedom (posed by the mall and the reopening of Freedom Penitentiary), the language of fraternity emerging in Huidobro's act of reading the traces of the past (the anarchist tunnel) as a fraternal genealogy links to the question that the philosopher Jacques Derrida poses: "What does fraternity still name when it has no relationship to birth, death, the father, the mother, sons and brothers?"[38] This "still" is maybe the question that the tunnels bring to the present of injustice. This is something that the text does not deal with in a direct fashion, but it is a question that traverses the realm of the inhabitable underground of tunneling, where architecture is not connected to a form of housing. This foregrounds the problem of a constitutive outside that the figure of the tunnel expresses, an outside whose human correlate is the prisoner (the outcast who is relegated to the zone of the noninhabitable).

It is as though the escape's form of inhabitance refers to a language that operates as a tunnel between modes of thinking about freedom outside the domain of property—freedom as a passage that is "made," but as a kind of making that arises in words in 1989 as a book that tells the story of those who do not tell it (*contar*)—in Spanish, to tell (or *contar*) the (hi)story of those who do not count (*que no cuentan*). This is a peculiar form of performative communication that opens up language to a form of passage. The verb "to tell" (*contar*) is another tunnel, tied to the series elaborated throughout the text as an excavation: to tell a history (or storytelling) whereby the act of telling forges its legend, to tell the story in the sense of tallying or accounting, counting the anarchists' blows to the bedrock, the work that would later be erased and yet remains in the tunnel. This facilitates a reading of what constitutes the language of the oppressed as an erased work, later to tell an underground history to History, since the escape involves those who do not tell this story as historical subjects (the ones who do not count as subjects of freedom—the prisoners of Libertad, the prison).

Within this layering that unites history and historicity, as a minor literary language, the complex, textual fabric contains multiple threads, urging readers to denaturalize the narrative of progress once posed as the norm that erased the violence that founded the new prisons (Libertad and the Mall). The narrative *La fuga* is produced at the moment when a new continuity (progression) in the administration of violence is produced and tested, thereby naturalizing the transitional architecture's attempt to domesticate past violence and the violence taking place in the present. The obsessive reiteration of the encounter between escape tunnels from 1931 and 1971 seems to suggest or evoke a mode of aperture that signaled the incompleteness of the very form it attempted to close. It attempts to counterpose a reading of the place that could bring about another realm of temporality—one that was incommensurable with the new structure of freedom. This creates another temporal schematic that structures *La fuga* in the form of a work punctuated by different escape attempts from prison, thus problematizing in the present in which the writing was taking place in the world of unfreedom that the consuming paradise attempted to deprive of visibility. Seen from this perspective, the narrative's unfinished character suggests a precarious construction of images that evokes the Benjaminian calendar of a discontinuous time from this narrative space of (minor) history to the new meganarrative of neoliberal modernization. The emergence of the tunnels involves a kind of discontinuity that interrupts the textual sequence, inserting spaces forever marked by the arrival of other voices (quotes) that supplement the void left by an entire heterogeneous sum of lives and lost histories. With this interruption and supplementation, the text stages the impossible work of trying to read what could not have been written.

Citing the Escape(s): Underground (Hi)stories and Minor Epic

Crossing of tunnels becomes a form of citation of a past, an interruption that comes from other times. In his book *One-Way Street,* Benjamin figured citation as an assault that suspended movement in the road, the spatial interruption of other voices. It seems fitting to ask: What kind of action is entailed by the textual interruption of the encounter with the 1931 tunnel into the text's primary action? How does the interruption coming from the past of the past allow us to think differently about the kind of museum configured in the text? How does the image of this crossroads between tunnels and histories function as a common language for stories that inhabit the underground of history? These questions prove central, since they show how this impossible museum in the language of *La fuga* is something more than a merely factual narrative; it involves what the cultural theorist Nelly Richard has called the poetics of escape, the possibility of reading escape narratives as being something other than mere political pamphlets.[39] The poetics of flight leads me to question other ways of configuring historicity from a past that, until *La fuga*, was like the tunnels—a language that resisted being turned into History but that invites us to think about the incommensurability provoked by this resistance.

In a certain way, the idea of tracing a minor epic—one that has been crossed or struck out (minor epic)—invokes a reading that continues to maintain the idea of an epic (as a form of configuring the history of the escapes as deeds of an epic dimension). Yet, following cultural theorist Gayatri Chakravorty Spivak, one could say that this could be read in a "strategically essentialist" manner, urging us to maintain critical distance from the danger of erasing these erased histories yet again through a monumental essential-ization. A minor ~~epic~~ register implies the insistence on building a history of past actions that rescues areas of the past that had always remained outside the different narrative frameworks of history. However, because these histo-ries and actions refer to places that were aimed at containing and controlling outcasts (in order to exclude them from what lay outside the walls), the act of inscription immediately becomes an area of struggle. Like the scaffolding or the impossible and invisible subterranean museum, the way the story of the escape is reconfigured implies an aporia because it attempts to fixate the past in the form of a (hi)storicization, but the form itself seems to resist, again and again, History as the narrative of the state (the prose of progress). It is a figure that assembles a form of passage (tunneling) and interruption (arrest). In-stead of being constructed in the form of a master narrative of the state or the political left, it deals with a register of minor occurrences in the Deleuzian-Guattarinian sense of a minor use of language and greater genre, "that which a minority constructs within a major language," understood here as the cre-ation of deterritorializing coefficients to open up signifying chains that were presumably closed, fossilized in the naturalization of a need to induce prog-ress and selective forgetting.[40] As such, bringing the escape route to the lan-guage of history evokes a deterritorializing instance of what the majority history of the neoliberal state attempted to resignify as inevitable progress.

Minor ~~epic~~ differs in various ways from the use of *testimonio* as a tool of political struggle in the sense posed by cultural theorist John Beverly in his definition "On Testimonio." In the texts analyzed here there is a political struggle that is trying to find its style (to be written), but the difference lies in the fact that minor ~~epic~~ keeps insisting on the necessity of figuring and rethinking the political as the configuration of a collective subject in a less programmatic sense than that seen in paradigmatic testimonial experiences like those of Rigoberta Menchú or Domitila Barrios. In the escape narratives studied here, there is an insistence on the collective as a political group strug-gling but in a moment in which the very sense of that collectivity has been lost. Those texts work in different ways, however, as a process of thinking the political, of inscribing certain unwritten shreds of political history in a lan-guage that would perform something other than just reconstructing a failed past. Deleuze and Guattari's theory of the innate connection of the minor use of language within a major one is relevant because there is a search for a collective to come, one that needs to avoid merely reproducing former hierar-chical binarizations and falling into an "attempt at symbolic reterritorializa-tion based in archeypes."[41]

I propose minor ~~epic~~ as the attempt to deterritorialize this loss of the political by means of a search within that which can be illuminated (reconfigured, re-created) within the past as a promise. This is what I emphasize by the function of the barred epic (~~epic~~) because it makes the reader immediately think about the process of reconfiguration of past actions as a form of constitution and destitution, an inscription of deeds that come from a place that differs from the typical epic accounts (imperial or state organic forms of historicization) while attempting to create a historicization of marginalized deeds that were systematically relegated to a zone of invisibility.[42] By spacing the signifying chain of an epic of progress entailed by the architecture of Punta Carretas as different ideals of progress and accumulation (modern and neoliberal states), *La fuga* deterritorializes hegemonic prose and places us, along with the tunnels, within a terrain of residue from other histories violently truncated (barred) to make this progress possible. In this sense, added to the naturalization of violence exerted by the logic of continuous progress, these remains of past struggles for freedom likewise involve, in the escape route, a kind of minor language as a performance that the prisoners bring with them in their inability to be indifferent to these spaces constructed from more than a decade of prior experience.

This leads to another characteristic of minor literature, which I connect with Benjamin's ways of reading Brechtian epic (redefining an emancipatory performance in art) and the kind of spatiality it involves. For one of the most striking gestures in Benjamin's reading is the way he poses a differentiation between Brecht and Aristotle's epic in terms of spatial description. He states: "Brecht opposes his epic theatre to the theatre which is dramatic in the narrow sense and whose theory was formulated by Aristotle. This is why Brecht introduces the dramaturgy of his theatre as a 'non-Aristotelian' one, *just as Riemann introduced a non-Euclidean geometry.* This analogy should make it clear that what we have here is not a competitive relationship between the forms of drama in question. Mathematician Bernhard Riemann refused the axiom of parallels; what Brecht refuses is Aristotelian catharsis, the purging of the emotions through identification with the destiny which rules the hero's life."[43] Benjamin distinguishes here between two different ways of configuring action (drama) in relation to the ways of conceiving space that are at stake.

As the cultural theorist Samuel Weber has stated, it is relevant to note that Benjamin is confronting Aristotle on two issues: the sense of drama as "conflicted, but ultimately unified and meaningful *action*" and also the notion of episodic plot that Aristotle only accepts if it "do[es] not compromise the unity of action."[44] In both cases (organic) action refers to a space that appears to be homogeneous and indifferent to the situation that is staged in it;

that is, both imply a sense of space as containment that reproduces an organic, unified, coherent form of action. Euclidean surface is, for Benjamin, a space based on the function of assimilation (what in my reading refers, clearly, to the prison ideal to contain and assimilate deviant forms of behavior). In the case of the Riemannian surface, however, space becomes a taking-place, an aftereffect of interruption that makes the situation appear like a place that emerges within the space of action. Instead of a homogeneous space in which action happens, organically, without interruption, place becomes connected to the very situation taking place, its circumstance. As in prison writing, action and space cannot be indifferent to each other; they cannot be simply equated either, for this would imply another form of assimilation that Benjamin criticizes.

Minor epic can be thought of as a form of narration in which interruption (instead of a homogeneous, unified action) is emphasized in a way that connects place and nonassimilable residual stories that cannot follow the idea of a progressive, coherent narration. Now, in the case of the escape narrative from Punta Carretas, interruption appears within the narrative flow as the reiterated arrival of the anarchist tunnel that produces a break in the main action every time it appears. It interrupts the narrator, opening up a fold that destabilizes the temporality of events, as if it were posing in a theatrical way the very problem of inscription of subaltern histories, described by Gramsci as always "fragmented and episodic."[45] Weber states that the pre-Riemannian, Euclidean condition of Aristotelian catharsis is a concept of space (as Benjamin writes of time in his text on history) as homogeneous and empty. Brechtian space (as described as Riemannian) is "neither empty nor homogeneous, neither infinite nor unbounded. It constitutes a singularly heterogeneous medium, a curved Riemannian space defined and punctuated by those interruptions of continuity."[46]

I would go further and argue that this emergence of place through the series of interruptions provoked by the encounter between times and spaces works like an interruption of Action in the grand epic sense, while still being posed in tension to it as a different form of action. What the minor epic would bring about is an interruption that takes place within the narration of an epic and that reveals the times and places that Epic needs to erase in order to exist (the areas of invisibility that would imply conditions of impossibility) without simply opposing epic to nonepic, action to nonaction. The question is: What kind of action does interruption entail in the configuration of space? As interruptions of a homogeneous discourse of State History, minor epic becomes a reflection on the complicated passage from actions that were made invisible (excluded) from their narration in a way that would demonstrate the multiple and irreducible temporal modes that constitute history. Whereas the Epic emerges as a stabilizing voice and temporal horizon in the history of the Western canon, the minor ~~epic~~ involves an appropriation that aims at a potential transformation to express something about the conditions of constructing history and literature.

In the case of Huidobro's text, one can read a double gesture in which there is both a desire to inscribe the grand event within an epic of the political left (at a moment in which the MLN was rejected from it) and a permanent form of interruption that takes place within textual space in the form of an arrival of other voices that compose an impossible unity of time (a nonhomogeneous temporality). The quotation that interrupts the author's voice reveals an instance of the oppression that composes the history of the prison and the different attempts to escape from its form of confinement.

Tunneling and the Impossible Museum

Benjamin emphasizes that in Brechtian epic the task is "to represent conditions," taking "represent" in the sense of an uncovering produced by interruption: "This uncovering (making strange, or alienating) of conditions is brought about by processes being interrupted."[47] If the tunnel performs something as a struggle for freedom that encodes political modes of questioning expropriation, the text would seem to perform its own takeover of genre, something that I read as the interruption of Action in a double sense as the epic of leftist heroes or the epic of state narration, without merely appealing to a total reconciliation or withdrawal from action. Within this context the punctuation of *La fuga* that is carried out by means of an insistent interruption brought about by the arrival of other temporalities (other tunnels) urges us to question the ambiguous area in the crossing between tunnels as a parallel to thinking as a form of crossing among different underground historicizations and literarizations in such a way that they distort the continuity of the dominant prose of history. At the same time, the minor character of the epic—in the Benjaminian sense, a history that denaturalizes the continuity of progress that systematically attempted to erase its own act of violence—furthermore runs the risk of falling into a mere romanticization of the evoked past. Romanticization would be a mode of catharsis, a way of inserting a period or an end; however, the spatial trajectory of the text points to the reopening of Libertad as a continuation of a realm of unfreedom that the architectural superposition of Punta Carretas camouflages in its peculiar form of opening.

The image of the crossing between tunnels shows how the writing style is marked by prison experience and how this affects narrative space itself, burrowing through it as a kind of (minor) history-tunnel. We could even say that this minor use of language—used to trace an entire area of erased histories that remember the prison escape—irrupts into the domain of the visible (sayable) of transitional architecture, bringing with it dislocated images of remains from other times, attempted escape routes. The images are dialectical insofar as they arise as a crossing of dislocated temporalities that create a tension between that which we cannot see in the mall—but which nevertheless is its coimplicated exterior, its erased and yet possible condition (violence, massacre, destruction)—and that which marks what would have been its condition of impossibility (escape, suspension of its impossible coherence, and so on). The images irrupt into the narrative, bearing with them what we cannot see, the inferno buried beneath the mall in a past and present of destroyed bodies (factories producing merchandise; past and present prisoners; the disappeared, mutilated bodies) and with this, the impossibility of reinscribing what is expelled from the major language as excrement and potential labor for the mall's success.

The narrative's recourse to images and a nearly encyclopedic accumulation of heterogeneous materials makes the text a peculiar, impossible museum for the remains of a political past that raises the problem (staged in the text) of how a book can become a site for a unique collection of repudiated and repressed matter by different prose styles comprising hegemonic history. The images and multiplicity of materials construct the text, postulating a kind of counter optics that attempt to recuperate, in the Benjaminian sense, what never was. This multiplicity constructs the idea of a text-space that equates to a museum but naturally implies what the museum made invisible as an ever-accumulative system of the state. This generates a greater textual drama seen in the writing style, which appears to act out the role of one who collects impossible emancipatory histories that the text attempts to reimagine; these histories urge readers to think about the kind of spatiality, temporality, and visuality implied by the countermuseum in its minor features.

In Huidobro's text the narrated story deals with a historicization, and yet from the beginning, it points to the impossibility of inscribing history within this site without bringing with it the prisoners' gazes. It is as though all language were the site of a struggle between the disciplinary apparatus that configures space and text (prison) and the interruption produced by the escape attempt. What emerges within the narration is a counterpoint between the prose of a major History to which the place refers in its architectural palimpsest (model prison and mall) and the act of inscription that *La fuga* implies or performs. The prisoner's act of reading and writing creates a different configuration of the place that attempts to construct its narrative from areas that aim to bring about the zones that are concealed by the mall.

Collectivity and Escape

Deleuze and Guattari say that for major language, space is an indifferent backdrop. For minor literature, space is always overpopulated with elements that make each action transform into a collective one in which there is no private space for the individual.[48] Yet, to what larger collective might the 1989 text refer? Perhaps the question of this collective, of the tunnel's extension toward an impossible escape, is what the permanent connection between temporal series poses as an interrogative.[49] In the figure of a "corner of history," temporality lacks a progressive, homogeneous linearity (there are divergent times before and after the tunnels cross each other) as well as a seemingly homogeneous space (that would integrate both tunnels). The spatial figure of a corner suggests an encounter but also a separation reminiscent of the figure analyzed earlier at the outset of the chapter "The Anarchists," which postulated two temporal series (civilian time measured by the prison sentence and the alternative time of the escape). In what kind of space can this inscription of a corner of history take place? The corner (built space) of history (temporality within a narration) seems to represent another kind of spatial surface that involves, simultaneously, another kind of temporality.

The emphasis lies on a difference (two paths, two senses of the political) that only shares the space of one word: *freedom*, which operates as the place in which the common becomes nonequivalent. The fraternity of brothers digging underground tunnels reaches a form of disjunction in the corner because it is narrated as a point where roads meet and part ways (histories, projects, fates): "Without knowing it, we had built a corner of history. They escaped down that path. We will escape down this other path. . . . We had advanced twenty meters and seventy centimeters in our tunnel, but it could be said that we were thrown back to a 'time' coordinate in 1931."[50] The crossing and separation of the (spatiotemporal) paths is expressed through an impossible site in which the prisoners' advance (20.7 meters) simultaneously implies a temporal return.

The encounter reveals another temporal layer in which the time of freedom relates to an incommensurability among times and paths as well as to chronological time (they advanced twenty meters and seventy centimeters while they were also thrown back to another time). The circumstance creates at once an encounter and a separation that interrupts the homogeneous, romanticized gaze of the oppressed while maintaining its precedence in the intensely described crossing between tunnels with an affect that does not belong to any political program; rather, it belongs to a unique language in the search for freedom, for its uniqueness rests on the impossibility of sharing the same space and time. In this sense, the crossroads as intensely affective moment for the prisoners in the text stages a way of sharing the incommensurable between different political projects that may urge readers to think about an area of subaltern affect—the singular mode of cornering in which a common language could make sense. Affect and language seem to operate in the narrative like a corner in which there is something inexpressible that the narrator associates with a search for freedom. The narrator repeats that the emotion he felt is impossible to communicate, but he immediately searches for a language that would express it, thus building in language (naming) *the corner* in which he traces a genealogy of diggers.

The persistent reappearance of this corner destabilizes the text's continuity, however, as if there were an insistence on bringing to light the incommensurable convergence between the affect involved in this impossible space of encounter (a site that is forever lost) and the language that emerges, always immediately, in an attempt to create a history. The text attempts to inscribe its singularity within an impossible continuity—one that I read as an anxiety about the present of the inscription of *La fuga de Punta Carretas* itself, or about the impossibility of conceiving that the underground image of fraternity would emerge, once again, in the present of 1989. The incommensurability between temporalities then becomes a kind of revelation (flashback) that returns, again and again, to the textual configuration of this place (the Prison of Punta Carretas) like a repressed element that the narrator wishes to recast in a present that was once again erasing the past through disavowal and censorship in the wake of dictatorship. However, this censorship is a form that the text itself seems to be reenacting by silencing certain key words that were essential to the very possibility of escape, such as dual power.

In the escape narrative, the moment that evokes the nontranslatable affect is immediately followed by a divergence of escape paths, where the 1931 tunnel is used for the escape but is not proposed as its model. Instead of drawing from the anarchist tunnel as a model to be followed (as a preexisting path), readers are told that the prisoners chose to continue excavating their route in another direction (a divergence), rather than using the anarchist tunnel as an area to store their tools. This would be another characteristic of the minor epic that opens up to a kind of unique underground museum of subaltern histories of or searches for freedom. It postulates another relationship to the exhibited object in a way that does not merely urge readers to contemplate it. Instead, it functions as another mode of interruption for what could be read as the romanticized figure of the crossroads between tunnels as a complete historical unity. To the divergence of paths following the encounter, the narrator adds a proposed way of connecting them for readers as the finite temporality of these escape attempts. Each escape attempt marks its past, finite, dated character within its specific political context (the impossibility of being a model for another era). Furthermore, the text posits the escape attempt as a promise, as an impossible freedom, forever yet to come but never having been. For this reason, invoking the surprise encounter in 1971 that interrupts the textual present (as an open past) with the 1931 escape (dead but also alive), this interruption seems to insist on this gesture of spacing times and spaces, disrupting the notion of a present closed unto itself. In this sense the text points to 1989 in a silent fashion, as if the question were how to translate its missing history (1972–1988)—from the date of the escape to the moment when the narrator remembers it.

The cultural theorist Gareth Williams has proposed thinking about subaltern affect from the notion of a crossroads between truncated temporalities that nevertheless urge us to establish new critical viewpoints, "with the past, and with the devastated affective residues of that past in the present, that would require a completely new relation between reflection and the historical formation of the social order; that would require, in other words, a new theoretical telos from which to think of the political histories of subaltern affect."[51] This is something crucial in the attempt to write a history of Punta Carretas from a different place that would not replicate the gaze of the architect, but that would question the limitations that these past forms of tunneling have in another present (the dated character of the escapes configured here). Returning for a moment to the difference posed between the science of the architect and the prison seen from the eyes of the prisoner at the beginning of the text, it is important to recall the word Huidobro uses to mark this difference: flesh. "It is impossible for me to describe the prison without emotion," he writes. "One thing is the science of the architect and another one, that of the prisoner. Let's try to enter the stones through the flesh."[52]

Interestingly enough, the flesh that is opposed here to the science of the architect who organizes the space to affect and administer the life of the prisoner's body reemerges after the first encounter with the anarchist tunnel. The narrator's discourse is interrupted by another voice that deromanticizes the emotion of the encounter with an image of the excavators' deteriorating bodies in the 1971 tunnel. It is as though the narrator had become an architect of sorts, trying to build a poetics of escape, which seems to forget the prisoners' physical deterioration while digging the tunnel. I argue that in the end of the chapter "The Anarchists," the (im)possible perspective of the nonarchitect prisoner (Huidobro could be seen as the architect of the MLN-T, a historic founder) is interrupted by the arrival of a quotation by Bandera Lima, a sugarcane worker and a foreigner, like many of the anarchists digging the tunnel in the 1930s. The appearance of this quote crystallizes the ambivalence that traverses the text as it both idealizes the past escape and avoids idealizing that political past as closed or perfect (self-sufficient). Following the deromanticization of the crossroads between tunnels (their divergence) comes a different form of interruption that emphasizes the prisoners' labors and bodily strain when burrowing their escape route: excrement.

This appears in the text after the underground crossroads (the escape that unexpectedly arrives at another escape), when there is another unanticipated turn, now from a testimonial by one of the 1971 tunnel's diggers, Bandera Lima, in his work *El abuso*. As mentioned earlier, Bandera was one of many Brazilian laborers who crossed the border into Uruguay to work in the sugarcane fields, living in absolutely miserable conditions. There he joined the MLN-T and ended up a prisoner in Punta Carretas, participating in the escape as one of the workers who dug the tunnel. The arrival of a quotation from Bandera's writing interrupts the poetic moment of the encounter between tunnels in *La fuga* and play an important role; it introduces the figure of the worker from another region, Brazil, which reiterates the continuous migration in search of survival (another territorial geography that is mapped by the figure of dispossession and the limits of the national borders). It also refers back to the anarchists who were largely foreigners fleeing persecution (Miguel Angel Roscigna was from Argentina, Gino Gatti from Italy, the prisoners from Spain).

This displacement, which hosts a deterritorialization in the figure of people who make it into *La fuga*'s narrative, becomes even more complex when the quotation from Bandera's text emerges as another crossroads that interrupts Huidobro's own poetics. It points to the origins of the MLN-T in the northern part of the country (Bella Union, Artigas), where the UTAA (Unión de Trabajadores Azucareros de Artigas) was founded to advocate for the legalization of the immigrant workers who had no labor rights, on a border where labor laws did not apply (no working hours, no contract, no rights). Bandera's quotation interrupts the poetics of the encounter by introducing a graphic image of the deterioration of bodies digging the tunnel. Tunneling emerges at the outset as arduous work that takes time. Yet the emergence of this other, minor narrative on the escape brings with it another meddlesome time, in this case a less emotional or idealized one, in reference to the lack of oxygen in the underground space and its repercussions on the excavators' bodies (intense headaches, diarrhea, and so on).

Whereas the space of the tunnels attempts to constitute a transhistorical language in the struggle for freedom, this romanticization is dispelled by the smell of shit when the excavators cannot reach the surface in time to take care of their bodily needs. This introduces another aspect of minor poetics that is crucial to prison life—the time of the body and, in this case, the time lag for the body caused by the working conditions when tunneling make it impossible to attend to bodily functions. In an interruption that introduces the scatological to the text, the question that arises once again is that of inhabitability. Here we see bodies fatigued by intense labor and working conditions, which begin to affect their health:

> A comrade had a bad case of diarrhea but didn't want to stop working. . . . And one day things got so tight that when he was scraping down there, he knew he couldn't hold it in. He dropped his tool and left at a quick pace, but when he came halfway down the path there was no other option.[53]
>
> When he got up there, *it was already too late.* We asked him, "What happened?"
>
> "Quit fucking with me! *I just shit myself.*"
>
> Of course, when we saw how he came down the tunnel, we cracked up laughing. It was our turn for the night shift. Believe me! In that tunnel there was a smell you couldn't stand, and that's when we didn't laugh anymore. We laughed at him, and we had to stand the smell for several hours.[54]

In this passage time plays in another manner, referring to the lapse between the tunnel and the body—the delay that leaves shit as its final image in the chapter titled "The Anarchists"—but from a voice quoted from one digger's memory, which now operates as a textual interruption. This quotation interrupting the poetics of the crossing between tunnels, now in the form of a deteriorated body (work), would seem to operate as a textual reminder that resists transforming the account into a romanticized poetics of escape by humorously configuring the harshest part of its logistics: working in an area without fresh air, which made the prisoners violently ill. The sugarcane worker's voice (in the underground) arises in this quotation in reference to the tedious work of digging the tunnel with human labor despite ill effects on the body (asphyxia, diarrhea, and so on).

This quotation, which interrupts the poetics of the anarchist encounter with another kind of countertime, now created from the visceral experience of mining the tunnel, would seem to stress their work—once the language of the oppressed—with the image of excrement filling the tunnel, in several senses. It is not coincidental that the episode deals with a sugarcane worker, the figure par excellence of an excremental life and unlivable conditions that gave rise to MLN-T actions. The scatological figure in the text is an unbearable exteriority for the structure of a working class and of a national grammar, just as anarchism has always proved problematic within the history of the political left and the national configurations of historical languages. The narrative's scatological and unlivable conditions emerge as work and as the figure of the laborer, in the voice introduced by the quotation that interrupts the textual poetics of the encounter and supplements the spectral museum with another kind of ghost and temporal structure: the worker's body and the impossibility of arriving at the surface on time.

The text seems to grapple with a different way of creating a figure of the oppressed, which forever remains a residue exterior to language, acquiring the form of the smell of excrement in this site. The language of the oppressed emerges at the end of the crossing between tunnels, through the figure of a body whose time dislocates the space of the tunnel, thus reminding the reader of its uninhabitability. The final image of excrement reverses any possible romanticization of the escape by ending with the bodily consequences of the prisoners' arduous search for freedom. In short, it poses the figure of a temporal lag between the space of the underground and the time of a body that cannot be synchronized to its uninhabitable conditions. The choice to conclude a highly emotional chapter on this note is interesting in terms of the role of affect, placing us at a point in which abjection, as the philosopher Julia Kristeva has written, does not refer to a particular object but to an unnamable form, "the place where meaning collapses."[55]

The signifying chain between abject pasts within a History dedicated to eradicating this ambiguous excrement from the political past encounters the impossibility of closure in this concluding point between tunnels. The tedious, unbearable labor of excavating the tunnel amid this stench and lack of air is now aligned with the crossing of histories. Subaltern affect highlights the incommensurability between a highly poetic moment and its interruption by bodily deterioration, thus conjuring up a reminder, once again, of a necessary change of optics within the prison. The underground becomes a kind of trap for this body, thus interrupting its poetics, rearranging the focalization of the text that still attempts to reach the flesh (to build a history from the prisoner's gaze—flesh). The image of a body that runs toward the surface to reach the cell and use the toilet generates another interesting image as it interrupts any sort of idealization of the underground of this past. It reminds readers of an area in which the narrative continues to refer to nonassimilable excrement in history whereby it forms part of the poetics (the excluded) and also the remainder of labor and bodily destruction from the lack of air in the underground of time.

A similar play occurs the last time the anarchist tunnel appears at the end of the narrative, pointing toward an interruption that again arises from the surprise of finding the tunnel, bringing readers to the night when 111 prisoners make their escape through the tunnel. Implicitly referring to the chapter "The Anarchists" (since it returns, once more, to narrating the encounter with the 1931 tunnel), this final section of the book is titled "Freedom" and begins with the image of the anarchist tunnel. Here the narrative seems to cite itself, drawing from the title of the first chapter to name this section "Two Generations," echoing the description of the historical crossing between tunnels. This chapter narrates the moment of suspension that takes place during the prisoners' escape through the tunnel when they stumble across a surprise: the anarchist tunnel. Here a kind of unique museum appears, which only lasts an instant: the moment when the men running through the tunnel read an inscription—a sign left by the diggers to mark the crossroads between their own tunnel and that of the anarchists—stating, "Here, two generations, two ideologies, and the very same destiny meet: Freedom." The narrative states: "My eyes will never forget the traces from their tools, so visible and clean-cut, crossing with ours at the peak of the archway."[56]

Appearing as a quotation of the sign in the underground museum, this intersection provokes them to remember these living, visible traces, and once more the word choice refers to a crossing. The sign emphasizes separation, an ideological differentiation (two ideologies), and a continuity that appears with its insistence on the word "freedom." Here freedom explains a major crossing, for it is used as the title of this last section of the book when the author narrates the final moment of escape: the passage toward the prison's outside. Like the title and the sign lost in the underground of the prison-mall, this quotation of the poster left by the excavators when seeing the crossing tunnels for the last time brings with it again the book's great, unnamed specter—"Freedom," as both an escape and the name of the other prison where many of the fugitives would later be incarcerated. The choice to end with the title "Freedom" suggests an incomplete escape (its promise), Libertad Penitentiary, the building raised off the ground by ninety-six pillars, and its future reopening when Punta Carretas was closed indefinitely. The quotation offers a final dialectic image that leaves us in the crossroads, heading toward a time of reading in which Freedom Penitentiary would reopen and Punta Carretas would turn into a symbol of neoliberal freedom.

Toward the end of this chapter, the previous narrative structure is duplicated at the point where the crossing between tunnels was interrupted by the finality of the workers' bodies, which once again evokes the image of the worker and time, in this case as a watch or clock (in Spanish, *reloj* may refer to both, translated here as "clock"): "Before leaving, the last one took one last look around and found a clock, forgotten inside the cavity of the shaft. The clock he and others used during those days to measure their time. The time of air shortage, of everyone's exhaustion. *He took it with him. He brought it with him.*"[57] This passage contains the forgotten figure of work, the time of work and body exhaustion, the patience and deterioration of every digger that is "brought" in the form of a clock, the measure of that time. The clock emerges here in this living museum as an object that stays behind as a forgotten remainder, but which is also taken with them as a reminder of the laborious process of building the tunnel, of planning their escape. Like the excrement, it is a remainder-reminder of an attempt to inscribe the time of the body and work within the space of the tunnel. This small artifact that measures the time of labor—but also of the prison sentence, the time in prison (the clock as a way of establishing equivalents that link the measure of work, the prison sentence, and so on) is inserted within the narrative, dislocating space and time yet again. If we analyze these sentences describing the clock, it would seem that when the worker takes it with him, it arrives at a present that is no longer intratextual, but at a present time of writing that marks a singular, enigmatic "now": "The clock he and others used during those days *to measure their time. The time of the air shortage, of everyone's exhaustion. He took it with him. He brought it with him.*"[58]

What is the space-time of this utterance "he brought it with him"? In a certain way we might consider that it indicates a Benjaminian "now" as the moment of danger, the "critical moment" that he sees as one in which "the status quo threatens to be preserved" and also as the moment in which "continuity" (the history of "progress") is established as the history of the present.[59] This "now" would indicate the instant of erasure in the destruction of bodies that remain unquestioned in the form of the mall and the reopening of Libertad, which in the text's insistence on the image of the body and manual labor refers to both the conditions in which merchandise is displayed within the mall (sweatshops) and the naturalization of a history of destruction as part of a critical question on who are subject to this freedom of consumption in the mall and to Libertad prison. A possible way of approaching the "now" in the utterance "he brought it with him" might be to use the word "toward" in this freedom of a time that remains open, undefined in the structure of an unfulfilled promise. It is there in the way in which the tunnel was unfinished—appearing in the text itself at the moment in which freedom, their final aim, would become a prison (Libertad Penitentiary) and a social utopia embodied in the free market (mall). However, this reminder-remainder in the excremental body of the expropriated worker and the watch that measures his time continues to be a problem—where the question becomes how to imagine, within that present, another form of thinking about the tunnels.

La fuga could be read as a commentary that questions postdictatorship freedom from the invisible times and spaces within the underground of a present that selectively erases obscure areas of the past. The now to which this tunnel, the book, is addressed involves a freedom that consists of other jails, pointing to an incomplete promise, a history that did not end for the world, which the crossing of tunnels urges readers to consider as a history of the oppressed. *La fuga* remains open, a crossroads between "he brought it with him" and the reader's time and space, staged by a peculiar form of listening that in this underground crossroads refers to listening to the reader's own act of reading. The impossible present of "he brought it with him" places time within a signifying chain: the question of a tunnel that conveys freedom through encounters between disparate times, to become a question on the modes of thinking about freedom for those who determine the free subjects of the mall. Here the statement "we advanced . . . but were thrown back" analyzed previously reemerges as a question for this present where progress is spatially marked by Punta Carretas's close and the double opening of the mall as the freedom of consumption and of Freedom Penitentiary.

The prisoners' advances and regressions point to the cyclical image of an infernal repetition (the time of destruction for deceased and disappeared prisoners) but also to the interruption provoked by the text in recycling Punta Carretas in a problematic, critical manner. The end of the final encounter between the 1931 tunnel in the 1971 escape refers to this watch (clock) that leads us to an impossible time: to the Benjaminian now, the critical fissure or spacing that interrupts the pseudo-continuity of our present itself—revealing the conditions in which the action it interrupts takes place. It is as though in the figure of the escape, when times impossibly coexist (the 1930s and the 1970s), the clock used to measure the laborious process of excavating the tunnel is now foregrounded in two sentences—"He took it with him. He brought it with him"—a temporal and a spatial reference. This temporal and spatial leap interpellates readers to reflect on the various times opened and closed within this open end, looking back toward a past in which the old tunnel reaches us today, interrupting the present in a Benjaminian way: "He took it with him"—perhaps to another ending point where the tunnel led him. "He brought it with him"—perhaps to the time that marks the act of reading for each reader.

At this instant the temporal destabilization produces a kind of expansion of textual space in which the 1971 tunnel arrives at the present, suggesting writing itself as a way of making a tunnel, whose open-ended question continues to be relevant to this word-site of language and creation, to freedom in or from their form of escape. We could also read "he brought it with him" in the context of a series of questions: How and when does an escape begin and end? How many escape attempts make an escape possible? In part, the writing style itself expresses this problem in the chaotic multiplicity of narrative voices, ranging from the first-person singular (the narrator's voice), to the first-person plural (the "we" of the political prisoners), to the intercalation of other voices that arrive in the text through quotations of other narratives and the press. Spatial multiplicity or amalgamation is seen even more in the obsessive recurrence of the intersecting tunnels from different times, a contradictory supplement that disrupts the homogenization and synchronization of times characterizing the architecture of the transition (as a spatiotemporal continuity that the heterogeneous, polyvocal, and contradictory narrative of the escape complicates).

I turn now to a final dialectical image from present-day Montevideo in which homogeneous, empty time is opposed to the calendar of the oppressed—a contrast that one can establish between the enormous clock that remains an ornament on the façade of Punta Carretas prison-mall under the word "administration" (*administración*) (see figures 1.1 and 1.2 in chapter 1), and the heterogeneous time that *La fuga* seems to configure in its open form (the clock/watch as an irreducible remainder that reminds readers of a time that keeps passing, a clock that keeps ticking). In the façade the clock's hands do not move; it is frozen in time, as though it embodied a perfect picture of the dream that the prison-mall staged in the moment of its transformation: the ideal of control over time that the fantasy of the "end of history" conveyed when administering History, and an eternalization of the present, frozen and empty, kept under the gaze of the word "administration." Perhaps this place could be fabricated with the new temporal figure of a clock whose hands are paralyzed and whose numbers are carefully erased—as did happen with the histories behind bars and the bodies that were never transferred to Libertad Penitentiary, in an eternal form of indefinite detention. Therefore this image of a frozen time under the word "administration" could be interpreted as the impossible dream of absolute management and detention of time itself, the transformation of the present into a frozen image to which the watch/clock from the underground (a nonplace) can respond, once again, with a temporality that reminds the reader of the time of work, violence, and deterioration of the laboring bodies.

The image of the watch (in *La fuga*), together with the peculiar destabilization of heterogeneous times for escape, refers to the key of the escape, in which the present is exhibited for its finality, bringing with it the bodies and labor of freedom as interruption, and likewise as a process in which freedom emerges as the possibility of repetition, perhaps by imagining that this narrative allows readers to enter into the question of inalterability: How might one repeat the gesture of the escape in a reading that is at once a re-creation and a reinvention of this aperture to a closed time? How might one think of the quotation of a history of escape attempts as a search for freedom while stressing the transition's erased architectonics of transparency in language and its obsessive recycling when erasing its destroyed bodies and their labor?

Drawing on the centrality of the image of the escape tunnels, I have attempted not only to investigate a text unnamed in criticism to date but also to explore a constellation of alternatives in literature, to imagine different spatiotemporal layers from the standpoint of the transition. Taking the central case of Punta Carretas as a node that allegorized its aim to become a symbol—an organic totality of meaning expressing the architectonics of the new time of market freedom—the literary afterlife of the prison in the underground escape allows me to reflect on *La fuga* (the book) as another form of tunnel that traces a pact no longer bound to the narrated past but that urges readers to grapple with the question of making these encounters readable, of imagining the juxtaposed figure of the escape in this present of the mall-prison. Arising within this register, now in my own writing, is another tunnel that leads us toward a text in which literary words also become an area of questioning traversed by crossings and quotations. For in both the work's writing style and the act of reading, these interstices urge us to question how we might think of a minor epic as a calendar for a political history erased by successive destructive acts and massacres throughout the twentieth century—ending, like Punta Carretas, in the form of an invisible ruin, a mall turned into a prison for a new freedom and democracy (of consumption).

3

The Workforce and the Open Prison

Awakening from the Dream of the Chilean Miracle in Diamela Eltit's *Mano de obra*

> What has the century left us? . . . A collection of general essays, a series of scenes perpetually about to be staged. . . . For Chile, the twentieth century will, I think, *remain imprisoned* in a narrative that was thoroughly contaminated by the military coup of 1973. *The coup will be the visible landmark around which the centenary will coalesce to form a labyrinth.* A circular arrangement that allows a clear glimpse of the programmatic escalation of the different types of violence that have occurred in the last hundred years. . . .
>
> It would be interesting to manage to imagine literature traversing the advertizing slogans that name it—with touching ingenuity—as unique, the ultimate, the new. *Or perhaps the best thing would be to close the door so as to watch from behind the curtains the formation of that great "mall,"* thereby protecting oneself once and for all from a system that, while maintaining social inequalities and imbalances, seems based on a single premise: *"I buy, therefore I exist."*
>
> —Diamela Eltit, *Emergencias*

In these remarks from Diamela Eltit's *Emergencias*, language and place are central to Eltit's reflection on the temporal placement of the coup and its aftermath, which are figured by two crucial spaces: the prison and the mall. In the first paragraph of the quote, historicity is connected to the image of the prison, which affects the narratability of the history of the whole century. At the same time, this mutilation of the possibilities of narrating a past emerges in the second paragraph of the quote in another spatial figure—the mall—referring to the limitations of literary language once it is progressively subsumed under the market and the euphoric reiteration of novelty marking a present time that is stripped of historicity and therefore of its potential for transformation. Eltit uses the figure of the mall as if it were a great wall or fortress providing a sense of safety and security against inequality and injustice. The image in the second paragraph of the quote follows the imaginary of the mall that I analyzed in the first section as an emblematic place, the architectonic fantasy of postdictatorship freedom, limited to ideals of security and surveillance as the freedom of redemocratization. Imported as the architectural incarnation of the fantasy of the end of history, the mall dramatized the anxiety about containment (domestication and adjustment) of a heterogeneous group of affects and temporalities left by dictatorships—a spatializing container, the present as fortress. Within this universe the question that emerges is how literary language can interrupt that unquestioning habitation without becoming merely one more refuge or fortress. How can literature, imprisoned in the marketplace, stage an escape when, as Eltit writes, "the neoliberal project is the real, contemporary official Chilean story"?[1]

In the second paragraph of the epigraph, Eltit mentions two possible actions for a writer—either to find refuge behind the great walls of the mall (a fortress) or to write the novel *Mano de obra*.[2] The option she chose is obvious, as this chapter analyzes the novel she ended up writing. Her novel is one of the first literary accounts of the supermarket and labor in postdictatorship times. It is the first written from the imaginary perspective of a supermarket worker. Without literally referring to it, the novel ends up configuring the structure that Punta Carretas Mall acquired, as it fictionalizes the place of the hypermarket in the form of a maximum security prison. It undoes the structural fantasy of Punta Carretas Mall as the resignification of a prison that was now to become the symbol of freedom. Eltit emphasizes what cultural critics noted in the 1990s—that the mall worked as a continuation of mechanisms of control and surveillance that a certain part of the population needed so they could move around safe and secure. *Mano de obra* redoubles this notion, however, for it does not just denounce the world of "unfreedom" that postdictatorship architecture concealed in its dreams of control. It also poses a counterpoint between the imaginary of surveillance and a fragmented history of emancipation and protest that, robbed of its prose, enter into the text as fragmentary, episodic titles waiting for sense to be made of them.

The idea of an afterlife of confinement is less obvious in this chapter than in previous ones because *Mano de obra* does not narrate the transformation of a prison but the figuration of the neoliberal marketplace as a prison that confines history and memory practices. Playing with ambiguity, *Mano de obra* makes the reader see the structure of supermax prison within the architecture and life in a big supermarket. Configuring the main trope of this book (neoliberalism as an open prison) in a literary way, the novel takes the image that Argentinean architect Juan Carlos López constructed when expressing his surprise at looking at the Punta Carretas prison for the first time and seeing in its structure the very diagram of a mall: "a mall," as he said, "of prisoners" to a point of critique. Eltit's novel moves within the horizon of this uncanny resemblance—the point in which the most familiar starts to be felt as its opposite, thus making it possible for us to read López's impression in a very different and critical way.

In addition to the task of historicization that leads us to connect the present of the supermarket with its condition of possibility, *Mano de obra* problematizes the way in which memory practices can and cannot take place within the supermarket. The main character of the novel, a neoliberal free worker without any rights, can be read as an allegory of what historicizing within the mall—the time and place of the end of history—might look like. By focusing on the worker's process of thought, the main topic the novel explores is the operation of memory within the marketplace and the forms in which a memory of political struggles carried out by workers in the past become disconnected from the present by the invisible forms of violence at stake in the organization of the space and time of the market. Continuing with the problem of how to escape from a present that is posed as a prison of freedom, this chapter therefore approaches imprisonment in a nonliteral form by making us see the worker itself as the prisoner of a situation.

If the fortress of the mall confines workers and customers to a form of surveilled and controlled freedom, then the novel raises a singular question: How can a literary figuration of this new space of confinement "free" history from being confined to its own end? If the mall and supermarket embody the dream of the end of history, how can a writer figure a constellation of awakening from such a dream? What form would this awakening take? Finally, what sense can the verb "to free" acquire when applied to signifying chains previously enclosed or confined within the single narrative of market freedom, when the realm that is about to be reconstructed has not been part of the prose of the history of freedom? Using cultural theorist Gayatri Spivak's powerful proposition of creating a theory of change from within signifying chains, we can explore how imprisoned and surveilled freedom in the postdictatorship period is interrupted by Eltit's insistence on bringing fragments of nonlinear, subaltern (erased and lost) attempts to escape from such freedom.

Maybe by focusing on the "free" worker of postdictatorship times, Eltit is already telling us something about the problem of awakening that is at the center of the novel; she forces readers to imagine how the history of the neoliberal experiment in freedom could be written from the monologue of one of its workers. Here literature itself is destabilized, and it is no surprise that *Mano de obra* has been seen as a turning point in Eltit's narrative style itself, moving from a more experimental avant-garde form to a different configuration of the relation between art, political imagination, and memory practices. *Mano de obra* sets up a dialogue between the contemporary hypermarket (figured as a prison) and the 1911 workers' revolt and massacre, posing the question of how to articulate the heterogeneous fragments and series of lost histories into a single narration—that is, how to transform a schizoid universe of unrelated elements into a constellation of awakening.

In "Las dos caras de la moneda" (The two sides of the coin), a talk given while Eltit was writing *Mano de obra,* she poses more questions regarding language and history: "I ask myself: how could we refer to Chilean political history when this history is simultaneously personal and corporeal, without falling into testimonial vertigo or the predictable exercise of constructing an intelligent or distant gaze?"[3] She continues: "When one does not come from the social sciences or politics or a specific discipline that examines sociopolitical events in detail, I think that, from within my literary place, it is perhaps in the word '*golpe*' (coup) that a key to approaching the history marked by the events of September 11, 1973, in Chile could lie."[4] Eltit here poses a question of how literature (as a place—*mi lugar literario*) can become the site for thought about historical imagination in an era defined as posthistorical, an era obsessed with the genres of memoir and the testimonial (museification, memory boom).

Following the idea of literature as place, I argue that words can be approached as sites from which other modes of historicization can be experienced (attempted), ones that can be thought of as modes of digging and tunneling that open up different layers of the past imprisoned by the mall. The possibility of reinserting into textual space certain fragments that the ideology of the "end of history" attempted to domesticate and monitor leads Eltit to a change of direction with the publication of *Mano de obra* in 2002. The novel caused a sensation among readers; some critics interpreted its use of key neovanguard elements (characteristic of the narrator) as a gesture toward realism.[5] Although it uses characteristic features of the Eltitian universe (rescuing the expropriated historicity of the marginal and minor), the text shows for the first time a desire to engage in a reflection on the history of emancipatory and revolutionary movements. It does so from a hitherto unconstructed location: the supermarket, prime site of the "adjustment" promoted by the Chicago Boys' so-called neoliberal miracle in Pinochet's Chile. Thus the supermarket (or hypermarket) and the workforce conditions of the postdictatorship neoliberal universe enter Eltit's text in a curious way, because the layout of different spaces in the text incorporate the characteristics of what I referred to earlier as the architectonic of the transition, but in a problematic, critical way. In *Mano de obra* the narration of the history of the left occurs through a double gesture: quotation and awakening, both connected to the word *golpe*, at once absent within the text and contaminating the whole history.

The novel is divided into two sections: the first is set in a supermarket, the second in a house shared by a group of workers. Each half of the novel has an overarching title that divides the text: "El despertar de los trabajadores (Iquique, 1911)" (The awakening of the workers) and "Puro Chile (Santiago, 1970)" (Pure Chile). Each chapter of "El despertar de los trabajadores" is split into subsections by the use of titles and dates culled from socialist, anarchist, and other radical newspapers and pamphlets from the first decades of the twentieth century. These assume a dual function as both subtitles and quotations; dates and places can be read as building an alternative calendar marked by a history of struggles previously erased from the temporality of the world both of the neoliberal hypermarket and of the dictatorship that made this world possible. The organization of the quotes follows no chronological order; they appear in the text as if they were out of historical sequence. This makes us look for connections between each title and the content it subtitles, marking a dialectical tension reiterated again and again throughout the section. Also, the subtitles of the first half of the novel contrast with those of the second, which are followed by neither places nor dates. They refer to events of daily life and the process of deterioration experienced by the group of supermarket workers sharing a house.

We can therefore establish a contrast between the titles-ideas of the first section—"The Proletariat," "Direct Action," "Light and Life," "The Voice of the Sea"—and the banalities that composed the life of the workers in the postdictatorial world—"Sonia Cried in the Bathroom," "Isabel Needed to Put on Her Lipstick," "Gabriel and the Cashiers," "We Had to Wake Isabel," "They'll Cut Anything," "Sonia Cut Her Index Finger," and so on. The events refer to work-place accidents, addiction, prostitution, and the denigration of women's bodies, alluding to the lack of rights and laws that would protect the workers from absolute exploitation. The threat of losing their jobs makes each worker enter a state of slavery that the second part of the novel emphasizes when referring to some of them as *"encadenados"* (chained) to parts of the superstore. The subtitles of the second section ("Puro Chile") refer to what used to be the content of the publications whose titles appear in the first section. However, there is no sense of how a collective form of protest could be articulated beyond the schizoid form; the erasure of dates and places in these titles evidence workers' acquiescence to the reproduction of their misery. The cultural theorist Jean Franco has stated that "the group of workers represent a parodic version of the solidarity that is constantly reversed by the treacheries, complaints, and insults."[6]

Because there are no key events to mark, the subtitles do not have a date or a specific place. The question that remains is how to make sense of the connection between the temporal series and the events in the monologue (the beginning and the end of the century, both marked by a massacre of workers), which implies a connection between the past (enacted by the titles that refer to the space of the printed word) and the present (enacted by the progressive destruction of the life of one supermarket worker). In a sense the contrast between past and present relates to the tension posed between the subtitles (names and dated events) and the material reproduction of the life of the supermarket worker, who resembles an *encadenado* (a chained prisoner or slave). By playing with the figure of imprisonment within the monologue of the worker, Eltit replicates the idea that she raised when she wrote that the political history of the twentieth century "would remain imprisoned" in modes of narration forged in the aftermath of the 1973 coup.[7]

The novel urges readers to think of the neoliberal site of freedom (the hypermarket) as a prison, a site that confines not just a certain history of change but the forms of narrating and remembering a broader history of attempts of emancipation. The supermarket traces the limits of the protected democracy within the structure of the mall, which, figured in dominant narratives of neoliberalization as a secure site of protected enjoyment. As in the prison-mall and in *La fuga*, the political past that the process of malling attempts to besiege like a fortress emerges in the text in the form of the citation. In *Mano de obra* the titles act in two ways, referring both to actual events (marked by the use of precise places and names) and to a promise implied by the relation between a title and what it entitles. This demonstrates the problem of titling versus entitling. A crucial point here—a literary one—is that the counterpoint between titles and the entitled calls into question the citability of the past, which is replicated within the space of the monologue in the form of a reflection on remembrance and time-marking. The status of this citation and its dialectical relation to the text constitute a labyrinthine, enigmatic form, forcing readers to take responsibility for making their own way(s) through these spaces-times, freighted with silence, fortresses, others, battles, escapes, and corpses.

Although *Mano de obra* continues to work with the recurring preoccupations of the (post)dictatorial in Eltit's work (space, body, violence), it opens up a new thematic area: the political histories of the left. Although sharing the great invisible nucleus of the 1973 coup, these histories generate a question about the continuity of modes of destruction and political violence that, as the first paragraph in the chapter epigraph states, mark the twentieth century as imprisoned by the impossibility of coming up with different ways of thinking about politics. By posing this question, *Mano de obra* introduces a different theme than that seen in two Eltit works that were crucial to the configuration of a literature on the dictatorship and the postdictatorial universe: *Lumpérica* and *Los vigilantes*. In these texts there is an organization of space that is both controlled and completely segregated. In *Los vigilantes* we have the privatized space of the city (monitored, surrounded, making the city "*un espacio instransitable*" (an impassable space) and the houses "*una fortaleza*" (a fortress).[8]

The space of writing (in the form of a one-sided correspondence, since we are never given the replies of the absent husband/father) and the space of dreams are the only areas of expression in which the protagonist feels herself to be alive. As the cultural theorist Idelber Avelar has pointed out, *Los vigilantes*, Eltit's first novel written in the postdictatorship period, has an apocalyptic tone that *Lumpérica* lacks, even though *Lumpérica* was written under the dictatorship. He adds that *Los vigilantes* seems to leave us in a dark, apocalyptic zone that dramatizes the impossibility of finding an outside, an exit.[9] Similarly, the cultural theorist Francine Masiello has stated that a central question in Eltit's textuality is "the survival of art and the conditions of creativity in an age of surveillance."[10] In a sense it could be argued that while *Los vigilantes* centers on dreaming, which was denigrated in the discourse of political realism that marked the process of redemocratization (the utopias are exhausted, stop dreaming, come down to earth), *Mano de obra* centers on waking up. That is, while in *Los vigilantes* a protest against the spread of Western values is found in the dream site in which the protagonist takes refuge, in *Mano de obra* the figure that is key to interpreting the text is awakening ("El despertar de los trabajadores").

Thus it could be argued that *Mano de obra* marks a new zone of literature for Eltit, one concerned with how to rewrite a political history of the Chilean left that would explore the awakening of a world abandoned by the dictatorship (crossing the fortress of the mall from its literary configuration, full of voices of the past). At the same time, how can awakening be meaningful if it is not approached from the standpoint of two formerly dominant pseudo-Hegelian paradigms of postdictatorial political discursivity? In other words, without reiterating either the paradigm of maturation—which saw revolutionary politics as infantile, adolescent, abnormal, and now "overcome" (without mentioning the connection between this overcoming and the massacres of the dictatorship)—or the end-of-history paradigm of the 1990s in which political partisanship was overcome by the triumph of capitalism as the only possible form of life, jettisoning any possibility of structurally transforming a system of exploitation and inequality.

One way of battling this political and philosophical conundrum emerges in *Mano de obra*, which explores the question of how to relate the figure of awakening to a history of the left and its others—that is, of the zones that don't qualify as Chilean but that are the material basis blotted out by the Chilean miracle, a history of the destruction of workers' bodies and times that has been rendered invisible by the economic success-mongering of a bloody dictatorship. Provocatively, Eltit suggests a parallelism between the famous massacres of workers who organized against the unlimited exploitation of their lives (their time, their bodies) and the daily massacre of a worker with no rights, who is disposable in the postdictatorship period. I believe that between *Los vigilantes* and *Mano de obra* there is a shift similar to the internal critical and political distancing from surrealism that led Walter Benjamin to his *Arcades Project*. This is paralleled in Eltit's work in the shift on the historicization of politics, which is treated differently than in the CADA (Art Action Collective). Benjamin writes that "whereas Aragon persists within the realm of dream, here the concern is to find the constellation of awakening. . . . here it is a question of the dissolution of "mythology" into the space of history. That, of course, can happen only through the awakening of a not-yet-conscious knowledge of what has been."[11]

Mano de obra appears to show a similar shift in that (utopic) dream marked by impossibility in *Los vigilantes* that emerges in *Mano de obra* as an exploration of ways of awakening from various dreams (perhaps also from the utopian revolutionary dream, since it emphasizes the formative, laborious act of struggle more than the fetishization of revolution as a historical rupture after which life will begin anew). In the section of *Mano de obra* that dramatizes the life and progressive destruction of the supermarket worker under the title "El despertar de los trabajadores," Eltit opens a parenthesis to the fetishization of the neovanguardist rupture (break, coup) and turns to a humbler but also more problematic (and no less vanguardist) question: How to theorize a process of change whose origins are radically heterogeneous?

How to organize a movement from an irreducible polyphony of voices? In Benjaminian terms this involves rethinking and reading the image of a history that has been massacred, robbed of its prose, in a way that attends to the faults and limitations that constitute that political past without reiterating the gestures of historicism or historiographic positivism.

By using the Iquique massacre as a parenthesis that titles half of the work, Eltit introduces an element that has been doubly excluded by the national and global imaginary of/from the time of progress in Chile (the nationalist imaginary of the early twentieth century and the mall as fortress in the globalizing imaginary). These remainders of the past that the text activates typographically as a title with a date and place serve as an enigmatic reminder of what does not count in history—the material of dismissible existences that uphold the miracle of progress—and a reminder of the forces that impede the narration of what has been left out of history. Here we face, once again, the problem of how to think and write the poetics of a history of that which was and is always included as excluded from national and global sites of progress. Defetishizing the theology of the economy of miracles, the "un-Chilean" of Chile appears from 1907 on as what was left out—its miners (immigrant miners from Argentina, Bolivia, and Peru also massacred in Iquique); all that was massacred by the dictatorship and the available, replaceable supermarket laborers with no rights. However, in its use of newspapers, *Mano de obra* also introduces and underlines a process that interweaves a form of Chile that not only encourages reflection on excluded and marginalized groups (miners, Indians, women, children) but also questions other zones of Chilean history that center upon the crucial theme of the nationalization of copper. This was perhaps the most controversial achievement of the Unidad Popular, since, for the first time, the protection of Chile required (in the imaginary of struggle against dependency, and within the resultant logic of national liberation) expropriating international capital in the name of which the protection of Chile had been defended.[12] Beginning with *Mano de obra*, Eltit's work turns toward zones of history that are more difficult to explore since doing so involves rethinking layers and zones of the past that had been excluded en masse from her previous work and from the political history of the left.

Mano de obra's experimentation brings us back to the minor ~~epic~~ critique of the present (mall, marketplace, configured as prison), which proposes, as an escape, the opening up of the mall's assumptions about time and memory to a heterogeneous multiplicity of other times, other layers that the fortress includes as its outside. As stated in chapter 2, the function of the barred word (minor ~~epic~~) is to make the reader think about the complex process of reconfiguration of past actions and the struggle over its meaning. This opens up zones in which difference simultaneously exists and doesn't exist, in which liberty in the neoliberal marketplace is an open prison in which the post of the postdictatorship never arrives as the passage from less to more liberty. *Mano de obra* approaches the open prison at the point we left off in *La fuga*—work, the deterioration of the body, and the insistence on creating alternative calendars as avenues of escape. Thus the clock discussed earlier is now constructed in the neoliberal supermarket as a utopia of unlimited exploitation of labor. It is on that edge that the text's structure causes readers to think of other crossings similar to those seen in the escape: How to listen to the echoes of what was expropriated from the time of historic prose? How to imagine the labyrinth of political experiments that cannot be subsumed into the form of a (Chilean) "consciousness" but which nevertheless constitutes a schizoid range of mute voices. These voices give weight to the question raised by Benjamin of how to think about a calendar of the oppressed, a calendar of remembrance and commemoration of what history does not register, which implies the trace of a different way of conceiving historicity.

The Awakening of the Workers: Reading the Quote, Writing a History

The title of the first half of the novel—"El despertar de los trabajadores"—is followed by a parenthesis around a place and date: "Iquique, 1911." We can read the title, place, and date that head the supermarket section as signaling a constellation of historical events that include the founding of the most important newspaper in the creation of a working class, *El despertar de los trabajadores* (1912); the massacre of nitrate workers that preceded it (1907); and the foundation in 1912 of the Partido Obrero Socialista (Socialist Workers Party), which became the Communist Party of Chile a decade later. The newspaper *El despertar* began as a response to the Iquique massacre, which occurred when a large group of saltpeter miners gathered with their families to organize against the intolerable working conditions in the mines. The workers (some of whom had migrated from Argentina, Bolivia, and Peru in hopes of improving their standard of living) spent all day in the mines, for which they received a voucher (*ficha*) instead of money, redeemable only at the company store.

Iquique was the epicenter of the nascent miners' union; it was there that the miners met and proposed terms for the amelioration of working conditions, calling for better safety measures in the mines, better pay, payment in money instead of vouchers, and the right to education and health care. The foreign and Chilean investors who owned the nitrate fields refused to recognize the miners' union, which then launched a general strike. To protect capital, the Chilean government declared a state of siege in Iquique. The workers responded by taking over a public school, the Escuela Santa María de Iquique, and refusing to leave until their demands were met. At this point the Ministry of the Interior solved the problem by ordering the massacre of the workers occupying the school.[13]

The legal and physical state of siege came to a bloody end when the military, stationed in the public square in front of the school, opened fire with machine guns (perhaps even using gunpowder made with nitrate extracted by the massacred miners). That evening, the local governor issued a press release forbidding the printing and sale of any periodical or newspaper. Between two thousand and three thousand miners and their family members were killed, while many others other remained unaccounted for.[14] Before the military coup of 1973, this was considered one of Chile's largest massacres of union members. As the Chilean historian Isabel Jara has stated, although the massacre was one of the most emblematic repressive incidents in Chile's working-class history, it had no place within official memory. It was never mentioned in school textbooks, nor in official historiography—only in the working-class press and in the oral history and folk songs of some leftist groups.[15]

Later, the founding of the newspaper *El despertar de los trabajadores* became a link between the massacre and the formation of the Socialist Workers Party.[16] José Emilio Recabarren, known as the father of the leftist press and of the Chilean working-class movement, envisaged the publication as a tool for education, which workers could use to begin forging a space of counterculture, instead of just reacting against exploitation.[17] Recabarren believed that an alternative press could play a key role in the creation of a working-class consciousness that would not remain limited to the mere act of going on strike. *El despertar* thus became a forum for the development of a proletarian culture (and not just a group of protesters).[18] The publication transformed the site of the massacre (the space of the school) into a project that became the site for the construction of a potential working-class culture. At the same time, it is important to stress that Recabarren was later expelled from the Chilean Communist Party. The party places this constellation in an impure zone evident even today in the scant bibliography on the connection between his struggle against the growing orthodoxy of the party and Recabarren's suicide.[19]

Clearly, by alluding to *El despertar*, Eltit allows us to open up a truncated zone of a past that never was, a past that was aborted. Her title exhibits it as a space of possibility, of unfulfilled promise. Eltit complicates the reference to the massacre by openly connecting it to the title *El despertar* because instead of just recalling the massacre, which was the endpoint of the miners' strike, the act of titling the first section of the novel "El despertar" suggests a reading that replaces the political (re)action with a more complex and irreducible process of imagining a political formation (*Bildung*).[20] The political organization of the workers (the creation of a working class) depended on the possible development of an alternative cultural and educational process. The title therefore gathers together associations with a process that was multiple, complex, and chaotic. This is shown by the different subtitles that reference publications not subsumed under the voice of the Communist Party (publications by anarchists, socialists, and so on) that compose the section under the form of an irreducible multiplicity in the title *El despertar de los trabajadores*.[21]

The evocation of the aftermath of the biggest massacre of workers in twentieth-century Chile before the coup of 1973 connects to the problem of awakening in the present of the supermarket, the aftermath of the dictatorship. This dramatizes a duality regarding the formation of a working-class consciousness, never transparent or unified, but still a (limited) space in which exploited workers gathered in their multiplicity and complexity. In a way, bringing the present into the schizoid monologue of the supermarket worker facilitates another way of critically approaching the history of that "consciousness." This approach involves the interplay between the polyphony that the different titles set up in their disagreement (the different political ideologies that the titles suggest: socialists, anarchists, communists) and the role of the title in gathering them together (replicated, as an enigma, by the schizoid monologue of a single supermarket worker at the end of the twentieth century). This makes reading the novel an act of re-creating other zones of the past, erased from the printed world of dominant historiography. In this sense the subtitles make readers aware how little they know of these histories, thus forcing them to imagine ways to connect erased and lost past(s) with a present in which awakening becomes enigmatic.

The figure of awakening alluded to in the section title acts as an alert that challenges readers to determine how to read a figurative awakening in the events that take place in the novel in relation to the cheap labor force depicted, placing us within the postdictatorship site par excellence: the supermarket.[22] We may ask ourselves how this awakening is connected to that which it supposedly entitles—that is, the process of the supermarket worker's deterioration. Through the play on the deterioration of the worker's body, Eltit forces us to see, in a succession of glimpses, the ways in which the paradise of the so-called Chilean miracle is a nightmare, enslaved in the world of the free neoliberal market and trapped within calculated forms of remembrance.[23] Eltit dramatizes the problem of awakening in the form of a monologue in which temporality emerges as both an obsession and an illness for the worker. This creates a counterpoint between the worker's inability to remember things, as he spends more and more time in the supermarket, and the idea of a possible calendar of past struggles (suggested by the titles). As the worker spends both his days and nights at work, his organs cease to function and his language enters a form of delirium, punctuated by flashes of panic associated with a temporal illness. This unveils the key issue of the text: the problem of marking, registering, and recalling time, of citing the past, that is connected to the notion of awakening.

Marking Time in the Supermarket

In the section entitled "Acción directa (Santiago, 1920)," the narrator explicates his illness many times: "I am possessed, I declare, from head to toe, by a *symptom that is entirely work-related, a temporal illness*, that has not yet been included in medical annals. Although I touch the products, I cannot recall the order and place that they should occupy on each shelf. I am the victim of a disease which, even though not strictly organic, compromises each of my organs."[24] The correlate of the spatiotemporal disorder expressed as a "work-related symptom" (the failure to coordinate the seeing and touching of the products) is a language problem. The beginning of the chapter exposes this in detail, as the narrator posits a relationship between his temporal illness and the emptying of language that connects different temporalities (work time, bodily time, commodity time); his disease corresponds to his problem recalling and recollecting, locating, naming and reading:

> At an incommensurable distance from myself, *I order* the apples. The geometrical contours *in which metals acquire their incisive destiny* are already *undrawing* themselves. I am *infected,* I am traversed by *weakness.* This huge drowsiness keeps me exhausted and *defeated before the impenetrable linearity of the shelves.* I stare attentively (even though I know I shouldn't) at the commodities; however, I *cannot manage to retain* them *or recollect* them so as to annex them within the professional memory that I need to employ with the products. Now, at this precise and disgraceful instant, I do not know for sure what they are, *what name* they have, and *what site* has been assigned to them in the supermarket. . . . Amid *fragments of uncertain images* and delivered into an absolute chaos, I think, as I already said, about the *legibility of the products.* In an instant they all crowd my mind, but immediately *they all fall downhill, slipping and falling* from the abyss of my disabled internal eye.[25]

It is interesting that the word used by Eltit to describe the worker's work-related symptom as a temporal illness is *retener* (to retain), a word that refers to memory practices and that in Spanish has different sets of meaning in both spatial and temporal senses. *Retener* can be understood in a temporal sense as the practice of memorizing (retaining an event or a memory) and reading (retaining a passage); it can also refer, in a spatial and legal sense, to the act of temporary detention (imprisonment) by the police. In the first meaning, *retener* can be understood as an idea of remembering that follows the fantasy of a metaphysics of presence—that is, of bringing the past forward as a present that was and that can be recuperated as such. In the second meaning, *retener* evokes a prison imaginary in which detention implies a provisional lack of freedom of movement while the suspect is kept under scrutiny to see if she or he will become a prisoner or a free person.

The question for the analysis of *Mano de obra* is how these two meanings and spaces are treated in an ambiguous, always polyvocal form, as if the novel's configuration of the supermarket as open prison was also dramatized by the different correlates of the word *retener* as well as by the instances in which the borders between the different zones of meaning are blurred. As the novel progresses, we witness how the deterioration of the worker takes the form of physical and mental paralysis, an inability either to move or to recall locations and names in his memory. In a strange way his work-related illness seems to have to do with the work of retaining, in that the more time he works (and the more exhausted he feels), the more unable he is to remember things and the more the supermarket resembles a prison in which the subject is deprived of a variety of experiences. In this sense the problem of temporality appears repeatedly in relation to a problematizion of retention (as in memory) and a sense of being *retenido* (detained in prison).

After mentioning his inability to recall names and dates, the worker associates retention with the past, in which he used to spend hours memorizing the supermarket catalog. The retrospective fantasy of an act of remembrance, like a catalog in which commodities were legible and locatable in his mental mapping of the supermarket, can also be understood as a (metaliterary) questioning of the way in which one can read the names and dates in the titles. The use of *retener* can be read in tandem with the series of titles, showing the problem of transforming the left's past into a catalog of deeds (fetishizing the history of working-class struggles as a unified and homogeneous consciousness). In both cases the word *retener* makes us think of the historicist dream of remembering as cataloging (objects, deeds) through a process of adding up names and places—what Benjamin criticizes as the historicist attempt to see the past "the way it was."[26]

Every act of remembrance is mediated by re-creation through language. The worker's fantasy of recalling the past as an idealized presence of things in his mind (as if they were objects stored there, as in a supermarket, objective things without history) can be read as a form of historicism in the supermarket. However, what other temporalities emerge that cannot be reduced to the form of this fantasized ideal of retention as bringing-back? This question is crucial if we consider what the titles evoke: the necessity of creating a calendar of modes of violence and oppression in which the temporality at stake is not the one registered by the prose of history (the history of progress and development). A calendar of the oppressed would imply the possibility of imagining other temporalities, ones in which progress is figuratively arrested, while also being inscribed within a spatial continuity—the calendar. In this sense retention shows the capitalist dream of temporality par excellence, a fetishism working within the very act of remembrance itself: to think of the past as a present we can retain, possess, and repossess, as in a miracle (a time outside time).

What is missing is the fissure within that past, the trace of what is not within that which "was"—something that frustrates the dream of a controlling consciousness able to recall and use the past. It is the longing for a present that suggests the frustration of its own present, another form of loss that the ideal of retention tries to camouflage or avoid. Derrida's emphasis on the difference between trace and retention allows us to envisage another way of connecting the series of past(s) and present(s). Retention and trace are incommensurable because retention involves the idea of holding something present into the becoming past; that is, the idea of a present that is or has been fully present to itself erases the very structure of the deferral.[27] In other words, it involves an ideal relation between past and present as a kind of transparent, unproblematic translatability. The trace makes us think about a problematic translation in which the past and present are always already fissured, delayed in themselves. It is within this structural opening that the problem of awakening becomes more complex in the novel because the emphasis is placed not on the recuperability of a past but on the ways in which remembrance could take place in connection with the "awakening of a *not-yet-conscious knowledge* of what has been."[28]

"El proletario (Tocopilla, 1904)"

A constant theme in both parts of the novel (the supermarket and the house) is fear of losing one's job, something that creates not only fierce competition among the workers (betrayal, survival of the fittest) but also a fear of the street, of being sent out on the street where there are lines of people waiting to sign up in search of jobs.[29] This generates a precarious work environment that causes the worker to spend more and more hours in the workplace. With no contract and obliged to spend almost the whole day and night at work, labor becomes slavery and the worker literally becomes a prisoner. The problematization of an increase of hours worked in relation to the supermarket as emerging prison and to labor as a form of slavery appears in a key chapter, titled "El proletario (Tocopilla, 1904)." The chapter starts with time as problem but turns to the anxiety that the worker feels whenever a shoplifter enters the place: "More hours. Later still. However, I am still behind my barricade. . . . Hours are a (dead) weight in my wrist, and I don't bother to confess that time plays in a perverse way with me *because* it does not really inscribe itself in any part of my being. It is only stored in the supermarket, it takes place in the supermarket. It is a trembling, infinite schedule that looms larger (still) when this particular new client enters, hypocritically."[30]

In this passage the worker's inability to register time refers to temporality as something stored, another commodity characterized by duality, in connection with money, as the hours are both a *peso muerto*, which can be read as both a dead currency (the Chilean *peso*) and a dead weight (a corpse). The play on this expression opens different associations in which the temporal problem connects to different forms of reading the role of money, robbery, and death while also referring to the role of inscription and affect, as time taking place in the supermarket is interrupted by the feeling the worker senses in his body when a particular customer enters into the place. This character connects indirectly to the title "El proletario," since the customer is excluded by the system and becomes a parasite who counteracts the productive machine of the supermarket by taking commodities without paying for them.

The emergence of this "particular new customer" in the narrative introduces another sense of time—a time of erotic play between shoplifter and worker. Seduced by the play of gazes that this particular customer starts as she or he looks for complicity, the worker also feels anxiety because he says he feels that he is just being used as a means to an end—that of enjoying commodities without paying for them. This other, more personal and intense sense of temporality is immediately interrupted by the idea of betrayal (the sense of being used for a pleasure he will not enjoy). He fears that the mechanical eye of the security camera will "retain" this interchange, so he controls his affect and reports the shoplifter, thus ending the erotic game and remaining faithful to the supermarket, the place that is, paradoxically, shoplifting his lifetime: "the camera retains the relevance of any precise sign (even the tiniest and apparently insignificant anomaly) which will be analyzed later—in a more than exhaustive detail—by the shift supervisor."[31] The word "retention" reemerges here, now relating to the recording machine that surveils (registers) every singular movement. The neutralization of the eye-camera permanently recording potential illegal activities creates a dialectical tension between modes of stealing. On the one hand, the figure of the solitary, proletarian shoplifter who attempts to act against the system that produced him or her as such, and on the other, the neutral recording eye of the camera that, like God, retains every movement to prevent illegal actions on the premises.

The dialectic that the text creates makes us think of multiple perspectives on theft, of the borders that compose legality and illegality, and of the sense of protection that is the rationale for the surveillance machine—protection for and from whom? There are two types of theft going on: the shoplifter, whom the text suggest is an unemployed person who goes to the supermarket to steal as a means of survival, and the multiple forms of robbery suffered by the worker who has no contract or rights, who lives in fear of being fired and under the constant surveillance of the mechanical eye of the camera that his supervisor will later analyze. However, the power of the text lies in its ability to evoke the connections between the different forms of *retener* (time, poverty, imprisonment), the cyclical repetition of naturalized modes of violence that produce an arrest in our thought, an impossible form of resolution. The chapter thus suggests the idea of the political subject par excellence, the proletariat, but contrasts it with the solitary form of a shoplifter and the surveilled worker, both seeking their own means of survival, both imprisoned within a situation that the text cannot solve but only figure within a schizoid language seen in the title that questions how an awakening from this nightmare can take place. A complicated network of allegiances connects the supermarket to the past, to the figure of change as something that never was, an enigma-word, also laden with betrayals and surveillance.

Analysis of the complex spatial structure of the novel hints at other ways in which the problem of awakening is posed and at the function of the supermarket as a supermax prison. The relevance of the camera that retains images, constituting a form of imprisonment, seems also to evoke the form of surveillance that Eltit sees as an afterlife of the dictatorship, the naturalization and camouflaged legalization of the application of violence to any attempt to subvert the system. The architecture of the supermarket reiterates the protected democracy and the military's impunity despite massive crimes. A similar dialectic is set up between the supermarket, surveillance, and the excess of light (further textual play on the cleanliness of the penitentiary dream). There is an ambiguity at work in the word "lights" (*luces*), one that we can read in relation to the Enlightenment and to the critical turn that Benjamin posed within both enlightenment and awakening. The more the worker inhabits the supermarket, the more blinded he feels by the bright lights and the more unable he is to dream as he is progressively deprived of hours to sleep. The dialectical play established among time, dream, awakening, seeing, reflecting/reflection poses a form of awakening to the obvious: How can one wake if one does not have time to go to sleep? How can one see when the light is too intense and weakens the eyes' ability to see?

The play on light exploits a semantic ambiguity similar to that of *retener*; Eltit uses the word *luces* (lights) to refer both to the lighting system and to enlightenment (the Enlightenment is known as *el siglo de las luces* in Spanish). This creates a zone of undecidability of meaning attached to *luces* throughout the text that is foregrounded in the worker's monologue in the references to the difficulty of reflection (seeing and thinking) due to the excess of lights: "This eye of mine . . . follows the order of the lights"; "this obsessive light cracks me up and makes me feel a persistent nausea. I am sick, I already said so. Unfocused, forgetful, and slightly absent to all that is going on in the interior of this place"; "the light is now my enemy"; "I know *the intelligence of the lights*. But I am sick. . . . I no longer have any expectation."[32] These statements play with the multiple implications of seeing, lighting, and reflection, showing the (blinding) effects of the lights on the worker and raising the question of how that might reflect the present. The question is: How can the present critique its own conditions and bring about a different form of questioning and connecting (imagining, reinventing) the past so as to make it shed some "light" on the present? Enlightenment here functions as a call by Eltit for a necessary critical turn—a questioning of the present that would go back and rethink the different enlightenments that were erased, massacred, and excluded from the Enlightenment supposedly possessed by the discourse of progress, maturity, and history. Following the distinction I posed in chapter 2 between Epic and epic, we could read here a similar play on awakening and the critical framing of enlightenment.

The double associative play of the word *luces* stages an ambivalence between a sense of freedom that is tied to the promise of a history of emancipation in which critique of the present is crucial, and the sense of light as increasing control and exploitation of those who are supposedly free (secured in the sense of being safe, protected) and enlightened by the lights (that keep everything under surveillance). If the play between the monologue of the worker and its (dis)connection in relation to the titles enacts this, the question of awakening acquires a more significant role as it makes readers question what sense an awakening of the workers can have in the present of the supermarket and how an awakening within that present would differ from the ones posed by the titles in the past. That is, how to connect that cleansed, whitewashed, surveilled present (protected from critique) with the shreds of (hi)stories that the titles introduce.

The titles re-create a critical form of ~~enlightenment~~, "othering" it with the impossible fragments of expropriated "histories"—the minor ~~epic~~ of a struggle to open up other forms and meanings for the words "rights" and "freedom." In a sense Eltit is posing a tension between layers of the present and the past, a tension that makes us wonder how a critical turn can take place from within that imprisoned present, the fortress of the mall, how awakening can take place. We can use social geographer David Harvey's description of malling as "the construction of safe, secure, well-ordered, easily accessible, and above all pleasant . . . and *non-conflictual* environments that promoted *an acritical attitude.*"[33] A critical attitude would mean, in this case, creating critical connections with the past that go beyond mere loss and that would be aware of the limitations of those discourses but would also insist on the necessity of rewriting and re-creating the foreclosed stories.

By connecting the ambiguity of *luces* (lights) to awakening in the text, we can read a form of protest against the violence of state and capital, a rethinking of the critical, undermined sense of other enlightenments that make us examine what a sort of *Bildung* can take place.[34] This is a critical project that runs the risk of falling once more into the acritical stance of leftist epics; however, trying to avoid the shortcomings in the historicization of emancipatory projects could end up closing off paths that a new form of cultural historicization of politics would open up. Thus the issue to tackle is: How does the narration of working-class historicization (and the tools one uses in order to approach it) always already tell us something about the present in which the question is posed? In the problematization of awakening that is strongly linked to Enlightenment consciousness, what looked like minor ~~epic~~ in the preceding chapter is treated here as a possibility of minor or future ~~enlightenment~~.[35] It is not an attempt to recuperate a lost essence, nor does it fall into the void of historicization, because it problematizes the notion of organizing a working class. The style here functions as a minor ~~epic~~ where citation works as the arrival of the noncoherent voices of an irrecoverable past. One has to pay attention to the textual space in which the theoretical problematization of awakening and ~~enlightenment~~ is staged.

Recalling Violence

After repeating that he is sick and in need of medical attention (although he does not have health care), the worker expresses a desire that synthesizes the overarching problem of labor: "*My desire (my last desire) is to fall down in the middle of an irreverent racket so as to drag an endless row of shelves* with me and make the commodities be the ones that bury me. But it is an absurd dream."[36] This death wish to be buried by the commodity system that he protects reveals another duality: on one side the desire to die (to fall into an abyss that would put an end to his misery), and on the other, an ambiguous end/death/fall. The language used here plays, like the words *retener* and *luces*, with the possibility of opening up different ways of reading and of connecting the series announced by the titles: metals (associated with Iquique and the miners), the *peso* (which can be read both as the Chilean currency and as weight), and death (which, added to *peso*—as in *peso muerto*—evokes the Moneda Palace, the site where the military staged their takeover and also the Iquique massacre).

The play of time-money-destruction is configured as different forms of violence that generate an incredible image at the end of the section when the worker is required to work twenty-four hours nonstop without overtime. The supermarket is about to feature its end-of-year sale. At this moment, he says: "The new year is coming. I count the minutes with my fingers. . . . The guards, fully armed, enter the supermarket and withdraw large amounts of money, and move toward the armored vehicle, carrying out a beautiful *war operation*. The arms, the stature, the decided gesture, and *the loot* in big sacks of money. *The year withdraws full of signs*. Prosperous year, and me, here I am, standing in the supermarket, guarding the strict circulation of money."[37] This quote unites the various series of polyvocal signs that have traversed the narrative and evokes many different associations for the reader: war zone, crime scene, circulation of money that, while relating to the present of the marketplace (through the continuous series of massacred bodies but accommodating different forms of killing), connects with the series from the past that composes the other side of the page—the titles.

The moment in which the worker perceives all of these different layers of space coincides with spending twenty-four hours on the job; he is *retenido* in the sense of being kept prisoner while witnessing the withdrawal of the money, which can be also read as the withdrawal of his expropriated time. The last words are symptomatic: "The bells ring, and an impressive beam of fireworks is unleashed. Twenty-four hours. Twenty-four (hours). Who cares about the imminence of dismissal. There is a need *to put an end* to this chapter."[38] The dismissal closes the chapter: *but what chapter?* The ambiguity of "end" and "chapter" in the novel at once suggests the relevance of textual space, as the readability of history relates to the practice of reading and writing in which the problem of awakening is configured. The final image of robbery with which the chapter (and the section) close embodies a possible reading of the political history of the twentieth century. The withdrawal of the gains of the day can be read in relation to the reiterated theft of labor and destruction of workers' bodies. With this, Eltit establishes a parallel between the daily destruction of the increasingly exhausted body of the worker and the body of certain parts of history, stripped of any possible critique of this process of destruction. The connection of awakening with this possible arrival lies in the dual meaning of the word "robbery." It points toward the expropriation of historicity mentioned at the beginning of the text (that which the dates-places try to re-create as a necessary critical rethinking of emancipatory struggles) as well as toward the figure of the quotation itself.

Here, *fin* (end) emerges as the last place in which the ambiguity seen in *retener* and *luces* is played out, this time in connection to the modes of thinking of violence and action. In the "Critique of Violence," Benjamin discusses the distinction posed by philosopher Georges Sorel between political general strikes and proletarian general strikes, the former implying the conservation of the status quo and the latter a destruction that seeks to create a new society from scratch. This is addressed throughout the section "El despertar de los trabajadores" through the reference to Iquique and the strike that was stopped by the state massacre. The Chilean philosopher Willy Thayer approaches the Iquique general strike as moving within a Sorelian notion of reactive measures (stop violence with violence). However, Eltit complicates these two sides (conservation of the status quo versus creation of a new society) by highlighting how the different systems of violence emerge as both impure and differentiated. She seems to be suggesting a different way to approach violence, avoiding the binary extremes of destruction/construction by pointing toward the problem of the transformability of the political experience.

This new approach to violence can be read in tandem with the problematization of the idea of awakening, which the text poses while questioning the two dominant ideologies of the moment (the ideal of the mature and the awakened consciousness of right and left). The notion of awakening is innately ambiguous, which complicates the theoretical binarism that used to rule the narrativization of political violence on the left and right. This raises the possibility of thinking of another narrative space, in which these binaries could be displaced in a critical way. In relation to this point, Derrida's reflections on Benjamin's classic text on violence shed some light on *Mano de obra*'s rethinking of politics and of the rewriting of political (hi)stories:

> It belongs to the structure of fundamental violence in that it calls for the repetition of itself and founds what ought to be preserved, preservable, promised to heritage and to tradition, to partaking (*partage*). A foundation is a promise. Every positing permits and promises, posits ahead; it posits

by setting and by promising. And even if a promise is not kept in fact, iterability inscribes the promise as guard in the most irruptive instant of foundation. Thus it inscribes the possibility of repetition at the heart of the originary. Better, or worse, it is inscribed in the law (*loi*) of iterability; it stands under its law or before its law. Consequently, there is no more pure foundation or pure position of law, and so a pure founding violence, than there is a purely preserving violence. *Positing is already iterability*, a call for self-preserving repetition. Preservation in its turn refounds, so that it can preserve what it claims to found. Thus there can be no rigorous opposition between positing and preserving, only what I will call (and Benjamin does not name it) a *differantial contamination* between the two, with all the paradoxes that this may lead to. No rigorous distinction between a general strike and a partial strike (again, in an industrial society, we would also lack the technical criteria for such a distinction), nor, in Georges Sorel's sense, between a general *political* strike and a general *proletarian* strike. Deconstruction is also the thought *of* this differantial contamination—and the thought *taken by* the necessity of this contamination.[39]

By appealing to "differantial contamination," a certain undecidability is inscribed that refers to the instance that separates, spatially and temporally, the retrace that makes it impossible to fix the signified as eternal or transcendental (something I illustrated in the words *retener* and *luces*). A powerful process of transformation can take place in the act of remarking and remembering in connection to awakening that places us between the general proletarian strike and the *Bildung* (and other forms of violence) that came afterwards.

In this sense the interstice in Eltit's text constitutes a space between titles (subtitled), between the textual and historical space and the space of the supermarket in literature. Temporal and spatial indeterminability was characteristic of awakening in Benjamin as a process that cannot be delimited with a precise beginning and end (he differentiates between awakening as process and awakened consciousness as the dream of enlightened reason). Eltit offers this sense of a process of permanent (endless) awakening. From a controlled past, framed in the prisons left in language by the 1973 coup, she creates the possibility of multiple crossings toward those emptied titles, a search that leads us in the opposite direction perhaps to the quotes (from Iquique toward Santiago) given that it assumes going from Santiago (from the supermarket) to Iquique, from the present to the past.

The text is bounded by the two biggest massacres of the twentieth century in Chile: Iquique and the coup. However, Eltit stages a different view of those events through the experience-event of "El despertar." This implies a building-*Bildung* in terms of a formative-educational ~~enlightened~~ counterculture that complicates the Sorelian distinction between destruction-creation, for what kind of act does this *Bildung* imply as a performance that reacts while acting? Where can we trace the border separating the formation of a counterculture (that implies forms of violence and exclusions) and the creative destruction that would introduce a new culture? I bring in Benjamin's figure of awakening instead of defeat because, in his discussions of Brecht, he is more interested in the problem of the *transformation* of latent elements within the capitalist desiring-machine than in following the more purist, Adornian break within the philosophical critique of dialectics.[40]

I think that examining Benjamin's position here allows me to adopt an approach that does not erase the implications of what one is criticizing or the constitution of oneself as a critic. This approach posits the act of being a critic as being part of that which we criticize but from which we try to escape through the performance of critical acts. I offer an attempt to think about the idea of a *transformability* that is connected to historicability, something that is latent in the dreams of education in which we dwell as university teachers—our impure forms of engaging with a tradition that, for better or worse, has to do with the opening up of others' paths to "enlightenment."[41]

The idea of a space of awakening that Benjamin develops in the "Convolutes K and N" of The Arcades Project is permeated by a rich duality in which awakening is seen as an act of remembrance that not only takes place in reading and writing but also in the body and architecture. On the one hand, awakening refers to the space of history ("here the concern is to find the constellation of awakening . . . it is a question of the dissolution of mythology into the space of history [*Geschichtsraum*]") that implies a textual realm and project: "Just as Proust begins the story of his life with an awakening, so must every presentation of history begin with awakening; in fact, it should treat of nothing else."[42] On the other hand, awakening takes place in a space. The philosopher Samuel Weber emphasizes that "awakening is essentially spatial," adding that "the person awakening never wakes up in general, but always in and with respect to a determinate place. The locality in turn is never closed upon itself or self-contained, but opened to further relationships by the iterations that take place 'in' it."[43]

In *Mano de obra*, awakening is posed in relation to the space in which the text is written—that is, the space in which the space of history, as a textual event, occurs as well as to the act of reading as the possibility of crossing borders instead of being *retenido* (detained) by the fantasies of retention analyzed earlier. Thus awakening involves a double play between the possibility of remembering "what has (never) been," the truncated past, that which never was (the possibility of reading that which was never written, never retained as a full presence in the catalogue), and the process of learning to remember what is closest to us in a more physical, material way. As Benjamin wrote, "awakening is the great exemplar of memory: the occasion on which it is given to us to remember what is closest, tritest, most obvious."[44] As the phrase "Hay que poner fin a este capítulo" ("One has to put an end to this chapter") coincides with the literal end of the chapter, it can be read as the literary text reflecting on itself, on its own place, asking also how literary space can become the site for a different way of thinking the history of buried emancipatory struggles. This is another way of approaching the role of the mysteriously quoted titles of the working-class press—as an insistence on the necessity of reinventing ways in which language could become the site of a critical project. It seems to show the role of awakening within the realm and task of literature in neoliberal times (to awaken from the market's power over literary matters and genres).

Mano de obra foregrounds the issue of awakening connected to the promise and necessary rethinking of the different unwritten sides in a history of emancipatory projects. Eltit stages this problematic by evoking the "The Awakening" as a publication that existed in the past as a process (in a historical sense) and as a duality that forces us to rethink the role of the quotes in terms of the quotability (iterability) of history. This is shown by the dual meaning of *El despertar* and "El despertar," the historical past (as a constellation formed by the Iquique massacre, the publication, the foundation of the Socialist Workers Party, and the creation of a proletarian culture) and the promise of an endless project of emancipation that would need to re-mark (rewrite, re-create) that which never occurred in the past. *Mano de obra* offers the possibility of a critical act of reading that uses repetition to connect the uncovering of an oppressed past and oppression in the present. Eltit's novel uncovers different processes and means of destroying and exploiting the workers through style and (as) content, in the dramatization of a repetition of destruction and in the different methods for massacring the bodies of workers throughout history.

The constellation of awakening as a dialectical image (shock) shows us another way to think of history and space that is neither the "advancement" of "what has been" (as a promise of that which never took place), nor a staging of the writing of history itself.[45] Eltit's style in *Mano de obra* allows us to see the passage from the deterritorialized quotation to its inevitable reinsertion within a different context. This makes us think of ways in which we could see the coimplication between the waking body and the impossible (fissured) space of the truncated past in spatial terms. Both senses are implied and inseparable in a counterpoint between *El despertar*, the title of the publication (referring to a constellation of events), and "El despertar," the title of the supermarket section. Connected to the act of reading, awakening suggests a never-ending process of interpretation of the past as a promise since, as the cultural theorist Eduardo Cadava has written, "the moment of awakening must be repeated endlessly because no one is ever fully awakened." It implies a "spacing that prevents the now from being awake to itself."[46] That is, the repetition of the act of awakening, where reading works as a mode of crossing the borders between past(s) and present(s), dramatizes the promise of emancipation in a present that becomes writable and readable. This results in a tension between singularity and repetition, which any promise carries within itself. *Mano de obra* poses a necessary rethinking of the literary as a horizon where the problem of interruption suggested by quotation needs also to be approached as a problem of reconnection, in all of its ambiguous possibilities and dangers.

In chapter 2, I advanced my idea of "minor epic" as an attempt to problematize and connect the postdictatorship of the 1990s with the zones that are bringing back some figures of dictatorship in the present. What I have been suggesting with the analysis of the narratives about the prison and the supermarket that focus on the prisoner and the worker is a mode of reading in which both narrations of past and present are interrupted by that which was always constituted as an outsider by national and global discourses of freedom of the market. Within that map the minor epic causes the interruption of a pure poetics or literarization: it introduces what we do not see, the hell below the mall (the exhausted subjects in the sweatshops), and with it the impossibility of simply or transparently reinscribing what is excluded from the (major) language—its excrement.

Mano de obra shows the impossibility of attempting to inscribe in language the destroyed or massacred remnants of the past, remnants that, by the very act of truncation, open up as a promise yet to be fulfilled. In this sense the work, written like an escape/fugue, confers on us a triple task: configuring the supermarket of the present as an open prison; contrasting the present with a buried history of working-class struggle; and questioning the key phrase "work force," as the space between the novel's own title, *Mano de obra*, and the awakening of the workers, both related to the problem of temporality and marking (historicization). By focusing on key words that link temporality, spatialization, and discursivity, *Mano de obra* can be read from a crossroads somewhat reminiscent of the subterranean encounter in *La fuga*, except that now escape is impossible. Once again, we can think about this on two levels. One of these links light in the supermarket to the surveillance that makes the supermarket a prison; on this level we find a reference to the enlightenment in its connection to the form of prison, vigilance, domestication.

On the other level, light in relationship to the Enlightenment also refers to the zone outside the supermarket evoked by the titles and subtitles, a sort of counter enlightenment, an impure one but one implicated in the past in a formative way. I am proposing here to read political history as a differential coimplication between these projects. It is perhaps this Russian doll captivity in which every movement seems connected to a form of imprisonment that introduces a necessary question about the way political history in post-miracle Chile can be seen as a closed world, an open prison. However, the titles and subtitles are there, as if alerting us to an outer edge. They are not an absolute outside but a space marked by the border between the supermarket and the past erased by it. At one point they are being watched by the world of the supermarket, but they are also being brought in by the writer as reminders/remainders, scraps of a struggle in worlds that were also imprisoned after the great massacre at Iquique. In this sense the text urges us to rethink the notion of violence and destruction as directed at the textual zone and at the literary act that we see here as a performance of historicization.

4

Freedom, Democracy, and the Literary Uncanny in Roberto Bolaño's *Nocturno de Chile*

> It all makes me think that we will enter the new millennium under the admonition of the word *abject*.... September 11, 1973, soars over us like the penultimate Chilean condor.... Sometimes I have the impression that September 11th wants to train us. Sometimes I have the impression that September 11th has tamed us in an irreversible way. What would have happened if September 11th had never existed? ...
>
> It is the end of the military presence, but not the end of the quicksand and silence that the military presence has installed in Chilean civil life, which makes one think that it will last for eternity or for such a long time in the space of a human life that it is close to eternity.
>
> —Roberto Bolaño, "Una proposición modesta"

Roberto Bolaño made these remarks after one of his first trips back to Chile after the end of the dictatorship, a trip that he described in interviews and articles as having caused him a sense of strangeness linked to the uncanny. In fact, one of the articles is given the ironic and ambiguous subtitle "A mi casa no más llego" (I just arrived home) that suggests a certain cynicism related to the experience of being "back home." In the many accounts the writer gave of this visit, the nation is figuratively presented as a home/house that has turned into an open, invisible, prison, a spatial figure that relates to the main topic of this book: postdictatorship as an open prison. Bolaño gives fragmentary accounts of this experience in essays and conferences, referring sarcastically to a Chile that is imprisoned by the mute and invisible effects of the dictatorship on the future of history, on civil life, and on the geography of the sayable.

Borrowing the title of an article written by the journalist Samuel Valenzuela, "A mi casa no más llego," Bolaño frames his sense of having arrived in Chile in an irreverent tone connected directly with one of his most controversial novels, *Nocturno de Chile*. His first experience in postdictatorship Chile takes place on a *fundo* (an estate) located outside Santiago. He describes the place as a former site for literary gatherings that was subsequently transformed into a museum, a restaurant, and at the moment of his arrival, a vineyard. It constituted "the Dadaist stage of my first meeting in my homeland."[1] It seems that the multiple functions and temporalities of the place Bolaño first visited (literary soirées, museum, restaurant, vineyard) played a key role when he was crafting *Nocturno de Chile*, in which the history of Chilean politics and literary practices is radically questioned. Taking the uncanny as a mode of reading history, Bolaño uses the house to represent the nation and to question literature as confining forms of "othering" historicization. The uncanny feeling of going back home seems to lead the writer to explore the idea of house/home/domesticity in areas that go usually unexamined. *Nocturno* starts and ends with the literary figuration of the house of the nation as a prison, but a prison that becomes visible only from a certain perspective.

I would like to pose now a dialogue between Bolaño's remarks in the first and the second paragraphs of the epigraph, which figure life after the dictatorship as an open prison and explore more directly the relationship between the (open) prison and the geography of the sayable. The passage questions the very possibility of placing in language a history of emancipatory and liberationist practices, pointing to an invisible form of imprisonment that confines the possibility of historicizing the past in ways other than those allowed by two decades of dictatorship. Here Bolaño discusses his visceral reaction on hearing conversations between leftist politicians on television:

> I got the impression (*possibly a fantastic one*) that some of them, specifically those who were favored by the majority of the electorate, were *behaving like recently-released prisoners* who were still *under the thumb, more imaginary than real, of their former jailers*. . . . And this is where the word *abject* comes up again. A harsh and burdensome abjection that at times seems irremediable. It is true that the left committed countless crimes, either actively or by omission. To demand that Chilean politicians on the left (who I suspect have actively committed very few crimes) recite a permanent *mea culpa* for Stalin's concentration camps is an outlandish one by any standards. But that is where political discourse seems to be headed. Never-ending penitence that replaces any exchange or defense

of ideas. . . . The left committed verbal crimes in Chile (a specialty of the left in Latin America), moral crimes, and probably killed people. But they didn't put live rats in any girl's vagina. They didn't have time to create their *evil*, they didn't have time to create their forced labor camps. Is it possible that given time, they would have? Of course it's possible. Nothing in our century's history allows us to suppose a rosier parallel history. But the fact is that the concentration camps in Chile were not the left's doing, nor were the shootings, the tortures, the disappeared, or the repression. All that was done by the right. All that was the work of the military regime. Nevertheless, we will go into the third millennium with politicians on the left apologizing, which isn't so bad, and is even, if you think about it, a good thing, as long as *all* the politicians apologize.[2]

Given the disproportion Bolaño refers to here between the mea culpa of leftist officials tamed or imprisoned by the neoliberal consensus and the silence of the Chilean right regarding its crimes, it is intriguing that he chooses to focus his literary historicization of the twilight of the twentieth century in *Nocturno de Chile* on the uneasy conscience of an ultra right-winger. The novel narrates the feverish deathbed confession of Sebastián Urrutia Lacroix, an Opus Dei priest who collaborated with the Pinochet regime while working as a literary critic and poet. With the author's characteristic humor, the novel stages a ghostly revenge, a peculiar kind of martyrdom by the imagination that creates a space for what never took place. If we approach the novel in dialogue with Bolaño's impressions of the uncanny on the return to his homeland, we can read it as a critique of how the history of postdictatorship Chile only spoke one language—a domesticated one in which left and right shared the same home, leaving noisy unarticulated voices outside the geography of the house.

In *Nocturno de Chile*, Bolaño recounts what could perhaps be the official right-wing mea culpa and accuses the neoliberal left (the "Concertación" coalition) of lacking courage. A fact that is not insignificant but is not mentioned by critics is that *Nocturno* was published in 2000, exactly three decades after the victory of the Popular Unity coalition (of 1970).[3] Following the notion of alternative calendars, the novel could be read as a unique form of commemoration of the Popular Unity government activated by opposition to the cowed self-laceration of the left that Bolaño identifies in his "Una proposición modesta." The entire novel focuses on what the author describes as the great national silence: the right-wing conscience (home) pursued and haunted by the ghosts of its hunting. The text is organized around the spatial figure of the house. The priest's conscience-memory is split between his obsession as a critic and writer with enlightening readers in his newspaper column (education/domestication/ housing) and his inability to control certain ghosts that haunt his memory, disturb his peace, and provoke the text we are reading. Clearly the obsession in the text with the problematics of home and with immunization of the household can be read as a reflection on the idea of protection that was the Pinochet dictatorship's legacy. The notion of "protected democracy" was the military regime's dream of controlling and predetermining the future architecture of democratic politics. The system of "protected democracy" was devised by a group of conservative judges, who presented a draft proposal for it to the Council of State (created in 1976). It was a deeply authoritarian piece of legislation that included, among other things, eight-year presidential terms, limits to the powers of Congress, and mechanisms to ensure the power of the armed forces over future governments. These provisional rules stayed in place for a decade.

The Chilean sociologist Tomás Moulian has defined the outlines of "protected democracy" in the following terms: transfer of sovereignty to the market; obliteration of the notion of historicity by weakening the discursive systems that offered alternatives to neoliberalism; naturalization of the notion of change or transition to include the idea of an expansion of current practices, thereby eliminating the idea of a transformation of the social structure; and a technocratic notion of government that depoliticized decision-making systems in favor of scientific discourse about the value of efficiency and pragmatism. Moulian suggests that in this capitalist counter-passive-revolution, the sign of Pinochetism in civil life (which would become entrenched in the notion of invariability that was the dictator's constitutional legacy) was its celebration of the success of the economic miracle in opposition to fear of failure. Thus the dominant ideology was disguised as ideology-free technology within a paradigm that saw the end of history as the end of ideologies—a time for action and not ideas.[4] In this sense the "protection" of a democracy involved an act of immunization by decades of military rule against the possible arrival (or return) of the unique form of Marxism that produced Chilean socialism.[5]

The play on architecture and the architectural in the trope of the house/home seen throughout *Nocturno de Chile* constitutes a literary reflection on the notion of protected democracy, one that focuses on the figure of the house as nation, a house that needed to be cleaned and put in order to become secure. This figuration also plays with the sense of protected democracy as the apex of an immunitarian paradigm in politics, the dream of a systematic, quasi-absolute determinability of the geography of the possible.[6] Protected democracy sought to determine beforehand that which could and could not happen, not only in the political economy but also in the realm of political transformation. In contrast to the immunizing logic of a guarded democracy that imprisons historicization (like the fortress-mall in *Mano de obra*), *Nocturno* explores the notion of decay and illness, in the decline overtaking the fever-racked body of the protagonist, exposed to his own end.

The character of the protagonist Urrutia is based on the memory of a real person (José Miguel Ibáñez Langlois), a literary columnist for the conservative newspaper *El mercurio* who was the supreme arbiter of the Chilean literary canon for more than a decade. The novel opens with Urrutia's obsession over his lost peace of mind. His consciousness is haunted by the figure of a silent young man who intrudes into his thoughts unexpectedly: "I used to be at peace with myself. Quiet and at peace. *But it all blew up unexpectedly.* . . . I was at peace. I am no longer at peace. . . . My aim is not to stir up conflict, it never has been, my aims are peace and responsibility for one's actions, for one's words and silences."[7] The ambiguous specter that haunts his consciousness throughout the novel stands both as a double of the young priest (who comes to regret his support of the long massacre under the dictatorship) and as the specter of a leftist militant, who reappears at the end of the novel as a corpse.

The text starts with Urrutia's initiation as a priest and poet in the 1950s and finishes with his death at the moment of redemocratization and national reconciliation in the 1990s. "And then democracy returned, the moment came for national reconciliation," the priest says, irritably.[8] At this point we encounter another critical perspective on the literary staging of the architectonics of transition, coming from a different standpoint than in Eleuterio Fernández Huidobro (the prisoner) and Diamela Eltit (the worker)—one that, while trying to maintain peace of mind about the past, is overtaken by the inevitable recurrence of certain images connected with the abject, images that emerge from the "corners of memory" (*rincón del recuerdo*) of the protagonist's delirious mind. As if following philosopher Friedrich Schelling's definition of the uncanny, quoted by Sigmund Freud in his classic text ("Uncanny is what one calls everything that was meant to remain secret and hidden and has come into the open"), the novel is organized around a slippage between home and not-home, home and the unhomely, housing and haunting, the return of certain images that emerge whenever the character gets lost.[9]

When he loses his way, he stumbles upon visions of spatiotemporal zones that should have remained invisible, as if imprisoned outside the borders of the house that stands for the place of official historicization. This is established by a play allowed by the nuances of the word *perderse/perder* in Spanish, which refer to "*perderse,*" as in "getting lost" and also as "in perdition" (*perdición*) and "*perder*" as in "to lose or fail." The play with the word and act of "*perder(se)*" constitutes the difficulties that emerge within the labyrinth of memories of the priest; it is when he loses himself and gets lost that what should have remained unseen is figured as a countertextual instance that interrupts and deconstructs parts of the national *Bildung* (formation) of Chile to which the title *Nocturno de Chile* seems to refer. Organized around the irruption of that which should have remained concealed, the play on the uncanny in *Nocturno* is directly linked to a conflict between architecture and freedom in the figuration of specific buildings that are connected directly to national and international political history.

By focusing on the detour into metaphor that allows the untimely arrival of heteronomy, the novel establishes a metaliterary reflection on a supremely literary phenomenon (the uncanny), through a tension between the narrativization of the national *Bildung* and the moments of denarrativization, of breakdown or illegibility that create "a fissure between language and signification."[10] These instances of denarrativization do not mark the complete end or total exhaustion of meaning in the text but rather instances of incommensurability that urge us to think of a different way of conceiving prose. They are moments when the text betrays itself, moments of anarchy or abyss in the text that are also moments when it breaks free, when we wonder how the gap in meaning reconnects to the heterogeneous space of narrativization. They produce a defamiliarization of the house without directly getting rid of it, which is part of the priest-poet's fantasy in seeking a clear border between inside and out, a border that will keep both spheres uncontaminated. These moments stress the complicity of things the priest wished to keep separate, a visible zone and another disavowed one. *Nocturno* thus explores the demarcation of spatial and temporal borders in the (post)dictatorship world through the role of the uncanny in the house-prison built by the dictatorship over political history to exclude novelty (information that is not known) and privilege the notion of public secret. *Nocturno de Chile* stages the emergence of what was there all along but was supposed to remain implicit—which, as Freud says in his analysis of the uncanny in literature, is not about informational language but about aesthetics and perceptibility.[11]

This problematic culminates in the last episode in the book, which contains the most repressed material in the text: the three-story house in which writers and artists gather in the large living room located on the ground floor while an important secret torture and interrogation center run by the Pinochet secret police (the DINA) functions in the basement. One of the literary guests in the house glimpses a prisoner downstairs on a metal cot, an image that, as the cultural theorist Patrick Dove has observed, is a cliché, a stereotype among the ways in which terror is depicted nowadays.[12] I show how cliché is central to the uncanny in *Nocturno* and how different clichéd images affect the narration, producing an arrest that brings out into the open that which should have remained out of discursivity, out of the realm of the sayable. The clichés that recur in the text involve the stereotype of the ugly peasants whom the priest does not understand, the leftist militants depicted as pigeons, and finally, the prisoner lying on the metal cot.

The enjoyment of the obvious in *Nocturno* begs the question of what consensus this obviousness presupposes. How is obviousness constructed? From what standpoint is something obvious? What does the revelation of the hidden show about the constitution of what is given? This chapter analyzes how the novel shows different perspectives on domesticity through the figure of the house that metamorphoses along with the different economies (the *fundo*; the interior of the country; the protection of capital at the time of the Popular Unity reforms; the practice of secret detention and disappearances that made Chile the home-laboratory of the neoliberal global economic program). These uncomfortable images make us wonder about the nonfamiliar in and outside the house, how domestic economy is marked by textual memory.

Domestic Economy and Aesthetics

As the architectural theorist Mark Wigley has shown in detail, the figure of "the house" is crucial for approaching the contested relationship between thought, metaphoricity, and architecture in Western philosophical narrative. It operates as a mega-image of the familiar that configures the powerful fantasy of belonging and closeness, shelter, security (the abode of the family, the familiar abode, and the abode of the familiar).[13] Thus the house is not just one more metaphor but *the* metaphor that makes metaphoricity philosophically possible: "It determines the condition of the proper, from which the metaphorical is then said to be detached and inferior."[14] The "paradigmatic mechanism of domestication," the figure of the house implies the always implicit articulation of language as a problematic mode of housing "because it appropriates, making proper by excluding representation and establishing a 'proximity' to presence."[15] Wigley states that every tradition (a system of repetitions naturalized throughout the nation's history) "is organized around a certain image of housing."[16] The iterability that I analyzed in earlier chapters reemerges here in an architectural and discursive figure in which we see the attempt to maintain a sense of one's house being one's own and of ownership (domestic economy), which determines the process of signification. However, the houses *in the text* expose what is impossible for them—what the house keeps out and therefore what haunts it; that which haunts the house and attempts to hunt down and fix the meaning of the proper in the space of the property—owning the place of meaning.

In this sense *Nocturno*'s exploration of how and whether the house can be figured at all urges us to analyze and denaturalize different domestication mechanisms that "go without saying" or are assumed as obvious, as the home of thought for the nation. Thus the text passes from the familiar-domestic to the zone of what those mechanisms exclude in order to constitute themselves. In the process it uses cliché to examine who are the possible subjects who inhabit the interior and what conditions make that inhabitance possible or impossible. The use of cliché is an unusual literary gesture, because instead of valuing the new in the literary site, Bolaño seems to want us to think rather about the force of what we take as general, natural, non-novel. This harkens back to the theme of chapter 3: a Benjaminian awakening based not on absolute novelty but on the possibility of denaturalizing that which we suppose to be close. In *Nocturno* literary mechanisms of defamiliarization are applied to the perception of temporal cycles. The cyclical temporality of legalized violence can be perceived as processes of accumulation of capital that reiterate the maintenance of proper order in the house (which is protected from expropriation). However, cycles of expropriation emerge from other perspectives (for example, the prisoner's and the worker's) as periods of imprisonment, the other face of progress as eternity in which life and the material reproduction of existence become tedium, bodily decline, slavery. This temporal game is seen in the first great house of *Nocturno*, the site of the narrator's literary initiation and as our first encounter or collision with a series of inassimilable moments of denarrativization of Chile's architectural history.

The text begins with the literary baptism of Urrutia as a young man when he meets Farewell, a right-wing critic who dominates the nation's literary scene and whom Urrutia immediately adopts as the father and guru of his writing life. Bolaño narrates these scenes humorously, introducing images of fledgling and falcon, which become fundamental later in the novel to represent the suppression (extermination) of subversives.[17] The protagonist recalls "with the naïveté of a fledgling, I said that I wanted to be a literary critic, that I wanted to follow in his footsteps."[18] However, the response from the "Father" of criticism jars the young apprentice: "In this country of estate owners, he said, literature is an oddity and nobody values knowing how to read."[19] This generates a silence from the young priest that disconcerts the critic: "Perhaps you have an estate or your father does? No, I said. Well, I do, said Farewell, I have an estate near Chillán."[20] He invites the priest to visit it along with some leading Chilean authors.

After accepting the invitation, the narrator tries to imagine the place: "I imagined that estate where the critic's path was indeed strewn with roses, where knowing how to read was valued, and where taste was more important than practical necessities and obligations, and then I looked up again and my seminarist's eyes met Farewell's falcon eyes and I said yes, several times, I said yes I would go, it would be an honour to spend the weekend at the estate of Chile's greatest literary critic."[21] The imagery here synthesizes the drama throughout the text: the tension between literature and rural economy. The young apprentice imagines the literary house as a utopian space, a path of roses with no conflict between aesthetics and the soil, the opposing realms of neutrality and profit.[22] However, the utopian image of the literary house is interrupted by the hawkish gaze of the critic, setting up a contrast between the beauty of the roses and the bird of prey (the falcon). This points to a central set of conflicts in the text between land ownership and language, landed gentry and literature, the economy of bodies and disinterested (immaterial) aesthetics.

This duality is dramatized by the architectonics of housing, creating the first observation (reading) and description (writing) of Farewell's living room, which provokes some uncertainty in the narrator, for the room seems to be split between library and horror museum, between the *casa* (house/home) of language and the *caza* (hunting) of animals, between mental work (books, reading) and stuffed heads displayed as trophies (barbarism). "The expression 'living room' is woefully inadequate to describe that combination of library and hunting lodge, lined with shelves full of encyclopedias, dictionaries and souvenirs that Farewell had bought on his journeys through Europe and North Africa, as well as at least *a dozen mounted heads*, including those of a pair of pumas bagged by Farewell's father, no less."[23] Books and stuffed heads represent two types of accumulation that dislocate the narrator and imaginatively split his reading of the cultural house into two kinds of process: culture and hunting, housing and hunting (in Spanish only one letter's difference sends us from one function to another: *casa/caza*). In this gap, Chilean national culture is expressed as a series of asymmetrical dualities that go from the estate-house of national literature, the natural museum of civilizing massacre and the life of bodies that the priest goes on to find when he gets lost looking for the outside.

Disturbed for no explicit reason and also uncomfortable because the greatest critic of Chilean literature makes some passes at him, Urrutia starts to find the ideal house claustrophobic. He decides to go out for a walk so as to literally retrace what he imagines will be "the path of roses." However, in the novel's paired trick mirrors, the falcon's gaze that interrupts the dream of roses will be superseded during this walk by its unrecognizable but constituent double: the estate's rural workers, or peasants (*campesinos*). The narrator gets lost in the wood and has an unsettling encounter with some campesinos. At this point the fissure described earlier in the living room resurfaces in different layers of space(s) and time(s). The reading of architectural space at the beginning now becomes a portrait of the campesinos, whom the narrator perceives as grotesque:

> Rings under their eyes. Parted lips. Shiny skin stretched over cheekbones. A patience that I feared was not Christian resignation. A patience native to some far-away place, or so it seemed. Not a Chilean patience, although those women were Chileans. . . . A patience that seemed to have come from outer space. And that patience almost wore my own patience out. And their words and their murmuring spread out through the surrounding countryside, among the trees swaying in the wind, among the weeds swaying in the wind, among the fruits of the earth swaying in the wind. And with each passing moment I felt more impatient, since I was expected back at the lodge. . . . And the women just smiled, looked severe or feigned surprise, mystery giving way to illumination on their initially blank faces, their expressions tense with mute questions or opening in wordless exclamations.[24]

Here, instead of the literary rose, the young poet comes face to face with a world that perturbs him with its incomprehensibility and antipoetic nature. Impatient, he can only catalog these people as contrary to the beauty of the rose: as ugliness, the ugly, the monstrous and disproportionate.[25]

As Dove has pointed out, the patience of the campesinos is a subaltern affect experienced by those who "dwell within the boundaries of national sovereignty but who are not visible as part of the whole, not yet seen as fully Chilean" and who remain in a spatial and temporal limbo since they inhabit neither the world of "Christian resignation" nor the world of "teleological logic" of the waves of modernization.[26] Patience, as a subaltern affect-time that resists imagination by the narrator except in a negative way (what *is not*) makes him impatient. It is a crucial moment in the text, for the dissymmetry between faces, time, space, and language defies the imaginary geography of Chile when the narrator encounters, in those who inhabit the land differently, the un-Chilean nature of Chile just where he was expecting to see/find/inhabit a path of roses. What exceeds the world of the (Chilean) house emerges asymmetrical and inassimilable to its logic, either Christian or aesthetic. This nonresigned patience that the priest imagines as part of that unintelligible other seems to point to a heterogeneous time in the house's present, a delay that imperceptibly does something (it insists or subsists) and that creates a certain impatience in the narrator. It is perhaps this patient delay that does not inhabit the shared fantasy of a teleological unity that is associated with the desert, the nonarchitectural and uninhabitable site, the ungrounded (unpredictable and uncertain for the house) that generates the priest's impatience as he thinks of returning to the time of the house where others "were waiting for him."

However, it is worth asking why the priest is disturbed by this patience of the "un-Chilean Chileans," this way of being foreign that the priest does not understand, that challenges his ability to name it, his ability to link language to this most supposedly telluric (folkloric) place of Chilean identity (those who work the land and are closest to it). There is an insoluble contradiction in the image of a place in Chile inhabited by beings who are both Chilean and not Chilean. This repeats the "casa-caza" duality of the living room but brings in bastard, dissymmetrical, and unrecognizable elements (not embalmed this time but living and inhabiting the place of the roses), a split caused by the narrator's persistence in going to look for the path of roses, getting lost and coming face to face with what should have remained invisible, offstage. Running into the campesinos marks the first instance of dislocation of the ideal of the literary as place and introduces anxiety about the coexistence of heterogeneous elements that do not inhabit the same time and space. This becomes an instance of irreducibility and incommensurability but also of coimplication since the estate (the Chilean economy) could not subsist without that un-Chilean fragment of Chile.

Thus what appears in the open, in broad daylight, destabilizes the economy of that antieconomic fantasy, by interrupting and contaminating the rigid oppositions that cause the young priest to want to keep the path of roses separate from the campesinos. This does not imply that the priest does not know that there is a campesino workforce maintaining the house. That is not the point: it is simply the need to carry on acting as if they could not be seen, did not exist. *Nocturno* stages irruptions of images that take over the mind-text of the priest again and again, interfering with his logic, making it impossible to keep out what is making the inside possible. On returning to the city, he recalls: "My literary baptism had reached its conclusion. During the nights that followed, so many varied and often *contradictory images* crowded in on me, inhabiting my thoughts and my sleeplessness!"[27] These contradictions among images that will continue to appear in the text concern the indigestible elements of the house, which interrupt the young narrator's previous ideal of a path of roses. The image here functions as a Benjaminian arrest produced by contradictions. Rather than advancing the narrator's progress, the contradictions halt it at a problematic constellation. Instead of leading to the other side, his path is truncated, an aporia that the final confession attempts to surmount.

The Architecture of the Nation and the Arrival of the Monstrous: The Popular Unity Coalition, 1970

Like the living room of the estate, the war on communist-marxist-liberationist "subversion" is framed in the narrative by the imagery of architecture and hunting. The falcon that was used to describe Farewell's eyes now stands as a metaphor for the bird of prey that destroyed the safety of the nation (by hunting pigeons that should have been protected by the house—hunting as housing). Something similar now causes a split in the narrator, who turns from being a literary critic and poet to a national security agent on a mission to Europe. The peculiar thing is that this mission is codified as conservation of the architecture of the nation's interests (churches, houses of God on earth) in the face of its possible deterioration at the hands of time (destruction of architecture): "My task would be to go and see, to visit the churches at the forefront of the battle against dilapidation, to evaluate the various methods, to write a report and come back."[28]

This custodial task signals once again the notion of protection associated with the national security measures and colonizing processes. The narrator's first surprise on arriving in Europe is that the cause of deterioration of the great monuments "was pollution caused not by humans but by animals, specifically pigeon shit, the numbers of pigeons . . . having increased exponentially."[29] The solution the church comes up with is to train falcons and launch them from the church to devour the pigeons. The initial house (domestic interior/stuffed animals) becomes associated with contamination as a threat to the conservation of national and international architecture. Once instructed in the art of protecting and conserving architecture, Urrutia returns to Chile to find his peace shattered by the possibility that the Popular Unity coalition might win, which makes Chile un-recognizable; this monstrous fate implies state architecture being overtaken by the electoral victory of a socialist party that will later declare itself marxist. Immediately, the narrator wonders about the inassimilable or unrecognizable elements synthesized in the figure of the monstrous: "Chile, my Chile. What on earth has come over you? I would sometimes ask, leaning out of my open window, looking at the glow of Santiago in the distance. What have they done to you? . . . [A]re you going to change beyond recognition? Become a monster? Then came the elections and Allende won."[30]

The monstrous distortion of Chile is expressed in the narrative structure as syntactic insanity: the Popular Unity's disruptive three-year government is described in two pages with no periods. The punctuation goes wild with the arrival of the new government and the priest's decision to go home and shut himself up to read the classics of the Western literary canon. At this point the craziness of the text's architecture makes the act of reading itself maddening. It refuses to let us pause for breath, causing the same problem for the narrator as the campesinos—the difficulty of making sense when faced with a logic that does not fit easily into his Christian or aesthetic categories. The arrival of the Popular Unity government causes him to make two long but interwoven lists in his memory: a literary genealogy of authors (from Homer to Aristotle) and the economic and social reforms of the parliamentary socialist government. This takes place in one single sentence that is two pages long. It ends with the coup d'état of 1973, which marks the return to peace, normal punctuation, and syntax in the text. Here is an excerpt from those pages:

> When I got back to my *house*, I went straight to my Greek classics. Let God's will be done, I said. I'm going to reread the Greeks. *Respecting the tradition*, I started with Homer, then moved on the Thales of Miletus . . . Zeno of Elea (wonderful), and then a pro-Allende general was killed, and Chile restored diplomatic relations with Cuba and the national census recorded a total of 8,884,746 Chileans and the first episodes of the soap opera *The Right to be Born* were broadcast on television, and I read Tyrtaios of Sparta and Archilochos of Paros and Solon of Athens . . . and the government nationalized the copper mines and then the nitrate and steel industries . . . and the first anti-Allende march was organized, with people banging pots and pans, and I read Aeschylus and Sophocles and Euripides, all the tragedies . . . and in Chile there were shortages and inflation and black marketeering and long queues for food *and Farewell's estate was expropriated in the Land Reform* along with many others *and the Bureau of Women's Affairs was set up* . . . and then nearly half a million people marched in support of Allende, and then came *the coup d'état, the putsch, the military uprising,* the bombing of La Moneda and *when the bombing was finished, the president committed suicide and that put an end to it all.* I sat there in silence, a finger between the pages to mark my place, and I thought: Peace at last. I got up and looked out the window: Peace and quiet.[31]

The "madness" of the Popular Unity's three years in government (which saw land reform, reconfiguration of the idea of law and of the idea of who counts as Chilean—seen in the reference to the census) dislocates the organization of the text, leaving both syntax and architecture (national grammar, monumentality) in a chaotic state.[32] It is difficult for the protagonist to point to the main actions of the Popular Unity in the unit of the sentence, thus the absence of a period. Unthinkable, monstrous actions such as the nationalization of copper, saltpeter, and iron; the agrarian reforms and the expropriation of the estates (including Farewell's); and the opening of a Women's Bureau are counterposed to the Western literary canon, as if the literary-territorial expropriation committed during that chaotic political experiment were soothed by a demarcation of the imperatives of the literary canon.

The architecture of the text sets up an impossible frontier between Chile and the non-Chilean, by using intrasentence punctuation such as commas and parentheses but by being incapable of using the intersentence punctum, the period, as if doing so would echo the earlier image of the estate workers taking over the house itself. The period is replaced by "and," which generates a remorseless accumulation, producing a kind of chaos in the syntactic legislation of the text and in the act of reading itself, which makes us wonder where to stop, where to punctuate in order to breathe. At this moment, exactly halfway through the text, the novel is split in two like Farewell's living room (now expropriated, unrecognizable as an unlimited geography), by those two pages in which the period bringing peace can only arrive in the form of the coup, the bombing of the Moneda Palace, Allende's death, and the recuperation (reappropriation) of the house.[33]

The paradox of this fragment of textual madness is how the monstrous interruption of Chile by all that is unspeakably terrible for the priest can only be resisted and defended from the refuge of the European classics through which truly Chilean literature can be saved. By evoking the monstrous, Bolaño introduces the problem of the recognizable and the limits that reveal the nonrecognizable within the supposedly familiar as an act of reading and writing—the problem of legibility and what becomes unrecognizable from within the reading system. The monstrous transformations of the Popular Unity government were illegible at the time not only from the point of view of the right and the Cold War anticommunist block, but also from the Soviet and Cuban block, which was initially baffled about what kind of socialism this was—the Popular Unity's embrace of Marxism without revolution and with a parliament made them unrecogizable for the so-called socialist countries. On the one hand, the Popular Unity government was a traditional one in that it was ushered in via the electoral process and in its maintenance of a parliamentary structure (which initially enjoyed the support of most of the middle class). On the other hand, when it began land-redistribution programs and started to redesign the national economy, culminating with the expropriation of mining production from international companies, it became a threat. In relation to the trope of "the house," we could say that the problem involves the juxtaposition of two types of households in a single house, a blurry zone of unusual contiguity, since this was not a revolution that took the house by force and destroyed it, but an election won by a curious parliamentary socialist government. This makes that textual economy much more difficult (which is marked by the impossibility of maintaining the boundaries of the sentence).

Language and boundaries emerge in the textual space as expropriated from the usual standards that mark the double problematics in the text: economy and aesthetics, private property and narrativization. It is not accidental that the only explicit expropriation of an estate mentioned is that of Farewell himself, the bastion of national literature, which is progressively appropriated by another principle or meaning of politics (another type of housing). This is the process that the coup cuts off, interrupts, dislocates with its military assault, described officially as necessary to cure or immunize the body of the nation (military officials repeatedly justified the stunning bombing of the presidential palace as "extirpating the marxist cancer") and to protect the national house (establishing a protected democracy to prevent the marxist cancer from recurring in the future). However, the moment of destruction that arrives with the coup creates a problem rather than a solution in the text: the destruction of democracy in Chile is posed as the way to conserve the architecture of democracy (destroying the Moneda Palace through aerial bombing to conserve the Moneda), self-inoculating Chile against its potentially non-Chilean part. With the coup the military regime retakes the house, eliminates the cancer and inoculates the legislature to prevent its legal body being seized again. Properties are returned to their owners and a wave of expropriation of properties belonging to another population (the "subversives") begins. National architecture is restored but in a fractured way, because immediately peace becomes a nightmare, as seen in the image of the last house—a secret detention center where literature coexists with the torture of subversives:

> The following days were strange. It was as if until then we had all been dreaming and had suddenly woken to real life, although occasionally it seemed to be the other way round, as if we had all been plunged into a dream. And we went on living day by day in accordance with the abnormal conventions of the dream-world: anything can happen and whatever hap-

pens the dreamer *accepts* it. . . . We move as if we had no shadows and were unperturbed by that appalling fact. We speak. We eat. *But underneath we are trying not to realize that we are speaking and eating.*[34]

An element of the uncanny—the impossibility of differentiating between dream/nightmare and waking—is expressed here as the effort of trying not to think. There is a constant struggle to control thought in all areas: even speaking and eating must be performed without thinking that one is speaking or eating.[35]

From now on, this will be a fundamental part of the dictatorship's vision, which makes the zone of secrecy a public secret (seeing without seeing, feeling without hearing, and so on). The structure of the regime and the implicit pact that Bolaño says permeates the everyday life of the postdictatorship are based on a form of anesthesia disrupted in the text by the arrival of another house expropriated by the military junta from Jewish activists (who have gone into exile), in which "underneath" means a secret detention center run by the DINA—while on the visible ground floor, writers and artists congregate regularly. Thus the thematic constellation of the house as housing-haunting-hunting is postulated in this last abode in a more explicit and perhaps more intriguing way. By focusing the end of the text on this house that functions as a kind of symmetric double of the initial image of Farewell's estate (literary place/hunting/campesinos), Bolaño highlights the legality and illegality of expropriation, language, the body, and the problem of inhabiting the unlivable. The answer the priest offers when this history emerges as a murmur in the transitional period of national reconciliation also directly invokes the problem of the uncanny: "¿Para qué *remover* lo que *el tiempo* piadosamente *oculta*?"[36] "Why go stirring up things that have gradually settled down over the years?"[37] The original Spanish shows the contrast between concealment and disclosure that I argue is crucial to the novel's treatment of the uncanny in different forms of housing.

Coming to the Open: *Polis*, Public Space, and Interference

The last and maybe most repressed image in *Nocturno* of a house as simultaneously housing art and subversive human bodies reveals an incommensurable coexistence between the gatherings of writers and artists in the large living room (located on the ground floor) and the important secret torture and interrogation center run by the DINA (located in the basement). The artists and writers who attend the cultural gatherings think they know their hostess, María Canales, a would-be writer and the wife of a former CIA agent, Jimmy Thompson, now a secret agent of the DINA in Chile. Bolaño is using the story of the CIA agent Michael Townley, who worked in Chile for the DINA and was accused of masterminding the assassination of the Chilean ambassador to Washington, D.C., Orlando Letelier. Townley was also involved in the assassination of Allende's vice-president Carlos Prats and his wife, Sofía Cuthbert, in Buenos Aires in 1974. María Canales is the name Bolaño uses for Mariana Callejas, convicted as an accomplice to the assassination of General Carlos Prats.[38]

The artists and writers at the meetings believe Jimmy is an executive for a foreign firm that has opened a branch in Chile. An unforeseen encounter with a disappeared detainee occurs in the narration when one of the upstairs guests takes a wrong turn and gets lost. This detour leads to a collision with what should be another layer of time and space, which interrupts the flow of a chronological present of an anesthetized world. This collision provokes the opposite of anesthesia, the unforeseen shock of horror. The first description of the discovery reads as follows:

> A friend told me that during a party at María Canales's house one of
> the guests had got lost. He . . . was very drunk and went looking for the
> bathroom . . . but being so drunk *he got lost*. Instead of taking the passage
> on the right, *he took the one on the left*, then he went along another passage,
> down some stairs, and before he knew it, he was in the basement, it was a
> huge house with *a floor plan like a crossword puzzle*. . . . Finally he came to
> a passage that was narrower than the others and he opened one last door.
> He saw a kind of metal bed. *He turned on the light.* On the bed was a naked
> man, his wrists and ankles tied. The man seemed to be asleep, but it was
> difficult to verify that impression because the man was blindfolded. The
> stray guest shut the door, feeling suddenly stone cold sober, and *cautiously
> retraced his steps.* When he got back to the sitting-room he asked for a
> whisky and then another and didn't say a word.[39]

It is interesting to see how an unexpected contingency causes the basement to become a labyrinth that allows the person to see another fold of time in which what was concealed is revealed. The guest's apparent lack of reaction and his mechanical return can be understood as caused by the panic of being caught in that maze, but still his silent return poses a gap, the incommensurability of this parallel existence, that emphasizes the artificiality of normal life under the regime.

The act of retracing the path toward the world of light on the floor above is worked out in more detail in the novel's third description of the same situation:

> I also found out, years later . . . that the guest who had gone astray in the
> deceptive corridors of that house . . . was a theorist of avant-garde theatre
> . . . who didn't panic when he lost his way . . . he opened doors and even

started whistling, and finally he came to the very last room at the basement's narrowest corridor, lit by a single, feeble light bulb, and he opened the door and saw that man tied to the metal bed, blindfolded, and he knew the man was alive because he could hear him breathing, although he wasn't in good shape, for in spite of the dim light he saw the wounds . . . the battered parts of his anatomy, the swollen parts . . . and then [he] shut the door delicately, without making a noise, and started to make his way back to the sitting-room, carefully switching off as he went each of the lights he had previously switched on.[40]

In this description of the same event the lighting system acquires more explicit relevance: the light is immediately turned off, and the contrast between this mundane habit and the irruption of the hidden body is more shocking because we see the collusion in the maintenance of suffering on the part of the person who returns, like an automaton, carefully switching off the lights to go back to the visible realm of the sitting room. The return to normality is described as an adjustment of lights, which highlights the notion of (lack of) visibility that these images of the secret detention center convey.

Here the novel problematizes spatial juxtaposition through a temporal suspension that provokes the disclosure of what was hidden but not unknown. This revelation is not something new but something disturbing that should have stayed removed (out of the open) in another temporal mode (resignation) in order for life—or at least the life of "true Chileans"—to continue in peace, a peace that is itself controlled by anesthesia. The image of the guest retracing his way back suggests impotence and silencing; it points to a lack within the structure of either a space or a language of disclosure. The narrator attempts to conceal this point again and again when he repeatedly asks why no one said anything about it at that precise moment, thus posing a division between purity and impurity of consciousness, right and wrong, that overlooks the key feature of the military regime: to whom was the guest supposed to report the actions of the DINA in Chile when secret paramilitary activity was the essence of the military administration? The question acquires Brechtian overtones; to whom and where should one report this practice— the police? How do you report a crime in a country with no shadow, in the imaginary of absolute immunity?

What takes us from house to housing is figured spatially as that which must be kept out of the light of the living room, that which is part of the house but not part of its livable zone, that which must remain in a zone of unintelligibility. The topics that caused instants of arrest at other points (the campesinos, the Popular Unity government) cause the narrator impatience that he attempts to expiate with reasoning, explanations, justifications. The interference between the visible and what was supposed to remain concealed shows up as a series of temporal limbos in the narrator's mind: the delayed, irreducible time of the campesinos; the unimaginable time of Popular Unity reforms drawing another geography in which Chile is no longer Chile; the indefinite time of the prisoner held in secret, waiting, that emerges in language, detaining (delaying) the logic of supposed national reconciliation at the end of the text, accompanied by the patient indifference of María Canales, who from time to time suspects something when there is interference on the television screen (caused by use of the electric prod in the basement).

This question of what constitutes Chile and what does not qualify as Chilean in the house itself links to a larger series of questions about literature, about what is made in the text. This occurs at the end of *Nocturno* with an interesting play of voices between María Canales and the priest-poet-critic: "She said, That's how literature is made in Chile. I nodded and left. While I was driving back into Santiago, I thought about what she had said. That is how literature is made in Chile, but not just in Chile, in Argentina and Mexico too, in Guatemala and Uruguay, in Spain and France and Germany, in green England and carefree Italy. That is how literature is made. Or at least what we call literature, to keep ourselves from falling into the rubbish dump."[41] The question that was silenced in the first house, the estate (also a hunting zone) emerges as an assertion: "This is how literature is made" (as housing *and* hunting), and the priest takes the voice of Canales and transforms what she says into a universal formula: "not just in Chile," as if this justified the whole enterprise (this is how world literature and culture work). The insistence on grounding the house on the iteration of an international formula for accepting something uncanny works as a form of anesthesia to enable readers to keep reading comfortably, once they are told about the inevitability of literary tragedy. María Canales's assertion attempts to generate closure by naturalizing-neutralizing-anesthetizing the horror that delimits the disinterested aesthetics that the priest dreamed of in the first literary house (the estate) as a "path of roses" (now full of thorns but "inevitable" ones).

The phrase "that is how literature is made," repeated like a mantra for exorcizing the ghosts that accumulate, is later clarified in a curious remark differentiating natural and literary law: "Or *at least* what *we* call literature, to keep ourselves from falling into the rubbish dump" (my emphasis). I argue that the "or" in "or at least" is crucial within the dynamic of the novel as it points yet again to the problem of the critical consciousness erasing itself, causing us to wonder about the geography of the "we" that delimits that explanation of "how literature is made." This is shown in the final counterpoint between the disappearance of the two central figures in the text: Farewell and the Young Man (his ghost, the left-wing activist), in which Farewell acts as spirit and the Young Man as specter. At Farewell's wake the priest muses, "I asked his spirit (it was, of course, a rhetorical question) why things had turned out as they had for us. *There was no reply.* I went over to one of the huge bookcases and touched the spines of the books with my fingertips. There was a movement in a *corner of the room.* I jumped."[42] This image condenses the literary house, the library, the search for a fortress against time, and the search for a reason that will account for destiny; however, there is no answer. The library books are an integral part of the horror that has taken place in the house but they cannot respond. Instantly the specter of the dying young man appears, followed not by silence but by his last word, "no": "The wizened youth has been quiet for a long time now. He has given up railing against me and writers generally. Is there a solution? That is how literature is made, that is how the great works of Western literature are made. You better get used to it, *I tell him.* The wizened youth, *or what is left of him,* moves his lips, *mouthing an inaudible no.*"[43]

This "no," not mentioned by critics who have elaborated upon this point on this text, is fundamental to Bolaño's differentiation between the protagonist from whose point of view the narrative is recounted and his task as narrator, tortured by that "no" that differentiates or splits the house in a different way. That "inaudible no" introduces a sequential chain of bodies whose speech is not comprehensible to the priest but who nevertheless establish a *disagreement* about the anesthetizing-naturalizing "formula" of horror. What I referred to earlier as "minor," under the strike-out regime, leads us now to ~~literature~~ itself as a process of reflection on and distancing of projects that have become incompatible. First, we need to differentiate between two spaces: the novel as confession by the conflicted conscience of the right-wing priest-poet-critic who is one "Chile" and *Nocturno* as a disturbing commentary by Bolaño on the silences that persist (like invisible zones in the house), causing it to remain a prison. "This is how literature is made" is a desperate attempt to naturalize something that is otherwise likely to arouse an uncanny feeling. The (inaudible) "no" insists on bringing the issue out into the open.

On this subject the cultural theorist Sergio Villalobos contributes the notion of a "co-belonging" of literature and horror, indicating a moment of exhaustion of literature, a theme seen in various texts by Bolaño: "His novels express the exhaustion of the modern articulation between literature and the public space of reading that granted to it a particular social function (illustration, education, moral exemplification, etc.). I call this exhaustion 'co-belonging,' a sort of coexistence between literature and horror [that marks] an end to the high modernist belief in the power of literature to illuminate, represent and/or de-familiarize everyday life. There is nothing extraordinary or sacred in literature (prose and poetry) that might be considered as the salvation of humankind."[44] I believe that this theory of the co-belonging of literature and horror dramatizing the exhaustion of literature as an enlightenment project needs to be interrupted-complemented; in my view that inaudible "no" separates us from the naturalization of co-belonging in the priest and suggests that *Nocturno* is the place in which that act is denounced. Let us not forget that the denunciation of co-belonging is being carried out in the supreme literary genre: the novel. By that I mean that the exhaustion hypothesis leaves out the material conditions in which the questioning of literature takes place.

A further question emerges: What difference follows from the distinction between literature, as a practice denounced in the text, and the literary practice in which such critique takes place (*Nocturno de Chile*)? Perhaps the latter should be considered as the "literary" because, rather than expressing merely the exhaustion of literature, which implies the notion of absolute deterritorialization (the death of the literary), *Nocturno* reconfigures other possibilities by exploring the presentation of the obvious as an act of defamiliarization. The detour in the novel leads us to rethink the uncanny in the postdictatorship period (open prison), a question the text makes possible through the defamiliarization of the house throughout *Nocturno* and the relation of the house to the notion of immunity, which was so crucial to the health of the nation/household in protected democracy throughout the century.

Nocturno moves through the house as if elaborating the return of the repressed, which rules the text through the device of getting lost, which leads the priest to bump into what was supposed to remain out of sight. In this sense, getting lost and losing one's way are connected in the text to a restatement of the uncanny, which keeps bringing in, by chance, what is displaced by domestic political economy. Thus, despite the urge to control the path, images of the hidden burst into the text as an autoimmune moment in which *Nocturno* shows what the house's immunity displaces (which is both obvious and invisible). This insistence on writing political history from the place of literature seems to emerge as a moment of exposure to a moment of autoimmunity from the viscerally literary. I am thinking of Derrida's meaning of autoimmune as that which "enables an exposure to the other, to *what* and *who* comes—which means that it must remain incalculable. Without autoimmunity, with absolute immunity, nothing would ever happen or arrive;

we would no longer wait, await, or expect, no longer expect one another, or expect any event."[45] In a way this would be equivalent to Bolaño's fantasy in the epigraph at the beginning of this chapter about breaking with the implicit pact in which democracy is immunized by concealing the most obvious things.

In an autobiographical text that also reflects on literature ("Literatura + enfermedad," [Literature + sickness]), Bolaño refers to the relation between immunity and autoimmunity by describing literature and the act of reading as "paths that go nowhere, and that one nevertheless has to go down and get lost on to find oneself again or to find something, whatever it might be, a book, an expression, *a lost object*, to find anything, perhaps a method, with luck: the *new, what has always been there*."[46] A path that goes nowhere is an aporia in which the insistence on the possibility of an impossibility is linked to the possibility of recognizing the new in what has been (the promise of what has not been). Getting lost on that path refers to fate, the arrival of the incalculable that does not, however, completely erase the central problem of the text: the disavowal of the political economy that makes possible the (impossible) fantasy of the path of roses.

Bolaño postulates something of the sort in his "Literatura + enfermedad": "Mallarmé wrote that a roll of the dice will never abolish fate. However, it is necessary to toss the dice every day."[47] In a way *Nocturno*'s exploration of the familiar and defamiliarization through the device of getting lost leads us to question a key feature of the uncanny in Freud's classic text: the type of revelation implied by the ~~literary~~. What happens if we think about *Nocturno* as a site that exposes the co-belonging of a particular literary or aesthetic model and the horror of the politics of preserving the estate in terms of its insistence on articulating the word for what is supposedly obvious? It uses the force of the literary word to express the uncanny in another way—defamiliarizing the notion of defamiliarization as anesthesia, bringing the "inaudible no" into this zone.

Denaturalizing the Obvious

It is important to keep in mind that, as Samuel Weber has reminded us, the uncanny in Freud's classic text emerges as a problematization of an act of reading, a differentiation between the experience of the uncanny in literature and its emergence in everyday life.[48] Freud explains that the uncanny in everyday experience evokes the feeling of a return of forms of cognition that we thought we had overcome, "primitive convictions" and "infant complexes" (fear). It is not irrelevant to point out that Freud wrote the text in exile and as part of his obsession with World War I. Freud seems to be disturbed by a sense of failure *within* the very structure of progress, by the peculiar coexistence of multiple senses of temporality of things that he thought were past and gone but that reemerge, destabilizing the structure of knowledge. The uncanny, then, is the feeling that all the things we thought we had overcome thanks to science reappear, seizing us with dread: "Our conclusion could then be stated as follows: the uncanny element we know from experience arises either when repressed childhood complexes are revived by some impression, or when primitive beliefs that have been *surmounted* appear to be once again confirmed."[49]

Freud says that in the region of fiction, the treatment of the uncanny is "much richer" than what we know from experience because it "embraces the whole of this [experience] and *something else besides,* something that is wanting in real life."[50] I think that this "something else" has to do with the idea of a different construction of place thanks to the imagination in the region of literature. Freud suggests that the writer is a sort of seducer who promises us one thing and then takes us to another place: "he betrays us to a superstition we thought we had surmounted, he tricks us by promising us everyday reality and then going beyond it."[51] Later, he shows how the same thing can cause an uncanny feeling in one story and not in another. Using the examples from different works (Heterodotus and Hauff's "Story of the Severed Hand," Nestroy's "The Torn Man"), Freud analyzes how the quality of the uncanny does or does not emerge, forging a connection between the gaze (the standpoint from which one sees) and the situation. Curiously, he implies that literature acts a little like the Sandman who deprives of the sight we consider ours, hypnotizing us and causing us to see things that in the automatism of everyday habit we do not see. So the experience of the uncanny depends on the standpoint from which the situation is created. Thus the notion of a common space starts to disintegrate because something supposedly commonplace (a historic moment, an episode) can awaken our sense of humor, our cynicism or the uncanny, depending on how the narrator focuses our gaze, how he or she makes us see, a crucial element for arousing an emotional connection to the situation.

Returning to Weber's notion, discussed in chapter 3, that Benjaminian awakening involves waking up in and from a place, perhaps the uncanny prompts us to imagine awakening *from other places.* Factual impossibility is the province of fiction because it is there that the uncanny arises, according to Freud, in the most intense way because fiction creates a way of seeing that is not dulled or camouflaged by experience itself—seeing from other places, thinking from other places. The uncanny in *Nocturno* is a sort of optical illusion, in which Bolaño makes us look at the history of the nation, its *Bildung* and decline, from an almost architectural viewpoint. Bringing in the clichéd figures—the campesinos, the disappeared prisoner—is a reiteration of Benjamin's crucial concept of recognizing the new as enigma, an act of seeing the familiar from another place, a remembrance that re-creates the present. What the text may be saying to us is that in order to recognize the new, we need to examine our gaze, our way of relating senses of temporality from which we see and don't see, and the way in which seeing always implies a way of not being able to see other zones.

The last house (the salon-detention center) problematizes the materialization of horror in the public-private space, exploring the role of secrecy and cohabition not only during the dictatorship but also in the silences and not-silences after the dictatorship. This is important, because spaces of horror were used by the military in neighborhoods where everybody knew that something horrible was going on (torture, killings, and so on), but they also knew it had to be actively denied or repressed to keep living "as if" nothing were happening. Secrecy plays something of the role referred to by Weber regarding castration as an "almost nothing but not quite" or as a type of revelation that destabilizes the fantasy of the evident as an unfissured presence by suggesting something that is "both too evident and never evident enough."[52] This characteristic of castration as being unnarratable is something that describes the ongoing problem of secrecy and the public in (post)dictatorships. Weber continues that "the *Uncanny*, like castration itself, is less involved with a *what* than a *how*, with the mechanisms of repetition, recurrence and return, and here: with reflection."[53] Is this the gaze of the jailer that Bolaño talked about in the epigraph as still patrolling the house-country? The articulation of the public and the impotence generated by the micropolitics of fear, crucial to maintaining a normal life in the decades of military rule, are crucial to understanding the relationship between the architecture of the transition and the process of homogenization of spaces and times following the dictatorship.[54] The impotence that emerges around secrecy becomes the map or geography that sends us to the uncanny, thanks to emotions like fear and the articulation of those emotions through ways of seeing, systems of visibility and knowledge.[55]

In this sense the figure of the house as secret detention center demonstrates the type of juxtaposition examined throughout this book, bringing us to a crucial, controversial theme: the normalization of the practice of secrecy, a key feature of most recent dictatorships through clandestine operations (parapolicing, paramilitary). Bolaño explores how this naturalization of secrecy affects the way times and spaces are inhabited in the postdictatorship period. By revealing what was supposed to remain hidden, *Nocturno* makes us examine how we think about the revelation of a public secret. What is the difference between a public secret and making it public? The problem of the secret detention center that the novel leaves us with—one that represents a crucial issue in the present, where the problem of life under the dictatorship has returned—is the familiarization of ways of knowing, feeling, and hearing that involve their opposites: looking without seeing, listening without hearing, and on. Thus, as a prison that is not a prison, the present stays protected (like a house, like democracy); the novel presses us to inquire what new ghost zones the present may be maintaining outside itself, other times in which the unlivable resides.

What *Nocturno* does peculiarly well is to link the phenomenon of daily life during and after the dictatorship to literature, showing how it acts as a crucial problematization zone of this very issue. The problematic coexistence in Farewell's house brings up the crucial issue of how literature can add something to the examination of the everyday nature of horror. In everyday life under the dictatorship, the problem of secrecy is related to the uncanny, and the great achievement of *Nocturno* is that it takes us beyond the history of the dictatorship to link literature and horror (exclusion, massacring, destruction) to a bigger history (nation-building). Thus the image of the last house (of national/global violence) makes readers think about the practice of reading itself as a mode of housing and wonder how one is blinded by housing. In this sense it is from the scene or staging of the most obvious or clichéd that the uncanny emerges. Is not the cliché precisely the crucial point in Benjamin's awakening, described as a practice of seeing otherwise what is closest, tritest, most obvious? Is not the house/home that place of the supposedly closest, most familiar, most homely?

A central activity of *Nocturno*, as a novel, is making the obvious and the clichéd visible, but in such a way as to make it less obvious and to show how the military gaze is still dominating postdictatorial Chile (as Bolaño remarked). The notion of obviousness is linked to the notion of a public secret since both operate as moments of naturalization and closure of a process of circulation of the secret in a society. Obviousness implies a "we" and a "them" that is not so obvious when interrogated; what is obvious and to whom? What is the geography that makes the obvious obvious? In this implicit pact we find again the controversial and problematic "we" of the postdictatorship period, connected with an act of seeing in which it is assumed as obvious that the prison will come to be seen as a mall and that the transition to freedom of the market is the measurement of time. The issue of the borders and limits that are naturalized by these assumptions show how obviousness is related to the uncanny in terms of the standpoint of the viewer, a visual location that determines whether or not something will seem sinister. We could say that if naturalizing (familiarizing) history is the transitional global economy's attempt to make us feel at home everywhere, the theory of the uncanny allows us to question how familiar the familiar is and who composes the family able to recognize that place as "home." In *Nocturno* the issue of the ever-more-powerful and seductive superposition of tourism and services (hotels, malls) on former prisons worldwide takes on genealogical meaning, for the house (detention center) represents the neoliberal economy's laboratory of freedom.

I propose that the architectural abyss in *Nocturno* suggested in those three years of the Popular Unity government that lack a period (leaving it up to us to decide how to punctuate them) connect to my analysis of *La fuga* and *Mano de obra* in that all three raise the problem of how to cite (to make quotable) the past. In all three novels a type of parallel power emerges (dual power under the MLN-T, enlightenment from below in *Mano de obra*, parliamentary democracy with the Popular Unity) that threatens to bring about a kind of transformation that differs from the right's nightmare stereotype of the abrupt, revolutionary break (a sudden break the coup mirrored in its own retaking of the house). The problem of how to cite the past emerges in *Nocturno* in the tensions that disturb the conscience of the priest since the sudden break feared by the right was in fact made by the right itself in demolishing its own architecture (bombing the Moneda, suspending parliament).

Thus these literary texts seem to ask for a critical rethinking of the political past (a zone that involves a problem of spatiotemporal perceptibility) that the coups surgically removed; they all invoke a zone of indistinction and incommensurability (coimplication) between forms of politics centered on social transformation. In other words, what emerges from the three texts is that the open prison of the "post" in postdictatorship is still guarding a detour that connects to instances of *trans*-formation rather than demolition, of contamination between two forms of violence that philosopher Georges Sorel maintained separate (conservation or creation out of nothing). It is the contamination between elements that a certain concept of politics wishes to keep separate (friend-enemy), elements that the texts bring in as coimplicated, pointing to an idea of literary historicization of politics that stresses the inevitable relationship of the immune and the autoimmune. This is the force they introduce by playing with the effects of prison on historicization itself, making us realize that what is being imprisoned is potentiality itself, which can ruin (autoimmunize) the immune neoliberal democracy that was Pinochet's legacy.

In this sense *Nocturno* is a text about protected democracy (immunity and impunity) figured as an architecture that attempts to prevent (protect) the return of an event (its discovery, its irruption); the uncanny stems from the impossible attempt to control and immunize the entire future of politics. The text configures an abyss that is the asymmetric double of the autoimmune example of the house. *Nocturno*'s ability to say what has become publicly unsayable—its ability to make us see the seeing-without-seeing—shows the link between aesthetics and the dictatorship as instituting a perception, an exhaustive vigilance over what was seeable and sayable that persists up to the present day.

5 Memorialistic Architectonics and Memory Marketing

A decade after the malling boom, memory itself became the object of a similar process, a kind of "memory boom." Besides the creation of different Commissions of Memory, the promotion of memory as part of the marketing of the state-market can be seen in the project for the creation of a "MERCOSUR-Memory," in which the regional market, promoted in the neoliberal context of the 1990s, starts to include memory as a tourist commodity, with the possibility of exchanging museum experiences and to obtain more profit.[1] Although I focus my analysis on the imagination of the clandestine in the transformation of key detention centers in Argentina, I open this chapter with an analysis of the transformation of the Buen Pastor Prison in Córdoba (Argentina) into the Paseo (Cultural) del Buen Pastor, a "cultural and commercial center" containing a gallery and arts center, shops, and restaurants. This transformation poses an uncanny resemblance with the case of Punta Carretas; however, in Buen Pastor the memory of horror was articulated as part of the site's narrative of refunctionalization, thus posing an interesting operation in which the practice of malling of the 1990s becomes a malling of memory a decade after.

The prison was built between 1897 and 1906 and, like Punta Carretas, became an uncomfortable space in the late twentieth century in a neighborhood that had a lot of potential for commercial investors. Plans for modernizing and repurposing the site began to be drafted in 2001. Demolition of parts of the building took place four years later, in 2005, and the commercial and cultural center was inaugurated in 2007 by President Cristina Fernández and the governor of the province, José Manuel de la Sota. The inaugural ceremonies included a show with music and illuminated dancing fountains. Promoted as a partnership between private investors and the state (the Archivo Provincial de la Memoria), the transformation was presented as an homage to the memory of the women prisoners who suffered in the prison. However, neither former prisoners nor human rights activists were invited to participate in the opening gala show.

An analysis of the transformation of the Buen Pastor Prison reveals a new phase of the afterlife of confinement, one that treats memory itself as part of its politics of marketing. Paying homage to the prisoners and victims of the past (something not seen in the transformation of Punta Carretas), Buen Pastor becomes a cultural and commercial "Paseo" (literally "stroll") that places memory itself under the surveillance of the market. A parallel can be drawn here with the whitewashing of prisons analyzed earlier in this book. There is a similarity between Buen Pastor and Punta Carretas (both are early twentieth-century prisons transformed into commercial sites) but also a slight difference symptomatic of a process of whitewashing applied in the later case to memory itself as a target for transformation. While Punta Carretas was turned into a prison-mall, in Buen Pastor memorialistic culture was imprisoned in the prison imaginary of the new, camouflaged commercial center. The newspaper *Clarín*, for instance, uses the image of the redemption of the site with the heading "De cárcel a espacio abierto para la cultura" (From prison to an open space for culture).[2] In a very different account of the transformation, *Palanca digital* posted an online conversation with ex-prisoners who protested their exclusion from the opening of what was supposedly a space of "remembrance" of the past.[3] From these opposite responses to the transformation (redemption/critique), a question about the transformation of Buen Pastor arises: For whom and from where are the processes performed?

The Malling of Memory? Buen Pastor Prison and Commercial Center

Buen Pastor Prison was a key center for detention of women political dissidents in the early 1970s, and it became a symbol of resistance after the successful escape of twenty-six prisoners in 1975, in the lead-up to the coup, when a state of emergency had been declared in the province (*medidas de pronta seguridad*). The fact that Buen Pastor was associated, like Punta Carretas, with a collective escape from imprisonment and was also turned into a camouflaged shopping and memory site allows me to approach the issue of the new economy of memory and the search for other forms of escape. The paradox is that "escape" implies the possibility of a different form of administering remembrance and forgetfulness from state-and-market, as if, in the era of the politics of memory, it was "memory" itself, as a human capacity, that was being confined, like the dissidents who had advocated structural transformation decades before. At stake here is the question of how a dissident practice of memory can articulate the possibility of imagining other temporalities.

The transformation of Buen Pastor into a mall used the language of the politics of memory in order to redeem the place by paying homage to the women who had been imprisoned there. This is shown by two plaques placed in the renovated site: one declaring that the site is an homage to the memory of the prison victims, the other depicting the transformation of the place as progress (from dark prison to colorful consumer site). The first plaque says: "Now that the Paseo del Buen Pastor is coming into existence, we would like to pay homage to all those women who suffered here the unjust imprisonment of the dictatorship and the horrors of torture and prison. . . . To the mothers, to the ones who suffered, to the ones who were here who should not have been here." The second plaque states: "Paseo del Buen Pastor. A work [*una obra*] of the Government of the province of Córdoba for everybody." Past and present, selective memory of the dictatorship and redemption of the place for the citizens of consumerism, meet in a language that was absent from Punta Carretas Mall a decade before. The commercial redemption of Buen Pastor also uses the language of memorial practices, transforming the site into a quotation where women prisoners are referred to as victims and mothers rather than political actors in either past or present times.[4]

As the anthropologist Mariana Tello Weiss has shown, the omission of the political in the plaques had an interesting double architectural counterpart that connects to the transformation of Punta Carretas Mall: the renovation of Buen Pastor not only erased the territorial marks of the repression (the cells) but also the traces of a poetic of freedom within the site (the window through which political prisoners escaped). Although the escape was organized by the Partido Revolucionario de los Trabajadores–Ejército Revolucionario del Pueblo (PRT-ERP), it also involved prisoners from another organization (Montoneras) and the help of approximately two hundred people from the community outside the prison. Of the prisoners who escaped, many later had to go into exile, others went back to prison, and nine were killed and/or remain disappeared. The erasure of the window that could signal the passage to other layers of prison life can be read against the state prohibition on taking pictures of the escape tunnel in Punta Carretas, highlighting the role of invisibilized acts of freedom in the reconfiguration of memorial practices and places. They point to the limitations and the limits of the transformation of the space into a place for memory—one that in this case performs a double erasure: the depoliticization of women prisoners, all subsumed under the stereotype of the mother and the suffering victim, and the erasure of any sign that would point to escape.

Unlike Punta Carretas Mall, Buen Pastor is run jointly by private enterprises and also by the Archivo Provincial de la Memoria, which is responsible for the defense of human rights issues. The dream of Juan Carlos López, the mastermind of Latin American malling, materializes here in an uncanny fashion, as this co-administration resembles his idea of the mall as a site of "social exchange," which in Buen Pastor emerges as prison, shopping center, and memorial site. The site speaks of the duopoly of state and market (of memory), which frames the renovation as an homage while getting rid of what is still uncomfortable. What forms of present(s) and past(s) are promoted by the enterprise of museification and marketing embodied by the discourses of architectural redemption of the place? Who stands to benefit from these processes of memory marketing? It is quite surprising that in a cultural and commercial site aimed at exploiting memory, the part of the building that was demolished was the cells where women prisoners were housed for much of the century. The architectural transformation resulted in the emptying or destruction of a space that was crucial for people's memory of the prison (the shape of the cells and the structure of the cell block). The creation of this vacuum angered some of the surviving detainees, who protested the erasures despite their fear of repercussions. In a kind of *escrache*, some of them attended the opening event and took the floor, interrupting the scheduled programming.[5] They decorated the barriers protecting the Paseo with ribbons bearing the names of the prisoners who were killed or disappeared after the escape, reciting their names and chorusing "presente ahora y siempre" (present now and always).

This constituted what Tello has called a counteract to the planned and scheduled event, and it posed a series of questions regarding the conflictual role of memory in the act of framing the narration of the past as a political one. The counterevent staged a different form of connecting past and present because, by bringing ribbons with the names of the dead women who had escaped, the survivors were paying homage to the disappeared, taking the poetic of the escape as their main trope of resistance to museification.

The protest becomes even more interesting when it is read alongside a video clip created by the authorities to represent the past and present of the place as a linear continuity (from the dark, old containment and repression to free consumption and modernization). In the video, prisoners are objectified in typical photographs depicting them in line, being registered at the entrance, suggesting that opening the former prison as mall is redeeming its dark past into a modernized space of consumption and free gathering, as if the lines of prisoners were lines of consumers using their freedom to enter the place. However, the video was counteracted by a documentary whose title points to the erased parts of the past: *Buen Pastor: Una fuga de mujeres.*[6]

Coproduced by Cine El Calefón and a group of ex-political prisoners who had participated in the 1975 escape, the documentary starts with two images of passage: on the one hand, the narration dramatized by the video clip in which the successful opening of the Paseo implied the passage from the dark history of the place to the new realm of consumerist freedom; on the other hand, a kaleidoscope of memories of the prison focuses on the window that was used for the escape three decades before. This shows another meaning of the word "Paseo," the "walk" of former prisoners who try to locate themselves in the transformed place so as to recreate the layout of the prison where they once lived. Recording the former inmates in the process of trying to locate themselves, the documentary shows a dialogue of competing memories, as the women argue about their memories of the layout of the place, the location of their beds, the bathroom, and so on. In a way we can see here a *tableau vivant* of what Eleuterio Fernández Huidobro attempts to do at the beginning of *La fuga*, as the documentary re-creates the place from the collective gaze of the prisoners, showing how certain marks become signals for the reinvention of prison stories.

As if to teach viewers another itinerary of Buen Pastor, a singular act takes place in the documentary while people are eating and shopping. Temporal layers mix as the women progressively transform the place into a site of struggle in which different diagrams of remembrance take place. Remembering the resistance of the past, the polyphony of voices that reinvent history in the present is an act of resistance to the present physiognomy of the place, not only as a space for consumption but also as one that confines the female inmates' history to the easy stereotype of victim and suffering mother. The new, clean, and colorful mall/cultural center becomes the backdrop for a collage that tunnels to a different narration in which the women's struggles in prison and the preparations for the escape encourage them to start to escape from the mall while the documentary goes on. This reaches a climax when one of the former prisoners being filmed, Cristina Salvarezza, starts writing graffiti on the walls and pillars of the former prison. Remarkably, all her graffiti refers to women inmates who disappeared after the escape. She inscribes the pillars with phrases such as "Here, Tota used to sing and Mariana danced," then she starts to sing and dance the songs she remembers. This creates a strange point of temporal crossing on camera where the memories of resistance in prison encounter a present in which resistance is being held captive in the mall that can act as homage only for victims.

The remembrance of a repressed prison history within the mall becomes a source of inspiration for the present in which the neutral museification of the past has become a form of imprisonment in the logic of marketing. What is interesting here, as Tello points out, is that the survivors introduce a kaleidoscope of past images that resist easy categorization as mother, militant, or suffering victim. They resist the stereotypes in which their pasts have been frozen by the politics of memory marketing, as if escape had to take another form in the present, one able to create some space in previous signifying chains that left no room for variation. In this sense the documentary counteracts the afterlife of confinement in Buen Pastor by introducing another set of echoes of the past. By bringing back escape to a signifying chain that fixed easy labels on them, the ex-inmates create a constellation of images of an irrepressible past of affects and struggle. In Buen Pastor the marketing of memory that confined the past to a set of comfortable stereotypes provoked former prisoners to transform the site of memory into the place of a struggle over meaning. The insistence on bringing up escape was a struggle over the place and politics of memory itself. After these protests the former escapees successfully lobbied for the Archivo to allow them to place a plaque remembering the escape, thus opening up a form of historicization that does not limit their imprisonment to a passive form of suffering and recuperating the search for freedom that led to their escape. The struggle to add other meanings continues.

Other Territories of Memory: Topologies of a Clandestine Past (Escraches and Memory Sites)

The act of citing the dictatorial past and its history of political violence has played a significant role in inscribing the "post" of postdictatorship in architectural space, cultural critique, and testimonial-literary space. Each act of citation involves a way of connecting or disconnecting layers of past and present time, implying forms of preservation, destruction, or recovery that make us wonder about untranslatable areas within the different practices (the contrast, for instance, between the prison cited in the mall and how this emerges in the memory of the prisoner with the image of the escape). At an architectural level, the act of citing played a key role in López's postdictatorial commercial architecture. In the construction of the neoliberal city, citation functioned as a culturally correct gesture for maintaining the past, generating a sort of spatial prose that represented a new chapter in history.

In this sense architect Estela Porada's citation of Punta Carretas Prison involved an act of preservation of the past that did not interfere with the new function of the site as space for consumption. The citation of the prison operates as a fetish capable of generating increased value. Abandoning its own history, the prison ends up subsumed under the new economic system implicit in the mall. The escape from Punta Carretas called for another type of citation, however—the emergence of invisible (and invisibilized) subterranean materials, lost for good but textually re-created in the figure of the escape as a type of subterranean museum containing what was systematically relegated to oblivion by the official discourse of History (histories of anarchists in the 1930s and of Tupamaros, still active in the 1980s).

The narrative re-elaboration of the escape in the transition period began to give way to a different dynamics of citation, one that starts to take place in the urban texture itself. The cultural theorist Francine Masiello has differentiated between two forms of citation: the conventional and the alternative. The conventional citation would preserve tradition, whereas the alternative citation would interrupt tradition by opening up another location. The first of the two "tends to deaden the possibilities of cultural critique, canceling free oppositional spaces so that they all appear to echo some earlier form, reinforcing the stability of temporal order, genealogy, and paths to the future. Traditional citation fixes the relationship between the State and its opponents, between North and South, East and West, city and country, men and women."[7] The second can be linked to the protest escraches as a way of "finding an alternative citational system to register their opposition to the cover-ups that had prevented the circulation of truth. They thus produce a version of public memory with an independent course of its own and, in the process, surpass the inadequate efforts of politicians to rectify human rights violations under the measures available by law."[8]

By using inscription regimes (such as graffiti, posters, and banners), the escraches that emerged in the 1990s insert language into space, thus pointing to the problem of the creation of (hi)stories as fragmentary constructions of place. At the same time, the escrache foregrounds the generally unquestioned or imperceptible connection between words, territory, and property, denouncing impunity as a private area in what is supposedly a public one (the street and the underground city of the dictatorship). The escrache emphasizes the idea of the street as a space where citizen intervention and plotting of other stories takes place, where "taking place" embodies a double meaning as both an event and a claim on space. The process of appropriation and transformation of ex-CDCs (clandestine detention centers) has taken the form of escrache to a different level, one that establishes a more permanent intervention.

The Argentine military state relied heavily on CDCs to detain, interrogate, and exterminate militants in the 1970s and 1980s. Although it is impossible to determine, it is known so far that approximately some 342 CDCs were established during the dictatorship. Since the early 2000s, different Commissions on Memory in Argentina have petitioned for the transformation of some of these sites into human rights museums and memorial spaces/sites. Marking a new beginning in the territory of memory, the administration of President Néstor Kirchner gave an unusual support to the struggle surrounding human rights groups' denunciations of detention and extermination centers. The administration reopened the struggle against the "Punto Final" (or Full Stop) Law by relegislating human rights violations during the dictatorship. Since then, some of the more notorious CDCs that have now been transformed into memorial spaces are the Escuela Superior de Mecánica de la Armada (ESMA), Campo de Mayo, La Perla, Escuadrón de Comunicaciones 2, El Faro, La Escuelita, Batallón de Arsenales 5, Batallón de Infantería de Marina, Chalet Hospital Posadas, Viejo Aeropuerto, Base Almirante Zar, El Pozo, and Mansión Serré.

The ambiguity and uncertainty about how to name these places, whether as museums or memory sites or memory spaces, is indicative of the problems that arise when planning new functions for them. The very act of naming spaces whose borders and times seem to be incommensurable with the present time in which the transformation is taking place involves political and ideological choices. At the same time, the Commissions on Memory have also been creating museums of memory in different cities of the countries analyzed in this book, such as Rosario and La Plata in Argentina, Montevideo in Uruguay, and Santiago in Chile. The creation of these museums runs parallel to the transformation of former CDCs, thus giving shape to a more global language that justifies such museums' existence as spaces in which to safeguard the horrors of the military dictatorships in the Southern Cone in the same way as there are museums for the Holocaust, apartheid in South Africa, Vietnam, and so forth.[9]

Although these museums/spaces are crucial, there is something disturbing in the homogenization and naturalization currently taking place in the museification of memory and also in the serial manner in which the process is being carried out. A marketing of horror is emerging in which the tourist industry has found a new product: memorialistic practices. This raises the question of what kind of temporality is assumed by turning memory into an artifact or museum object. Is the fact that such museums are called museums *of memory* (instead of museums of recent state authoritarianism) to be understood as assuming there will come a time when there will be nothing memorable or worth remembering? How do we link memory museification to the horrors that are still taking place today and to the ones that this museification excludes or fails to take into account? How do we define the beginning and the end of memory? For whom and from where are these processes of transformation performed?

Sometimes, as in the case of the ex-CDC Villa Grimaldi (now a Peace Park) in Chile, the global subjects who most visit the sites are U.S. and European tourists or academics doing research on trauma studies. There is a sort of global obsession with the idea of museification of past forms of state violence that has been transforming trauma into a hot commodity, while leaving unquestioned the violence occurring within the state-global economy of time. It is worth asking how the transformation of ex-CDCs can contribute to a different, more critical approach to the genealogy of the global imaginary. This would mean locating these territorial idioms (the singularity of each site within the network of CDCs) within the broader national grammar of the global economy and temporality, and examining how the extermination of political dissidence is a condition of possibility of the global economy in which the CDC becomes a site for global tourism.

The process of appropriation of ex-CDCs (which in Argentina is referred to as "recovery") is, like the escraches, a process of intervention that draws attention to the temporalities implicit in the period of dictatorship and post-dictatorship and creates a topology of the dictatorial past. It could be said that the emergence of a network of appropriated memory sites supplemented and transformed the task of escraches, by problematizing the notion of museum and by creating a discursive and visual language capable of generating (hi)stories about what had been marked as "outside" official discourse. The escrache attacked the property of history and impunity by problematizing the public space of the street, questioning what is "common" by improperly appropriating the street as a page to be graffitied or inscribed, and this process reemerges in the struggle over museification and language in the appropriation of the ex-CDCs.

The CDC-museums, although operating as escraches, rearticulate the relationship between territory and language as practices that are not possible without the state's intervention. Because turning the CDCs into museums or memorials involves a lasting appropriation rather than the ephemeral street inscriptions of the escraches, it raises a question about the relationship between territory, inscription, and the state, because there cannot be appropriation of such sites without the state's approval. At the same time, once the site has been designated, the narrative to be created about it implies the creation of a language that questions the ruling discourse about the postdictatorial state. This is what distances the street practice of escraches started by HIJOS (Hijos e Hijas por la Identidad y la Justicia contra el Olvido y el Silencio) in the mid-1990s from the process of appropriation of ex-CDCs. The recovery of the CDCs poses a series of crucial questions already seen in Punta Carretas Mall and Buen Pastor regarding the notion of citizenship, the idea of property (appropriation, property, impropriety), the possibility of telling and creating (hi)stories about disappearances, and the new limits such histories would set.

Sites like ESMA or Buen Pastor, for instance, can only be appropriated if there is a relationship with the state, which therefore frames the mechanisms of signification and limits what can take place there. Thus a question arises regarding institutionality and legality, seen in the struggles in the literary texts analyzed in this book over the historicization itself of what was kept outside historical prose, a historicization that requires a type of legality to be able to emerge. The transformation of the CDCs raises some important critical questions regarding law, the rights to sites, their possession by the military state, and their afterlife. The state was transformed under martial law by the operation of CDCs as secret and illegal machines. Who makes up such a state?[10] The struggle for the appropriation of sites involves examining what sort of legality and relationship between citizen and state is articulated when a collective historicization of this kind emerges, and what areas the language of appropriation fails to reach.

Once again, citation becomes both crucial and problematic. Since the creation of the Instituto Espacio para la Memoria (IEM, or the Space for Memory Institute) in Argentina in 2002, the theorization of memory and place has started to focus on the relationship between memory and legality, memory and public speech.[11] This presents an interesting frontier where patterns of transit and transformation are using the languages of personal memory to construct another history. This opens up the possibility of rethinking the category of the public and the areas it never reached (reaches), making it necessary to pose the following questions: For whom can a site be conceived (marked) as a memory site? How is memory structured in terms of social class? What remains out of view in the sites? Considering what constitutes the public in these sites makes us see the need to examine the link between historical memory, social class, and denarrativization processes, for processes of exclusion and disappearance of individuals in the past are being echoed once again in contemporary appropriation processes of CDCs.

The creation of a topology of memory currently taking place in Argentina and other Southern Cone countries implies the need for critics to problematize the state's role as narrative machine that homogenizes and organizes the processes of construction of the sites' histories. It also implies the need to denaturalize the connection between historicity and spatiality, between creation of history and the public, between historicization and legality. As critics, taking into account subjective-testimonial memory and public history, we may insist on reading the ex-CDCs by attempting to differentiate between the binarisms the state promotes and new approaches to memory, historicization, and citizenship that problematize the notion of democracy created by impunity and clandestinity.

Naming and Resistance to Museification

In Huidobro's and Eltit's texts we saw the political implications of imagining an alternative schedule capable of fictionalizing the history of political violence by giving narrative voice to what is made invisible by architectonics. In some way the struggle for the appropriation of CDC sites brings up a similar set of questions regarding the disappeared: how does one imagine a history of disappearances from the impossibility of what will never be here again? This is a process that, according to the sociologist Elizabeth Jelin, requires avoiding literal or easy answers.[12] How can we think about the past in the meeting point between territory (its materiality) and the discursive emptiness it dramatizes without presuming that there is a way of bringing back a presence that can fill the void?[13] Certain groups are resistant to the category of museums of memory. What does this resistance indicate? What type of politics of memory is being rejected by questioning the global language of memorialistic museification?

Undoubtedly, at the heart of resistance to museification lies a resistance to opening up the past of the CDCs, which takes us back to the peculiar living museum I analyzed earlier in the chapter on La fuga. The resistance to museification of memory points to the insoluble nature of a past the museum wants to make present as object by fetishizing it and placing it out of ongoing history. The repurposed CDCs highlight the ways in which certain pasts have not completely passed, as demonstrated by the disturbance they cause in certain political quarters. The fact that threats and even disappearances continue to occur shows forces much more sinister than marketing, bringing back unsettling memories from the past to the present. The military feels threatened, and there is a widespread perception that insisting on the past hinders present progress—the argument that defined the transition. Coauthors Jens Andermann, Philip Derbyshire, and John Kraniauskas have argued that, despite our critiques of the objectification of memory, rummaging through the past continues to be a risky practice because a clandestine network of kidnappings still exists, as seen in the disappearances of key witnesses like Luis Gerez and Jorge Julio López and human rights activist Juan Puthod.[14] Both Gerez and Puthod turned up alive, while López remains missing.[15] Bringing up the clandestine practice of the military state continues to constitute quicksand.

Returning to the issue of the afterlife, it is worth considering at what point a secret detention center or a prison becomes an unsettling presence that has to be destroyed. This leads us to analyze the relationship between ruins and historicity and to problematize the official narratives about such spaces. Undoubtedly, certain territories (such as former prisons and CDCs) show an excess that causes unease. Although such sites cannot speak, they represent a potentially uncontrollable proliferation of discourses. The ESMA in Argentina is a central site in this regard. In 1998, President Carlos Menem ordered the naval school to be transferred to the Puerto Belgrano Naval Base, calling for the demolition of the buildings on the old location, to be replaced by what the IEM has described as "the construction of a space for public use where a 'symbol of national unity' would be located." Notice here the drive for the architectural demolition of a site that was part of an earlier wave of modernization and the most important CDC during the dictatorship (essentially the only one operating throughout the whole period of military rule). Peace is constructed here as reconciliation: the space of the massacre is re-dedicated as a symbol of national unity. This is undoubtedly a territorial supplement to the amnesty law called Punto Final (Full Stop Law) that ended the possibility of the military juntas being brought to justice. Menem's decision to destroy the ESMA and create a symbol of reconciliation heralding a new era goes hand in hand with his administration's legislation of impunity—that is, of a self-legitimation of justice as forgiveness for the massacre of political dissidents.[16]

Menem's decision was challenged by human rights groups, leading to a standoff that was not settled until the Supreme Court of Justice declared Menem's decree unconstitutional in February 2001. The city of Buenos Aires asked the federal government to return the ESMA premises and to authorize transformation of the site for "educational purposes."[17] In March 2004, President Kirchner approved the creation of a "space for memory and for the promotion and defense of human rights" on the ESMA site. In December of the same year the city government formally regained possession of seven of the buildings, among them the officers' quarters (Casino de Oficiales), where the CDC operated during the dictatorship. In March 2006 other parts of the premises passed back to city control, and in 2007 the navy moved out completely and the idea of creating a museum of memory emerged. As the photographer Marcelo Brodsky has shown, the idea of transforming the ESMA into a museum of memory was changed over time into the idea of a space for memory that will have a museum as part of it.[18] What does this change in nomenclature say about the reinsertion into history of an area that was, by definition, hidden (clandestinized)? Noticeably, it opens up a certain indeterminacy regarding the reformulation of a complex past that until then had been stabilized by the category of museification. Why so? Why did the transformation of the nomenclature become so important at the moment of making the clandestine visible?

The ESMA was the first recovered CDC, and it was there that the tensions about naming the territory as a museum first surfaced. It is as if the CDC could not be subsumed under the category of a museum because it involved a series of unstable and unsettling issues for the present, which the museum tries to make light of as things/objects of the past. In *La fuga* the act of putting into writing, of entering what had been systematically erased from the records of historical prose, poses a problem that the text expresses as the possibility of a different kind of museum—an invisible, subterranean one. Something similar can also be read in the case of appropriation, naming and transformation of the ESMA, which is motivated by a desire to acknowledge the history of disappearances and to create something more than a mere exhibition of a former military extermination site. This wish for something more is what causes the shift from "museum of memory" to "space for the defense of human rights"—a shift that opens the site up to continuity in the present time in which the act of naming itself takes place, a speech act that places it within a topology.

The overlap between prison and mall reveals imaginaries of control and social cleansing (regeneration of deviant bodies and histories). The overlap between prison and museum poses the question of how to contain and adjust a disturbing part of the past in which the museum seems to be repressing a certain form of historicity by framing and stabilizing identities and regimes of signification. It is symptomatic that the choice of museification is always made or articulated by the state. This makes the struggle against the reduction of memory sites to museums a dramatization of the conflict over the spatial and temporal resignification of political extermination territories and the modes and limits set by the state in contributing to this process. It seems almost impossible to neutralize the image of the past generated by the museum as a space whose functions and origins—like those of the prison—lie in the architectonic fantasies of the modern state. Too often, museums contribute to staging the state's horror catalog, as shown by Jens Andermann in *The Optic of the State* with regard to the launching of the "desert campaigns" in Argentina, a nineteenth-century process of "national" regeneration involving an earlier set of disappeared, subversive bodies.[19]

In *Museum Memories* the cultural theorist Didier Maleuvre has stated that "the ideological dimension of museum exhibition invalidates the idea that art can be neutrally exhibited," which raises the question, What kind of ideological valuation occurs when the exhibited is no less than the mise-en-scène of the largest massacre of political dissidents in the twentieth century?[20] Tracing the museum's origin to the period of secularization of culture and nationalization of collections in the aftermath of the French Revolution, Maleuvre emphasizes that the museum implies "a historical production of history" (a historical act that stages a break in the conception of history) and a site for the "protection, preservation, exhibition of what a community agrees to identify as works of artistic or historical value."[21] This process implies the disciplinary logic with which the museum operates, like the prison that "isolates its inmates in categoric cells," thus taking part "in the process of societal rationalization that controls beings by immobilizing their identity, or by simply postulating an identity—identity being already a precipitate of social immobility."[22] In this sense, making a museum out of a former CDC suggests the idea of the twofold prison as crucial concept not only because of the redundancy implied in its Chinese box shape (a prison inside a prison) but also because of the type of imprisonment implied by the treatment of a former CDC as historical object.

The problem here is not so much the rejection of the idea of the museum itself (which implies fetishizing the museum without considering its history) but the way in which naming the site as museum produces a discomfort symptomatic of something else. Resistance to the museum can be seen in the substitution of other titles such as "sites" or "spaces." This is one of the first ways in which the complexity of dealing with the clandestine is expressed. The act of naming becomes a space of struggle and uncertainty when the thing named refers to such a major site of extermination of political dissidence, involving the forced or passive complicity of the population. The ESMA was a veritable factory of a micropolitics of fear, as Gilles Deleuze and Félix Guattari called the fascist machine. The micropolitics of fear shows the difficulty implied in putting the clandestine into narrative or into language as a territory that has been made explicit (marked). There is an incommensurable gap between the territory and the creation of (hi)stories about it.

There is also a problem defining CDC borders, the spatial, visual, sonorous, and temporal delimitation between the CDC's inside and outside, between what is visible and what is made invisible, what is heard and repressed in the neighborhood and the social time implied, imposed and repudiated by the CDC within and outside its borders. This macropolitical area of affects imperceptibly generated by the CDC brings up the problem of naming and the resistance to the disturbing notion of a museum of memory, since such a museum deals with a constellation that cannot possibly be defined as object. The now recovered CDC evokes repressed (but connected) layers of the past and the present and the past's modes of afterlife.

For instance, in the case of ESMA, if we referred to the site as being itself the museum object (that is, to the CDC as a museum and object at the same time), what would be the implicit idea of collection here? It would have to include the clandestine circuit to which ESMA belonged, with its real estate agency selling properties expropriated from detainees, its role as training camp for other CDCs, and its role within the geography of the neighborhood. If we outlined ESMA's path as CDC, where should we set the beginning and the end of its itinerary as museum object? How are we to connect the history of the Navy Mechanics School with the navy's clandestine operation coexisting in the premises, which was seen without being seen?[23] If ESMA operates as a prison without having visible bars, can we consider the outside of the CDC, the neighborhood where the ESMA is located, as also part of the collection that makes the center clandestine? This is not a minor question if we consider that it is the inside-outside of the CDC that expresses and exhibits the peculiar dynamics of seeing/without seeing that made the site a clandestine space that was simultaneously located in a visible and audible territory (trucks entering and leaving the site, screams during torture, shackled persons, burning of corpses, and so on).

These spaces or sites pose a question on the teleological beginning and end of the museistic process (of history and memory, of the postdictatorial) focusing on the problematic or clandestine afterlife of that past in the present. This makes us try to imagine what type of social temporality embodies the CDC, what constitutes its outside and future. It points to the duality of the civic-military state that set up these centers in Argentina, paralleling the prison system in a schizophrenia of confinement and paralysis that created a different type of human material: the disappeared person who failed to qualify as prisoner. In the resistance to museification, there is something I read as related to a different form of containment in the CDC that fails to respond to the museum-prison scheme, something that implies a different modality of power and the extermination of what is not considered human material.

As the psychologist Hugo Vezzetti has said, the CDC considers the disappeared as an exterminable community where surviving or not surviving depends on the almost sovereign or deified determination of pure chance.[24] The legalization of the disappeared by transfer to a normal prison (allowing the person to reappear as social subject) implied the resumption of the right to be a prisoner as opposed to the idea of disappearance in which a person was abducted, never to appear again.[25]

The Micropolitics of Fear: Tour around ESMA and Olimpo

Clandestinity was a crucial device of the Argentine military dictatorship. The political scientist Pilar Calveiro has described the Argentine CDCs as cores for the development of a power technique that differentiates the most recent dictatorship from previous ones by turning disappearance into a central, characteristic feature of the regime. This poses a series of questions as to how disappearance might continue to operate in a present where borders of the prison/nonprison are invisible from certain angles. In a way the spatial-temporal structure of postdictatorial historical narrative is reminiscent of the mechanism described by Michel Foucault in *Discipline and Punish* as the introjection of the gaze of the surveillant into the prisoner. This was refined by Roberto Bolaño in *By Night in Chile,* which explores the complicated situation of postdictatorial society in which the left remains chained to the gaze of the dictatorship itself, thus affecting narrative processes.

However, dictatorial punishments are unlike the type of introjection and discipline that Foucault distinguishes from the spectacle of punishment as a pedagogy that restores sovereign power. The difference lies in the coexistence of the legal prison and the practice of clandestine punishment which, following Calveiro's analysis, introduced a new logic of power.[26] In this new form of control over bodies-territories-gazes, the national security policies of the latest dictatorships in the Southern Cone created a unique disciplinary scheme—one in which punishment was publicly applied but as a secret. This is what the priest in *By Night in Chile* poses as the problem of seeing but pretending not to see, hearing but pretending not to hear, and so on. As cultural theorist Diana Taylor has shown in *Disappearing Acts,* "percepticide" was a deliberate project of the military regime, which used power as spectacle to reshape a perception.[27] There is no subject outside this logic; it became a way inhabiting space and time that continued to operate in the postdictatorship era.[28]

In the field of the appropriations and conversions of CDCs, it is interesting to examine the type of narrative and visual processes that were used to dismantle the habitus of this differential type of dictatorial punishment. Disappearance as punishment affected not only the disappeared and imprisoned population but also the society within which it operated, using a semipublic secret modality and a conception of politics that coimplicated civilian and military life. How was disappearance explored by the arts when CDCs came to be transformed into memory spaces or museums? As in *La fuga*, where the subterranean museum emerged as a twofold and truncated past that was still alive in a peculiar way, CDCs as memory sites link the present that is transforming them to the past that was hidden by clandestinity.[29] What would it mean to resist museification in these sites that were key to the dictatorship's illegal extermination of subversives? How can this resistance to the idea of a museum as an object-collection of the past transform the way an image of the past is created? I now turn to two final topics: the refusal to maintain a preestablished script in the tours of ESMA and Olimpo and the issue of narration itself as the key problem about the past; and the figure of the disappeared in political narratives of different types of rights.

ESMA constitutes one of the most emblematic sites among the clandestine detention centers in Argentina. Operating as a CDC even before the military coup, it was the largest detention center during the dictatorship.[30] Approximately five thousand detainees, a majority of whom subsequently disappeared, passed through its doors. The Naval School continued its normal operations throughout these years, providing the most obvious example of complicity with the center's activities. Prisoners were exploited for forced labor, falsifying documents, and managing real estate transactions for property seized by the government from detainees. ESMA also served as a space for antisubversive education, training military personnel on the (mis)treatment of detainees. After a long struggle the site was transformed into a "space for remembering and defending human rights" in 2004. Former detainees had lobbied for the establishment of a memory museum, a concept that was later transformed into the idea of a "space for memory and the defense of human rights." In 2006 a key book based on interviews of women held at ESMA states that once civilians gained control of the site, former detainees wanted it to express the struggle of those who were exterminated.[31]

In the case of ESMA the monumentality of the place lies in its military history; a visit emphasizes the intimate coexistence of the Navy Mechanics School and the CDC, further underscoring the proximity of the secret detention center to surrounding urban life. ESMA must be seen within the wider context of a systematic process to eliminate dissidence. The site's power exceeds its specific location, creating an experience that takes place concurrently within and outside the prison. Tours of ESMA highlight the absence of bars in the jail cells, allowing visitors to perceive the internalized terror that made it almost impossible to escape. One fugitive, Horacio D. Maggio, was killed after being recaptured, and his dead body was exhibited in the prison as an example and threat to other prisoners who might attempt the same thing.[32]

"Olimpo" was the name that the military personnel used to refer to the CDC that operated between August 1978 and the end of January 1979 in a depot of the Automotive Division of the Federal Police in the Floresta neighborhood.[33] Some detainees identified the same material used for the cell doors that they had encountered in Club Atlético, thus implying that Olimpo had been specially equipped for use as a CDC.[34] The utilization of Olimpo began after Club Atlético's scheduled closure at the end of 1977. This points to Olimpo as having constituted the third hub on an underground circuit that included Club Atlético and Banco. After a long struggle by Floresta residents, human rights organizations, survivors' and victims' families, the government declared the grounds a Historical City Site, and it became a "memory site" in 2004. Since then, many public remembrance activities have been held there, including discussion workshops, several film series, and a neighborhood library containing banned books from the dictatorship years. Olimpo does not exhibit the same sense of architectural monumentality as ESMA. It had only a brief run as a CDC and was vandalized by the police before they turned it over to the city—an explicit demonstration of the rage that this functional transformation provoked. One can still see the destruction wrought by the police before relinquishing the site. There are plans to remove the floor, as in Club Atlético, so that visitors can see what is left of the jail cells. This choice allows the site to evoke the structure of the CDC simply by showing the many floor layers that serve as a record of its former architecture. Like Club Atlético the terrain itself reveals the temporal layers laid down as part of its postdictatorial concealment.

Olimpo's past is neither cosmetically concealed nor made eternal. It expresses the incomplete character of the void; the ruin both speaks and at the same time remains silent about the past, without offering visitors a finished structure for a complete history. The fact that the site's jail cells were not remodeled reveals a reluctance to transform these spaces into sites for reconciliation. However, a neighborhood library is being built for books banned during the dictatorship. Each book will relate its own story on censorship, encouraging discussion about the materials held there. Also, workers at Olimpo are debating whether to install an exhibit on labor history and its transformations both during and after the dictatorship. The entire process of the Olimpo transformation reveals a commitment to the present rather than a museification of the past.[35] However, the figure of the museum does emerge within the site in the proposals to organize exhibitions on labor history during the dictatorship. The museum is not simply the opposite of a memory space; there are two different logics of reading, in which both macropolitics and micropolitics coexist.

In contrast to the malling of Punta Carretas, which centered on erasing unsettling temporalities and promoting the idea of a new (and controlled) market freedom, the ex-CDCs create a series of holes in the urban fabric. They suggest many questions regarding the clandestine, systematic extermination of dissidence that sought to put an end to any alternative idea of society. The proliferation of these kinds of spaces shows the ongoing struggle against becoming a city of impunity. They open up certain temporal folds that make the clandestine past visible, providing a bleak history for the conditions of possibility of the free market. These sites become critical for their very inability to provide a truth or a clear answer with respect to the past. In contrast to the whitewashing of Punta Carretas, with its messages advertising a "new time," ESMA and Olimpo emphasize a radical ambivalence. Neither site is a museum in the sense of a collection of objects; both are involved in a debate on how to avoid remodeling or recycling their own architecture.[36]

In ESMA there are only citations of passages taken from works written by survivors that stand in the middle of the void left after the place was dismantled by the navy. The task of recycling architecture in Punta Carretas was symptomatic of a society in which the past had to be held at bay by negating its temporality. One finds the opposite tendency in these two sites, where the architecture itself expresses years of terror without becoming objectified as a tourist fetish. Both Olimpo and ESMA avoid falling into the trap of promoting fascination with the torture gallery that lies within them (something I find problematic in Villa Grimaldi). Unlike the recycling that conceals the past in Punta Carretas, I find it significant that these sites have been maintained without remodeling. Raising a series of questions regarding the relationships between (post)dictatorship space and their complex set of multiple temporalities, their decay and their absence of monumentality, demonstrated by lack of a specific, definitive script for guided visits, highlights their complex and open character. In this sense the remainder problematizes another area of unstable ground in the geography of law and politics, a global-national-local problem based on the notion of citizenship that the civic-military apparatus passed on to neoliberal democracy. Tours of them generate uncertainty in the visitors, who are confronted by the haunting incompleteness that characterizes these ruinous spaces. There is something in ESMA and Olimpo that evokes not only the unpunished extermination of dissidence but also the society in which the CDC operated. What differentiates the CDC from a penitentiary is the uncanny absence of bars—something that makes the distinction between the inside and the outside of imprisonment take other forms.

Politicability: Territory, Citizenship, and Disappearance

According to the cultural critic Silvia Tandeciarz, in the struggle for memory sites it is "the uneasy coexistence of past and present, in the rub of dissonant discourses, and in the open and continuing dialogue those discourses promote that a new Argentine citizenry is being forged."[37] If we go further and argue that it is the notion of citizenship and its limitations that are being explored in the recovered CDCs, we can discuss how memorials, artistic production, and public debate contribute to this exploration. These processes can be read in complex connection with the processes of struggle against the disappearance of political activists before and during the last dictatorship. According to Vania Markarian's study of this process in *Left in Transformation*, the demands for human rights were gradually transformed into a language that had to avoid political activism and stick to the individual and biographic in order to be heard.[38] This logic connects to the boom of hypersubjectivism that took place after the memorialistic boom but, for the time being, I only want to focus on how the regime of struggle and defense of human rights victims affected a way of remembering that is still in dispute nowadays. The demand for the victims to appear alive became a demand for human beings' right to life, which gradually presupposed the deletion of the figure of the political subject. In short, to be considered a subject of human rights, it was necessary to "disappear" the militant status of the disappeared. With the gradual naturalization of this discursive operation, the human right to live was gradually separated from the human right to politics. This involves a change in the narrativization of disappearance, in which what is left out is not politics but rather what I call "politicability."

The idea of politicability is inspired by a series of questions proposed by the philosopher Etienne Balibar in his study of France's Declaration of the Rights of Man and the Citizen. He starts with "the apparently irreducible split" between the concept of equality and freedom in the configuration of the rights of man and citizen. "Equality" generally belongs within the economic or social field while "freedom" refers to the legal-political field. The question is how these are transformed into two almost mutually exclusive concepts. According to Balibar, this exclusion results from the axiom shared by liberalism and socialism that "the realization of *equality* occurs through State intervention, because it is essentially a matter of *redistribution,* whereas the preservation of *freedom* is tied to the *limitation* of this intervention, even to eternal *vigilance* against its 'perverse' effects."[39] From this irreducible split between equality and freedom, Balibar derives the paradox implied by two types of rights: the rights of man and the rights of the citizen, as if replicating the two previous spheres (the rights of man as "the right to existence, the right of peoples to self-determination" and the rights of citizens as related to the political, technocratic, and economic sphere).

However, he questions the split by suggesting an analysis of the founding text of the declaration of the rights of man based on the relationship "between the aporetical character of the text and the conflictual character of the situation in which it arises and which serves as its referent."[40] Balibar points to the twin traditions that frame the text's uncertainty: the contractualist tradition and the revolutionary tradition where the bourgeoisie and people ("non-bourgeoise masses") constitute alliances and confrontations.[41] He argues that there is no gap between man and citizen because "the treatment of equality in the *Declaration* is precisely the site of the strongest and most precise identification of *man* and *citizen*. . . . The *Declaration* does not posit any 'human nature' *before* society and the political order, as an underlying foundation or exterior guarantee. Instead it integrally identifies the rights of man with political rights and, by an approach that short-circuits theories of human nature as well as those of theological supernature, identifies man, whether individual or collective, with the member of political society."[42]

This is the key to Balibar's hypothesis about an impossible notion of "equaliberty," where equality and freedom are posed within an inseparable and differential relation (like man and citizen). Let us go deeper into the notion of equaliberty because it is crucial to the struggle for "memory" so far analyzed in places like Buen Pastor and Punta Carretas Mall, where a poetic of flight was intimately connected, in the present, to articulating the political in a present that confines memory to the stereotypes of victims and villains. Balibar's argument for resignifying the struggle for human rights as a right that includes the right to politics sheds lights onto the struggles for memory within and outside the past of the left of the Southern Cone. It brings up the problem of how to imagine or reinvent a memory of politics and freedom without falling into a stereotyped and acceptable politics of memory. In Huidobro, the past of the prison undermines freedom in a present where the dictatorship's prison was reopened in a show of impunity, naturalizing the criminalization of poverty and of politics. In the case of Buen Pastor, former prisoners questioned for whom the Paseo was being built, since the homage to prisoners was erasing their struggle against injustice. One of the forms of afterlife of confinement is a camouflaging of the past to avoid addressing injustice and the structural transformability of society, in a present that can see such questions only as a problem of the past.

Balibar follows the core hypothesis of an equaliberty where "equality is identical to freedom, is *equal to freedom*, and vice versa."[43] He insists on the impossibility expressed by this portmanteau word that "gives both the conditions under which man is a citizen through and through, and the reason for this assimilation. Underneath the equation of man and citizen, or rather within it, as the very reason of its universality—as its presupposition—lies the proposition of equaliberty."[44] An impossible key to this reading lies in the possibility that "the signification of the equation man = citizen is not so much the definition of a political right as the affirmation of a *universal right to politics*. Formally at least—but this is the classic example of a form that can become a material weapon—the *Declaration* opens an indefinite sphere of 'politicization' of rights-claims each of which reiterates in its own way the demand for citizenship or for an institutional, public inscription of freedom and equality."[45] Equaliberty would refer to that human right to politics, to politicability. It is the possibility of insisting on the transformability of politics, of both the geography and therefore the definition of politics (that is, transformability in terms of rights that could be modified depending on social class, race, or gender constraints).

In this sense, equaliberty, as a right to politics, implies a necessary problematization of the split between a human right and a political right. The split between the human and the political (as a category that is not inherent to what is human) implies that, in order to be a human right, the right to politics has to follow the guidelines established by the existing geography of rights. Human beings need to adjust to the constrained geography of the state (national/international) at any given time. If so, they can be subject to citizens' rights, which include the right to possess freedom. In case of failing to adjust to the definition of citizen for the state, human beings no longer belong in the category of political subjects, citizens, and therefore free subjects. What is lost in the constrained freedom and equality determined by the geography of rights is the potentiality of a different right and notion of politics—that is, of politicability. In other words, it is the possibility of transforming the limits of humanity implied by the notion of a right—the right to a political right as the right to the transformability of rights. This is reminiscent of Bolaño's vision of an imprisoned and restricted outlook created by the dictatorial apparatus in what is labeled as subsequent "political" life. The naturalization of the discursive transformation operating in the dictatorships highlights the notion of restricted democracy, which laid the basis for the subsequent redemocratization. Such naturalization implies the limitation of the human right as a right that is "alien" to the political right and as the only way of voicing expressions against the disappearance of political prisoners at national and international level.

To what extent is the relationship between human rights, citizen rights, and social class a topic that continues to be shunned by the work on memory and the defense of human rights? It is crucial to reconsider the problematic presuppositions about memory, its restrictions and potentialities when being transformed into sites of the citizenry mentioned by Tandeciarz.[46] Is it possible to insist on a politics of memory that problematizes the notion of politics as restriction? Is it possible to problematize the fact that there are only two options: the depoliticization of the disappeared (the dictatorial perspective) or the idea of a politicization that fails to examine the limits and restrictions of the notion of politics of the militant past? How are we to rethink the political based on the questions about the subjects who qualify for rights? According to the sociologist Emilio Crenzel, when the CONADEP (the National Commission on the Disappeared) moved away from the federal capital, they started to meet people who had never reported the disappearances of family members, either because they did not know that there was a commission operating in metropolitan areas, or because they were afraid, or because it was not easy to distinguish between dictatorship and postdictatorship in terms of practices of violence.

There is an anecdote about people from the interior who heard about the *Nunca más* (Never again) report and found characteristic features of their own daily life in its (hi)stories of dictatorial life, by "associating the violence described in the book with the violence they endure or that they have heard the police have inflicted in the neighborhoods where they live. For this group, time . . . passes beyond the changes in political life or the profile assumed by the State status."[47] Clearly, there are areas where that violence (the violence of lacking rights) continues to operate, areas where that "never again" does not refer to the past of the dictatorship but to the present in which people live. Has the transition reached this area? The dissymmetry of current times— hostile to redemocratization—brings up a series of questions addressed by Balibar when posing the figure of political and human rights as a problem.

This results in the emergence of disjointed temporalities, which fail to encompass civic activity during the transition. How do the "voices" of territorial protest become citizen voices (since they are "always already" configured by other discourses) without being problematized from the writing and the reimagination of history? What voices remain outside the geography of that which can be heard, perceived as dissonant sounds that violate the grammars already established by the left, the right, and human rights? Such voices are not the assimilated ones defending heroic activism; we need to think about what this type of voice silences, the areas that have been disqualified by both types of historicization. What type of unsolved temporality interrupts the sayable and visible as a specter, a spectral return of the disappeared, inserted into a narrative that disappears it again? Chapter 6 analyzes this type of irruption in two films that problematize the clandestine and its afterlife in the Buenos Aires of the 1990s: *Buenos Aires Vice Versa* (directed by Alejandro Agresti) and *Garage Olimpo* (directed by Marco Bechis). Both directors show the tension between architectonics and temporality by exploring the regimes of tellability and visibility in the space-time of Argentina's "re-democratized society."

6

It Goes without Seeing

Framing the Future Past of Violence in Postdictatorship Film

In previous chapters I analyzed how retaining the prison structure as the base and cultural heritage of the new mall created an optical problem in various different critical and literary discourses. Texts by Diamela Eltit, Fernández Huidobro, and Roberto Bolaño set up the relation between place and gaze in such a way as to show the prison and the consumer world as coimplicated in the regime of neoliberal freedom. I have focused on ways of imagining the borders that separate, differentiate, and also confuse the space of the market superimposed upon the prison, raising the question of who can see what from where, from what social location. I wanted to show the complexity of relating past and present; the dynamic, shifting relationship between the production of meaning about place and gaze; and the violence involved in assuming a homogeneous social unit, a universal gaze and space (the mall as the world of freedom). Displacing the gaze involves questioning the automatic, usually unquestioned, composition of place out of space, the transformation of a space into a place.

In their remarkable work on memory sites, sociologists Elizabeth Jelin and Victoria Langland have distinguished between the physical and lived spaces in which we usually move and the idea of place. In the latter, multiple social and political processes of collective struggle occur.[1] We saw this transformation of a space into a site of struggle for signification in the case of Buen Pastor, where former prisoners transformed their remembrance of escape into an act of resistance to the confinement of their political histories in the present. In that case, the documentary and the *escrache* were the tools the women used to disrupt the processes of signification and contest a system of stigmatization that was confining them in the present.[2] In this chapter I analyze the overlap between afterlives of confinement, displacements of the gaze, and the transformation of space into place in the medium of fictional film.

The questionable limits and limitations of what constitutes "post" in postdictatorship emerge in the problematic relation between "space" and "gaze" in two films from the 1990s that dramatize the official framing of post-transition Menemist Argentina: *Buenos Aires viceversa,* directed by Alejandro Agresti (1996), and *Garage Olimpo,* directed by Marco Bechis (1999).[3] We should note that the film titles themselves involve a problematization of place—the capital city Buenos Aires and the former clandestine detention center (CDC) Olimpo—by the addition of another function-word to both locations. With "viceversa," the title *Buenos Aires viceversa* evokes the possibility of another angle or way of seeing and connecting space and gaze. When "garage" is added to the place-name Olimpo, it suggests the slave workforce of prisoners at the CDC, which was an auto repair shop run by the federal police.

The transformation of place by name in the choice of both films' titles can be read against the background of the Menem era's characteristic impulse to fix and adjust meaning. Former president Carlos Menem argued that the solution to the crisis of the Raúl Alfonsín regime involved a financial adjustment with the austerity measures of the Cavallo Plan. This was a legal adjustment in the pardons of 1989 and 1990 that decreed the impunity of the military as well as a historic-discursive adjustment to take control of politics, seen in the rise of nonparliamentary presidential decisions.[4] It is perhaps in this constellation of place, gaze, date, and historicity that the films can be seen as critical commentaries on how to forge a link to a past that was being actively erased. If the economic-legal-parliamentary adjustment consisted of fixing meaning from the unilateral presidential gaze (an ideal I earlier called synchronization, the adjusting of clock time), the films open up zones where meaning is less clear and well defined, presenting the years of the dictatorship as a crucial problem to be constructed through gaze and through space.

The problems examined in earlier chapters—the transition and its chronological instability, and the spatial problem of the border between the CDC and the world in which it occurred—are explored now in the critical nexus between place-time-eye.

Place and gaze are framed and problematized within the two films, which offer different readings of the relationship between spatiotemporal experience and the visualization of history. The afterlife of certain spatiotemporal experiences of dictatorships is approached in visual language. These films allow us to glimpse perspectives that undermine the construction of seeing, showing how it is linked to a training of vision during the decades of military dictatorship and how the perception of history in the everyday world can transform the gaze and the perception of place. The problem of resistance to museification is dramatized in the films as the possibility of decentering the dominant, official angle of vision, the play between framing, screen, and camera. In the bodily metaphor of surgery without anesthesia that Menem used to describe the economic adjustment policy, there is an almost metonymic naturalization of electroshock therapy (the application of pain without anesthesia), previously used to describe the "antisubversive" struggle but now with the objective of regenerating the body of the nation. Thus a feature of the imaginary of the 1970s is adjusted to the new present and naturalized as something automatic. The question then becomes how these films translate the formula of that naturalization (it goes without saying) into the formula "it goes without *seeing*."

Framing, which is an essential part of cinema's optical mechanism, is used here to problematize the gaze and the universe of constitutive constraints of postdictatorship freedom, beginning with the screen as a common space that is problematized on a metafictional level. Taken together as a problematic constellation, the two films explore certain afterlives of dictatorship space-times, questioning the relations between territory and vision in the construction of the impossible "us" (*nosotros*) of neoliberal freedom. The question is then how the films subvert the constitutive constraints of the 1990s' imaginary of success by introducing that which was supposed to remain unseen. Each film uses a different type of spatialization: in *Buenos Aires viceversa* the architecture of success of the deregulating the Menem administration is deconstructed in multiple ways, whereas in *Garage Olimpo* it is the secret or clandestine military city of the dictatorship that is the framing device.[5] Thus the afterlife of dictatorship and the spatial and temporal adjustments are examined in a visual field that is framed by the camera.

Encounters between the 1970s and the 1990s: Economic Politics and the Body of Doctrine

In their analyses of *Buenos Aires viceversa* and *Garage Olimpo*, the cultural critic Christian Gunermann and historian Valeria Manzano have stressed the dated nature of these films as a critique of the "city of malls."[6] In the case of Argentina, the mall-city became almost a spatial equivalent to Menem's adjustment policies. However, there is a structural difference in the temporal organization of each of the films: *Buenos Aires viceversa* problematizes assumptions about the city by playing with different mechanisms of visualization and timing. The film contains a series of different plot lines; the central one is the process of filming of the city, the production of a documentary on the Buenos Aires of the day. The other storylines involve the life of a woman addicted to TV news; two technicians who repair televisions; a boxer who longs to make money; a blind woman who gets separated from her blind partner and is tricked by a former secret police torturer who takes her to a motel and drives her crazy, accusing her of being a "filthy leftist"; and a young man (the nephew of the former torturer) who works in the motel and may be one of the children of the disappeared.[7]

The main plot involves Daniela, a child of the disappeared, who is looking for a job. She is hired to film what is going on in the city by an aristocratic couple who have not left home since the dictatorship. Daniela produces two videos: the first, as Gunermann shows, uses 1970s-style cinema verité as social protest, showing the poverty in the city that has become invisible because of the mall. This video provokes disgust in the elderly couple, who connect the gaze implied in Daniela's images with their disappeared daughter. After reprimanding her, they ask her to film the city again, with more attractive and "realistic" footage. Frustrated and furious, Daniela thinks she has found the "beauty" of Buenos Aires in a tree but when she goes to film it, a homeless boy appears, rendering the image opaque and short-circuiting it through poverty. Daniela asks the boy, whose nickname is Bocha, to move, but he mockingly refuses. This causes Daniela to burst into tears, at which point Bocha comes down from the tree and comforts her. An intense connection grows between them, and they become codirectors of the new video of the city.

This second production of a "realistic" Buenos Aires begins with a shot of the façade of the ESMA (Navy Mechanics School) and continues with other footage of city architecture, culminating in the final space—the mall—where the boy dies. It introduces the architecture of a way of seeing the city (we never see the entire video, but we catch glimpses of façades, churches, rooftops, squares, and fountains) that makes the elderly couple happy but that ends up in fresh trauma for Daniela. After the success of the film they have made together, Bocha tries to steal a video camera in a mall. The security guard, who was a torturer under the dictatorship, shoots and kills him. The mall emerges here as a crossing point between time periods that are linked to the geography of impunity and the criminalization of poverty. Bocha, who says he sleeps in the street in cardboard boxes, dies from a gunshot wound among the cardboard boxes piled up in a corner of the mall. As the cultural critic Martín Sorbille has demonstrated, the boxes are inscribed with the words "Made in China," referring to the economic policies of the time and connecting Bocha's death with this universe.[8]

Garage Olimpo offers a more obvious connection to the 1970s and less to the 1990s, since its time frame is limited to the dictatorship. It shows life in the Olimpo CDC as seen by a prisoner, María, and the connection she develops with Félix, a member of the *patota* (the task force that carried out kidnappings and ran the CDC). Before María was detained, Félix used to rent a room in her mother's house.[9] The story takes place both inside and outside the CDC, showing the daily routine and how it relates to the rest of the city in different ways. Although there is not explicit connection to the city of the 1990s in the film, Manzano has argued that *Garage Olimpo* translates the social, political, and cultural issues of the late 1990s in its representations of the past dictatorship, not only in the theme of disappearance after the impunity rulings but also in its stereotyping of the police.[10] Unlike classic transition films such as *The Official Story* (which, like *Buenos Aires viceversa*, examines the nation's official architecture) and *Night of the Pencils* (which, like *Garage Olimpo*, focuses on the clandestine), neither movie has received much attention from academic critics. Nevertheless, I am intrigued by how they connect the spatial and temporal imaginaries of the 1990s and the dictatorship in an oblique, subtle way, allowing us to reflect on how temporality and territoriality constitute different ways of approaching the gaze.

Reading these two movies together as a problematic constellation shows the encounter of disjointed and incommensurable temporalities in postdictatorship images of space. Thinking of both films as symptomatic of the era of adjustment allows me to discuss two images of the city and two different temporal series that are not typically connected but that are central to this book: the city of malls and the city of CDCs, the 1990s and the 1970s. Thus my analysis goes back to the beginning of the book but now focuses on the connection between the city of the CDCs and the city of malls (seen at the beginning as open prisons). In a sense we move from the question of how to read the space of prison from the prisoner's point of view to how to read the framing of the city by the camera's eye in these films. How do they generate critical views of the mall-city through its production of images about its pasts-presents? How do they express visually the incommensurability between layers of pasts and presents? The films open up an interstice between the economic austerity measures and the legal ones (the impunity laws), urging us to begin there. The montage of pasts and presents that have become invisible, thanks to neoliberal shock policies, allows viewers to examine what goes without saying—or, in this case, what goes without seeing.

Making the Nonvisible Visible: Optical Impotence and Deframing

As a teenager, Agresti witnessed the dictatorship, and Bechis is a CDC survivor; their work occupies a hinge position between the classic transition films on the dictatorship and contemporary movies produced by children of the disappeared, who identify with the category of postmemory film proposed by the cultural theorist Marianne Hirsch.[11] Situated in that temporal interstice, the two directors offer a 1990s' perspective on disappearance, at a point when ways of thinking and filming the afterlives of dictatorial violence were still relatively unexplored, thanks to the dominant imaginary of the 1986 Full Stop Law, revitalized by Menem's Impunity Laws (1989–1990). These sought to portray those who continued to "dwell" on the dictatorship as clichéd, resentful, and tasteless. Examining the construction of the gaze in relation to territory, the composition of the visible, and what is rendered invisible by such visibility, the films problematize the afterlife of the dictatorship by showing how it involves a kind of framing that works to imprison the gaze.

At the same time, the critical challenge for films that introduce the clandestine in order to "make visible" what passes for invisible lies in avoiding a phenomenological fetishization of looking. The emancipatory projects of the minor epic and the unsayable reappear here in the visual field of cinematography in the question of how to make the world of disappearance appear on screen. As I showed in the chapter on Bolaño, we need to avoid introducing a notion of unveiling (in the slang of the CDCs, removing the hood or blindfold ["quitarse la capucha" or "des-vendar"]) as if there were something objective and essential operating as truth that was once hidden and is now manifest. If we start from the premise that there is no absolute truth to be revealed (no truth that would become present by removing the blindfolds), the question becomes how the gaze can escape from the prison of the blindfold when there is no uncontaminated outside to be revealed, just as there is no uncontaminated outside for the prisons and CDCs.

Films, as sites of image-production that can create other ways of seeing, function to unsettle the gaze, bringing to light what we see without seeing, the conditions of possibility and impossibility that frame the relationship between image and historicity. It is crucial to read these images not as producing a truth that adjustment conceals but as examples of a decentering of the official framework that shows it to be an effect of a position, an image framed by a circuit. In other words, "unveiling" would reproduce the fetish of a single, concealed truth that, were it to be revealed, would solve the problem. Decentering the framework is just as problematic, since if the theme of these films is framing itself (the camera, the gaze, being made conscious), we end up with a radical finiteness of seeing that works retroactively on the movie itself, making us wonder what kind of framing is presupposed by this critique of framing. If there is not an absolute position from which to see the totality of a measurable, homogeneous time and space, what kind of space-time emerges in this problematization of framing?

Agresti's work creates a mise en abyme of the act of filming, because the process of filming and framing the space of the city is part of the film's plot structure. It makes explicit the relation between (hi)storicization, territory, and visuality (what space to film, from which standpoint, for whom). In Bechis's film this relationship is posed by the optical framing of the CDC and its borders and the theme of visibility, blindfolding, and hooding. The frames are problematized through a disconnection between images of the CDC and the surrounding urban environment that systematically ignores and invisibilizes it (the problem of a blindfolding-hooding of life outside it as well). This dramatizes a question about the type of Benjaminian awakening I examined earlier in this book—a process of making perceptible what is closest. This is paralleled in the movies by the problematization of the camera's focus and frame, which challenges the idea of making visible as the phenomenological fantasy of a truth always at hand, always present. The mirrored tension between territories and what Gilles Deleuze has called "optical situations" in these films points to a problem with time. He defines "optical situations" in *Cinema 2: The Time-Image*, as signals of a crisis in the action image when automatic action ceases and the frame that configures the situation becomes the theme of the work (as a premise that emerges as the site of reflection itself).[12]

We can trace a connection between Deleuze's description of the crystal-image (crucial to his series on time-images) with Walter Benjamin's dialectical image, because both deal with an image generated as an interruption of an automatic action (the sensory-motor framework that links perception and action). Starting with the idea of a crystal that expresses an insoluble tension, both theorists suggest alternative approaches to the temporal and political imagination. From this standpoint, Benjamin's dialectical image and Deleuze's crystal-image offer us a critical language with which to approach the relation between memory-image and temporality—the image that emerges as a point of irresolution between times. This language underlines two points: first, the incommensurability between times as that which habit and historicism attempt to erase with a common(sense) approach; and second, the possibility of avoiding the phenomenological or positivist idea of an unveiling that makes visible a truth or a raw fact from the past (privileged access to it from the idea of transparent consciousness and transparent language). In this sense the image becomes the site of a fissure that marks its own ending, the asymmetry between past-present that is delegitimized in every perception to make the present productive. Thus the perceptibility and production of historic imagination are exposed by a problematization of pasts that do not adjust to the present and vice versa.

In Deleuze's *Time-Image,* the "crystal-image" stages this problem as an expression of "the most fundamental operation of time: since the past is constituted not after the present that it was but at the same time, time has to split itself in two at each moment as present and past, which differ from each other in nature, or, what amounts to the same thing, it has to split the present in two heterogeneous directions, one of which is launched towards the future while the other falls into the past."[13] According to the cultural theorist Ronald Bogue, the crystal reveals not only the multiple and dissymmetrical nature of time but also the ways the virtual, truncated past (that which did not happen as an open promise in what did) "may be related to the ongoing actualization of time in a present moving toward a future."[14] We could say that this actualization urges us to approach the time in which the crystal-image is constituted as now (a fissured present), in which it points to the passage of time as a way of expressing legibility—in other words, of figuring an incommensurability.

At this point Benjamin's description of the dialectical image in his *Arcades* helps to supplement the crystal-image by focusing on the type of actualization the image produces of the past and present. The problem of how a past is actualized in this image does not assume organic (anthropomorphic) linearity nor the idea of actualization as fulfillment of a possible being imagined as based on the present as its form of resolution. On the contrary, the image appears in both Benjamin and Deleuze as a crystal that expresses another way of approaching the experience of a time that is not yet narrativized and that implies a relation of times that does not assume the form of an adjustment or resolution as subsuming the past under the logic of a present. It is the impossibility of assuming the implicit value of subsuming that produces the dialectic crystal-image as an instant of detention that figures what cannot be incorporated. In Benjamin the actualization that generates the image as a dialectical image (which produces a kind of relationship between past and present) refers to a "historical index" that "not only says that they belong to a particular time; it says, above all, that they attain legibility *only at a particular time.*"[15] Establishing a distinction between his image and what phenomenology postulates (the object-image placed opposite to a subject), he says that the "historical index" and the critical gesture implied by the image suggest another way of imagining time and politics: the detour, the misadjusted in the past and the present, which decenters the framing by which the image is constituted. For Benjamin the image does not refer to a visual object but rather to how past and present crystallize as the place or site of times that are neither assimilated nor similar: "image is that *wherein* what has been comes together in a flash with the now to form a constellation. In other words, image is dialectics at a standstill."[16]

In Deleuze the crystal-image is the present beside itself, expressed in its double, dissymmetrical constitution (the virtual-current past, the virtual-current present). This distance in which time is exposed through the suspension of the habitual opens up what Deleuze calls a "minimal difference" connected to an instant of "minimal freedom." Emerging as a counterintuitive leap is the idea of the image as expression of a contretemps that interrupts the habitual chain that constitutes the narrative of the history of progress. In the films the decentering that emerges when the body of the nation is "adjusted" leads to the production of images that deviate from Menemist types of framing, introducing other connections between less obvious layers of past and present. This attempt to figure an outside-the-box generates a center of indeterminacy or hiatus in the present that expresses not a gaze that informs us (gives us information) but an image as a way of thinking about time and about the way time reveals itself. In this interstitial space of minimal critical freedom, the images that emerge in the two films present a way of inquiring into the traces of the past in a present.

Buenos Aires viceversa

Although *Buenos Aires viceversa* involves a complicated set of parallel stories connected in different ways with the authoritarian past, two particular points in the film focus on the problem of space and gaze. One is the process of filming the city (which we only see in fragmentary flashes) and the reaction of the people who commissioned the videos; the other involves the space at the end of the movie—the mall—where a homeless boy, Bocha, is murdered by a private security guard who used to be a torturer during the dictatorship. After showing the renarrativization of the murder on the TV news, the movie leaves us with the connections between the mall, impunity, injustice, and the criminalization of poverty. The visual frame is questioned by the very act of filming, which becomes the central problem in the movie. An elderly, upper-class couple who stopped going out when their daughter disappeared hire Daniela to bring them images of the city (for them, the outside that they are afraid of). They want to "see what is going on out there," in the postauthoritarian city they no longer know. They are outraged, however, when she brings them images of a city they do not wish to see, images that they read as deliberately ugly and shocking. These involve poverty and subjects termed "*cabecitas negras*" (literally "little black heads"), historically a pejorative racial epithet denoting subalternity in terms of class (poverty), race (Indigenous features), and national origin (Latin American immigrants). The epithet is used to refer the non-European ethnic population. Upon seeing these faces, the elderly man loses his temper and says:

> MAN: To sum up, my dear, I don't think you understood what we asked you for at all. That stuff you brought us is nonsense you made up to shock us.
>
> DANIELA: That's the street.
>
> MAN: *That's not the street.* Be quiet and don't interrupt. That's not the street, that's not art, that's nothing. You just like to shock people . . .
>
> DANIELA: I don't understand why you're so angry.
>
> MAN: We're angry because girls like you are very upsetting to people like us. We used to have a daughter. And we don't like other girls ending up like she did. . . . I'm going to give you another chance. . . . I'll give you 500 pesos and in one week you're to go out on the street and bring us *things like normal people*, understand?
>
> DANIELA: *What people?*

The scene ends here, with the young woman's question punctuating the division between the two videos she brings. Although we only see momentary glimpses of her videos (in the background, never close up), the earlier version show a "backward" Buenos Aires. The new one highlights the city's architecture, beginning with the façade of the ESMA and covering squares, fountains, rooftops, and buildings (here people have been replaced by pure architecture).

The play of framing is important, because as we witness the dialogue between Daniela and the aristocrat about the first video, there are random shots of the television screen in the background showing a prostitute on the street, looking angry, reacting to something that is outside our frame of knowledge. A play of images is set up: the image of the living room becomes the frame for the images occurring on the television in Daniela's video, where we glimpse a woman who is perhaps looking at a point beyond us (we are blind to it). Needless to say, the idea of people that emerges is interposed on this woman, opening a chasm between the raised voice of the elderly man and the silent scream of the image, emptied of sound. The couple's first request for a video is ambiguous: they want to see what is going on, and that "seeing" involves people (they want to see people). However, after seeing the people that Daniela films, the word becomes an idiom: the couple want to see things "*como la gente*"—meaning proper, appropriate, "normal" things as opposed to inappropriate nonsense. Daniela responds by questioning the assumption of the idiom itself: "*¿qué gente?*" (What people?), highlighting the ambiguity of language that is taken for granted. In the context of the film, the idiom "*como la gente*" (like normal people) also highlights the kind of people who become visible in the video as unworthy of the image of the city requested. In the video, people are literally the main problem: What people? Using what type of frame? In what layer of the city?

As Daniela makes her first film, we see, through Agresti's camera, her camera filming the city. It is obvious that the people she is filming are reminiscent of 1970s protest cinema, people emerging from poverty, remnants who do not fit the Buenos Aires stereotype of the European immigrant (like the elderly couple, who stress their Italian heritage). These people come instead from the interior of Argentina or from other countries such as Bolivia or Peru. In the first video, race and class are the common denominator in the group of people Daniela films; it is they who constitute the city the elderly couple do not see. The question about people that emerges out of the angry discussion her images provoke becomes the fundamental area organizing the film: "things like normal people." (Silence). "What people?"

The theme of visible space, class, and race is crucial to the anger of the elderly aristocrat/aesthete. His understanding of people emerges as an implicit effect of ideology, as a pact (sharing the meaning of street-art-people) that Daniela's images shatter by questioning the implicit framing of the city and the people who are supposed to inhabit it. The spaces Daniela shows are the poor parts of Buenos Aires, public spaces with couples embracing, mothers with babies, and elderly people. This irritates her patrons because they wanted a video showing that everything is all right, that the daughter's disappearance (ambiguity) was worth something. This opens up an interesting space in recent cinematography in terms of the problem of the economy and needing to legitimize the deaths with a gain, a surplus (especially in a time of crisis and austerity).[17]

The articulation of the gaze—the main point of Agresti's film—seems to lead to the possibility of reflecting on the sense of belonging that goes without saying, as the reaction of the elderly couple shows. The gaze emerges as a way of grouping a sense of belonging to a group that in films is linked to a specific territory. The film suggests an aesthetics able to question and transcend the opposition between cinema verité (the 1970s documentary film we do not see) and art for art's sake (stage-managed images of the beauty of Buenos Aires), an aesthetics able to restate the relation of class, race, and affect. The film explores the continuity of the nation's foundational racism and the national imaginary's process of reorganization (regeneration). Underlying Daniela's first set of images is the figure of extermination, which the elderly couple want to rationalize in the regeneration the film does not show. They demand the imagistic reconstitution of another city, *like normal people*, through the architectural façade of the nation-state, an image without an interior. Here people have to be replaced by architecture, the successful city of the 1990s as a continuation of the turn-of-the-century city, which only appears backstage in images of the ESMA, cathedrals, public squares, the Obelisk, and so on. This is the vice versa that produces the beauty of a Buenos Aires "like normal people."

Vice Versa: Architecture and the Mall

Frustrated by her inability to find beauty for her second video, Daniela meets Bocha, a homeless boy, orphaned like herself, who teaches her to see another city. Their encounter is significant; just when Daniela thinks she has found the beauty of the city in a tree, that aesthetic ideal is marred by the appearance of the homeless boy, who spoils the shot. This affective process is accompanied by shots of the vice versa, a Buenos Aires seen through its architecture, its squares, its cathedrals, its rooftops. All this is punctuated by a new silence, as if to erase those who no longer count as people in the space of consumerism. When Daniela and Bocha go to the mall to spend the money they have earned with the second documentary, expectations are overturned. Bocha happens to see a stack of cameras in a store window and decides to steal one (possibly as a present for Daniela, who taught him to film). When Bocha takes the camera, a private security guard chases and shoots him, and the boy falls dead among some cardboard boxes. The images leading up to Bocha's death are interspersed with ones of Daniela listening to a piece of music that is her only memory of her dead parents. However, the music is punctuated by the silence of the crucial final scene in the mall.

The death is then narrated on the television news as the result of an altercation between a security guard and a drunken lower-class boxer. While the guard was struggling to defend himself, his gun accidentally went off and hit a boy walking through the mall. The last words in the film are those of the news report: "El boxeador se encuentra a disposición de la justicia" (The boxer has been taken into custody), leaving us with the impunity in which the mall and the TV report cross paths in the interests of the dominant prose of history that the film (re)produces. It is highly significant that this part of the film, which underlines the new impunity surrounding the (naturalized) criminalization of poverty, begins with a shot of the façade of the ESMA and ends with the death of a street boy in the mall. This sequence establishes two types of connection between space and gaze that assume the continuity of in-commensurable forms of injustice: the elderly couple expecting to see beauty in a façade from a flourishing Buenos Aires, and the desperate gaze of Dan-iela before the death of a loved one. *Buenos Aires viceversa* is the first film that juxtaposes a mall and a former CDC as crucial spaces that speak mutely through their architecture. The question now becomes how this progression harks back to the restructuring of the space of the market and the space of detention, which cross one another's paths in the unpunished destruction of lives that do not count and beings who do not qualify as being "*como la gente*" ("like [normal] people").

The mall scene articulates a series of open-ended images that question the logic of social class, impunity, the Cold War, television, and racism (Bo-cha and the boxer are both "*cabecitas negras*"). The impossibility of recon-ciling the scene with the discourse that appears on television (reinventing everything that was seen) makes spectators of the film—like the characters who observe Bocha's murder—witnesses to a double injustice: the killing of a child (who does not qualify as a person in the mall) and the transformation of the event on the national TV news that grants impunity for a new crime committed by an ex-torturer. The image generated is both dialectical image and crystal-image, because there are multiple temporalities shown in the space of an insoluble tension. The reconstruction of the facts in the dominant narrative makes the spectators participants in the impunity of the 1990s but also prevents any closure. The tension between images (the mall scene and the TV version) produces a sense of helplessness and claustrophobia. How are we supposed to react? What discourse should be generated? If the process of national reorganization implies an act of narrativization shown here in the conversion of the event into History (the discourse of news reports), what contrasts exist to that narrative?

The Olimpo Blindfold

This problematic is also central to *Garage Olimpo*, which plays off images of the CDC and the city, the border between the two that opens and closes, the possibility of clandestine acts by the state and the system of secrecy, helplessness, and claustrophobia they generate. The images analyzed here illustrate the problematization of the gaze that takes place in *Garage Olimpo*, which, as Manzano has pointed out, undercuts the 1990s' ways of seeing the past. The film's central theme is the gaze within the secret prison and the blindfolding or hooding of prisoners, creating a complex metonymic game between the CDC and the society in which it takes place. The gaze is staged through the blindfolds of the "post"dictatorship as a society that also sees without seeing. At the same time, by placing us within the nonvisible zone of the CDC, the movie makes us yearn to see its outside—the way of seeing but not-seeing and hearing but not-hearing that marks daily life outside and creates the border of the CDC.

In relation to the most well-known and widely seen movies about the world of the CDCs (*La noche de los lápices* or the more recent *Crónica de una fuga*), *Garage Olimpo* (released in 1999) is an outsider that has yet to receive much critical attention. It is, notably, the only film about the CDCs that uses the name of one of them in its title: Olimpo, which is now a memorial site. The word "*Garage*" added to Olimpo reminds us of the prison's identity in the neighborhood as a garage that was also an auto repair shop for the Federal Police and thus its double function: a garage as façade of a site that makes us think of the constitution of the gaze on the CDC from outside (the neighborhood in which it takes place and becomes invisible), and the slave labor of the mass of prisoners within the CDC. Bechis's film fictionalizes the internal world of the CDC that operated between August 1978 and January 1979 in the office of the Automotive Division of the Federal Police in a Buenos Aires neighborhood called La Floresta. Besides taking the name used secretly by the Federal Police, *Garage Olimpo* is notable for depicting the all-powerful might of the disappearers inside the center, stressing the absolute power the guards and task force members held over the life or death of the prisoners.[18]

Garage Olimpo begins and ends with an aerial view of the Río de la Plata shot from a plane. This framing is symptomatic of the film's examination of the militarized gaze—the Argentine Air Force plane flying over the Río de la Plata, an impossible graveyard of disappeared bodies. This introduces an image of what had been utterly banished from the picture: the plane carrying the bodies of prisoners to throw them into the sea, which, like *Buenos Aires viceversa*, problematizes the naturalizing frame of unpunished crimes (the mall in Agresti's film, the Río in Bechis's).[19] Produced shortly after the confessions of Captain Adolfo Scilingo in 1997, the first corroboration by a member of the military of the "death flights" performed from the ESMA, the movie opens with the omnipotent gaze of the camera in the sky, indistinguishable from the plane. The image of the graveyard-river is accompanied by the sound of a radio station giving the weather forecast (the climate, which is also the political climate) and the performance of the stock market (the economic climate).

Superimposing a narrative voice forecasting the weather and the economy on the image of the Río introduces the notion of predictability and calculability and an interesting ambiguity in the word for "weather" (*tiempo*), which in Spanish also signifies clock-time and historic time. Between gaze and language there is a rationalization of disappearance using both prediction (control) of historic time and calculations about the economy (disappearing that which might upset predictability). However, this link between disappearance, the economy, the political climate, and the river (mass grave) is open to interpretation by the audience. The film invites us to think about how we link image and discourse through reason, thereby confronting us with the violence of closure implied by narrativizing, punctuating, explaining, and justifying what we see and hear. In the sky/heaven (the Spanish word *cielo* can mean either) we have Olimpo (Olympus, a hellish heaven), the CDC referred to in the film's title and the connection to the deprivation of finality implicit in disappearance as a category. The next time the sound of the radio emerges, it will be inside the center, when the female protagonist is brought in and told, before the radio is turned on to drown out the screams of the torture session: "This is the world of sound for you. From now on you're not going to see anything ever again." The radio becomes a sound that connects inside and out via a pipe the camera shows us between the "operating room" (military slang for the torture room) and the street, where a man is staring at the sky while waiting for a traffic light to change so he can cross. Such connections in this film seem only to generate greater distance, an incommensurable gap between the hidden and the visible world, between inside and out, the world of the free and the world of the captured.

At a crucial moment in the film, the protagonist, María, is at work repairing a car stolen by the task force when one of the other prisoners gives her advice about how to survive in the CDC. Everything he says involves absolute control over the gaze: never act as if you can see when you see something; never look in your captors' eyes when the blindfold slips or when they take it off so you can perform some task; and, above all, disassociate the gaze from any expression of affect. Her mentor explains: "Here the thing is never to show you're afraid." This exchange about the gaze foregrounds the relationship between affect and survival, problematizing the borders and extension of the CDC as an (optical) diagram. This "seeing without seeing" belongs to a logic that affects everyday life outside, in which gaze and affect have to be disassociated in order to pass by the garage without seeing Olimpo, seeing-without-seeing, hearing-without-hearing. In the formulation of the gaze in this dialogue, in which the two prisoners have to avoid looking at one another while speaking, the border between inside and outside becomes indistinguishable. However, the status of that indistinguishability is complex, since it is an irreducible coimplication (instead of mere analogical continuity or a sharp distinction between inside and outside the CDC) that governs the asymmetry of images, faces, and sounds throughout the film.

The reflection on the mobile border of the site and the relationship between gaze and affect is acutely powerful when María, working on the same car with the same prisoner as before, sees a task force member go out and leave the door of Olimpo open. This is a moment of extreme tension that the camera exploits by filming the situation from different angles, showing the nearness of the street and the possibility of escape, but also how this open door causes terror among the prisoners. First, the camera lingers on the open door, which is letting in rays of sunlight from an outside that is near but that recedes into the far distance as the scene unfolds. The tension comes from the state of indeterminacy in the gaze caused by the various layers of the situation: seeing-without-seeing, seeing the open door but imagining it closed, or alternatively, seeing the door as a passageway to escape. The sight of the proximity of an outside mesmerizes the prisoners, whom the camera shows glancing at María. She then starts to walk rapidly toward the street, breaking into a run and crossing the flimsy border between the world of the disappeared (who are alive but dead, socially dead) and the outside, near but impossible, of the living. In this act of crossing over, María ignores her companion's lesson on the gaze and a momentary point of rupture crystallizes. The indeterminacy is maintained since the camera stays focused on the door (which is open for whom?) through which María immediately returns, dragged by her hair by the guard who had left and who now pretends to shoot her, shouting, "So you wanted to leave, birdie? You wanted to fly?" María loses control and screams, contradicting her friend's lessons once more by showing panic in her voice and her gaze.

A new layer is added to this series of inside/outside images when María is taken out for a walk by Félix, the torturer who is in love with her and who, in response to her escape attempt (which he reads as a betrayal), decides to take her to the other side for a while. In this excursion into the outdoors, during which María walks around the city like an agile ghost, the camera is used to great effect to produce a double tension, in confusing, rapid shots that alternate between inside and outside her viewpoint. With María we observe territories and situations in search of potential escape routes. When the camera angle changes, however, we see María walking through the relative outside of the city with the obsessive gaze of Félix functioning as an imaginary chain or shackle imprisoning her. From this perspective María seems immobilized, detained by a social death that goes beyond the exhaustive control of her captor.

The border established by the open door in the previous image is reinforced here. What was a relative outside-the-frame (what we did not see in María's momentary trip outside, when she tried to escape) now becomes the impossible outside that has disappeared. In this trip outside the CDC, the film juxtaposes at least two layers of cities-spaces-times without assuming a point from which the universes can be integrated: one is the city apparently back to normal with its rhythm and movement; the other is the city we see through María's eyes, which seems like a ghostly double of the previous one, showing or expressing that which must be kept invisible for its apparent normality to function. After some extraordinarily tense moments during which we wonder if María will manage to escape her captor's gaze, the tension peaks during the taxi ride back to the center. María asks Félix to run away with her and he refuses. The film ends with a double return: the return to the CDC, where María is put in the line of people who will be transferred (*trasladados*, meaning "disappeared"), thrown into the Río de la Plata; and the return to the airplane flight with which the movie began. After the walk through a sinister but relative outside, we move to the absolute outside of a disappearance that is no longer provisional but definitive, which transforms the final image of the river into a fluid graveyard.

The permanent play in the film between inside and outside the CDC comes from the type of frame it dramatizes. It shows a relative outside the frame (the moments in which what is excluded is imaginable as excluded by what we see, in a sort of analogical continuity) and the absolute outside the frame that is death. Deleuze considers the possibility of reading elements outside the frame as deterritorializations that function in a relative way when they refer to what is excluded by the frame, and an absolute way, when they refer to the open totality that would be the film itself. In this sense we could say that the problem of gazes that *Garage Olimpo* problematizes as a symptom of its own moment of production (the 1990s) involves the impossibility of an absolute deterritorialization in terms of an alternative political imagination to the one the frame makes possible—that is, the claustrophobic impossibility of imagining an outside to the film's images of impotence: the instant of the open door when María sees the light, the failed escape, the return, the flight, death.

In her analysis of the film, Manzano argues that it is still imprisoned by representations of politics typical of the 1990s; torturers and prisoners lack a political history because they appear to have begun living when Bechis starts filming them. However, there is a sequence of shots that signals, perhaps also in a claustrophobic way, a political universe. At the beginning, we see María's grassroots activism in a slum, teaching illiterate older people to read and write (a fact that causes the torturers in Olimpo to call her "la maestrita de los pobres" [little slum teacher]). Then there is a reference to the guerrillas, in the rather underdeveloped character of Ana, who plants a bomb in the home of Olimpo's top official. The moment of María's "transfer" coincides with a change of leadership at Olimpo. The supervisor is killed, juxtaposing his death with María's and creating another unresolved tension. Is the film establishing a sort of parallel between these two deaths? If we connect the operation at the end with the opening shots, in which the radio broadcast was an auditory backdrop to the image of the air force plane flying over the river, how do we link the visual and the auditory? Do they supplement one another? Do they legitimize one another? Are they discursively linked?

Garage Olimpo plays with multiple tensions that it refuses to resolve, problematizing borders and the notion of unveiling the hidden, leaving a kind of narrative vacuum instead of linking or synthesizing the different situations. The film creates a zone of ambiguity between impotence and escape and dramatizes the problem of disassociation between the gaze and narrative in the character of María. She irrevocably breaks the pact for behavior within the CDCs, filling her face with affect, expressing fear, transgressing the implicit logic of an impossible survival. In the end the prisoner who gave María the tips on surviving by controlling one's gaze is next to her in the truck as they are taken to their end, in the river-grave (a space in which they look at one another for the last time, with neutral expressions, as if they were already dead). Bechis places María's small transgressive acts of looking and expressing in that minimal kind of liberty. The film seems to insist on defending something that exceeds the possibility of survival, an excess that becomes incommensurable in this confusing protagonist who does not fit the usual images of activists in captivity as either traitors or heroines. María's characterization expresses a mode of indeterminacy within the stereotypes of the political activist.

The attempt to bring Olimpo to the gaze in contrast to its façade as garage confronts us not with a new resolution of that 1990s past but rather a search for points of escape that are doomed to failure from the moment the general frame of the film is given as the Río de la Plata (the mass grave, death). Thus the movie's problematization of the gaze cannot easily be translated into a political form. By attempting to make images of the hidden as a social diagram, the film does not bring new information or new content about the hidden (it uses what is known); instead, it obsessively questions the link between gaze and affect when politics is overdetermined by death. It shows the ways in which the gaze can produce (configure, figure next to) a transformation in the way of approaching and signifying what was formerly merely marked as nonvisible, a public secret, hidden. What remains is to take the displacement of the angle of vision that the film performs again and again in a sort of claustrophobic multiplication, to open a more robust critique of the possibilities of thinking the political.

The frame that appears in order to be problematized is thus the film itself as an unresolved whole, and its way of juxtaposing different temporalities of the 1970s and then exploring their traces in the 1990s. This is shown in the critical doubling between 1970s' and 1990s' images of María's face. In one she is gazing, terrified, at the injection of Pentothal, and in another she is sitting in the Armed Forces truck, casting Félix a look of fury for having brought her back to the center. There is also the image of María that was used to promote the film in the city of Buenos Aires in the 1990s. In it she is shown without eyes, since she is blindfolded, as was usually the case in the CDCs. This photo was the first image of a disappeared, blindfolded prisoner ever to appear outside a CDC, crossing-cutting the rhythm of the city in the late 1990s. If we generate a constellation between the drama of the gaze in the movie and the film's promotional poster, what are the implications of removing María's blindfold? How does the blindfold link to her inability or refusal to see without seeing, which breaks the prisoners' survival pact and accelerates the arrival of her own doom?

The Film Poster in the Mall-City: Social Blindfolding and the *Escrache*

The film poster of María blindfolded circulated around Buenos Aires almost like an *escrache*, sending us back to the mall-city in the marketing of the film itself. As Manzano has pointed out, there was an instant of indeterminacy when the film's marketing campaign morphed from promotion to camouflaged protest, an indiscernible point at which promoting the movie started to resembled a *pegotineada* (street postering) by the group HIJOS. The poster showed María's face, blindfolded, the title of the movie, and the times it was showing. The photo of a disappeared, blindfolded prisoner evoked disappearance, but it differed from the photos typically used by human rights' groups, which show the disappeared in their predisappearance lives, gazing openly at the camera (in family or civil ID photos). It also differed from the only photos known to exist of the disappeared in captivity: the ones taken in the ESMA because *Garage Olimpo*'s propaganda poster used a photograph of the impossible, whose crucial detail lies in the blindfold: the disappeared woman is separated from the vital possibility of sight and from our possibility of connecting with her through the gaze.

The promotion of the film used a forbidden imaginary, recalling the trials of the junta in which photos taken from the ESMA by disappeared ex-detainee Víctor Basterra played a crucial role in legally proving the disappearances. In the photos that left ESMA in Basterra's negatives, the detainees' eyes are not covered by blindfolds, which causes us, the viewers, to see the prisoners as their captors do. However, the *Garage Olimpo* promotional photo that circulated showed María with the blindfold, which creates an impossible face by deleting her eyes (to date there are no photos of blindfolded prisoners because of the very secrecy of the process). This raises an impossible question: how does one compose the idea of removing that blindfold at a time when impunity was being reaffirmed? On another level, the unmentionable association between the film's marketing campaign and escrache also points to the limitation of that historic moment, in that the only possible form of politics is to make marketing an inevitable universe with no outside, as in the CDCs.

The use of that photo, which united territory and image in a unique way (like an escrache, both marketing and interpellation), contributes to the film's role as a site of reflection on the border of the CDC and society (which is now exposed, with the blindfold, to itself as being blindfolded in more than one way) and the impossibility of recovery. The key to the status of the disappeared lies in the very impossibility of seeing a photograph of a disappeared person as disappeared, since the condition of being disappeared means not-appearing. By titling the photo of the blindfolded actress with the words "Garage Olimpo," we are invited to connect the blindfold and the CDC Olimpo and to question the figure of the blindfold in relation to ways of perceiving territory. As interpellation, the questions raised by this promotion-escrache, which took place in the Abasto (the district that held the former central market, now a mall), concern the seer of the blindfold and the name of the place: What blindfold constitutes us as subjects of the impossibility of that photograph of a prisoner? What blindfold lies between María's blindfold and the name of the place? In what sense can the blindfold be removed? Here we face a similar issue to the one discussed at the beginning of the earlier chapter on museums: What type of gaze and image of history do these inessential, impossible processes of unveiling reveal, appealing as they do to an act of reconnection between forms configured by the hiatus between past and present? What blindfold does this blindfold project to another time, the present of the promotion of Olimpo in the Abasto, which is the Olimpo of a present we cannot see?[20]

If we connect the Abasto mall into which the *Garage Olimpo* poster is inserted with the unpunished death in the mall at the end of *Buenos Aires viceversa,* we can perhaps see a link between the blindfolds that connect disappearance and the CDC and the relation between art and poverty, which the elderly aesthetes in *Buenos Aires viceversa* refused to see. While refusing cinema verité documentary, both films pose the connection between art and politics as the artistic drama of the present, not in the sense of critiquing the aestheticization of horror, but in the sense of questioning the very notion of unveiling and shock. Making art from and about what is kept secret means hard work and self-awareness. The political power to make contradictions visible is part of the problem in these movies, which show how seeing can be involved in the process of making something invisible. However, what is missing in citations of cinema verité and the documentary of the 1970s in these films of the 1990s is another possible way to frame the political. Both films suggest that art and politics need to think of their own situation as a minor act or action, for they question the connection between visibility, territoriality, and escape in a complex way, not by unveiling or making the invisible visible but by showing how that visibility is another construct, also imprisoned by a blindfold.

The disruption of common sense in both films via the problematization of affect, historicization, and gaze raises the question of what will happen if we remove the blindfold. There are different modes of blindfolding inside and outside Olimpo. Is the blindfold in the camp the same for everyone? Does the blindfold create a group? What relationship is created between that community and the possibility of seeing the same thing? The same questions apply to the CDC's outside. In the garage façade (which has bars and out of which army trucks suddenly appear), there is no physical blindfold, like a door, but there is a blindfold effect, a different kind of blindfolding: the sense of helplessness or the indifference created by the difference of being outside, being free. From where and how is the idea of indifference to the CDC produced? Both films point to a certain strangeness about space-history-gaze and the process of narrativization that seeks to create links between the seeable and the sayable. At the same time, between the gaze and the discursive decision in both films ("that's not the street, that's not art, it's not like normal people") that culminates in the intense closure that appears in the television and radio rationalizations of the killings, the perception of the incommensurable is generated, producing another meaning (another closure) capable of keeping the question open.

This incommensurability emerges in another zone, involving two last images that lift the national blindfold to the international dimension. The first involves the outside of Olimpo, now transformed into a memorial site, in which there is a picture of the face of Julio López, a survivor of the CDC who was disappeared again under democracy before he could testify as a witness in the trial of police officer Miguel Etchecolatz in 2006. This generates a curious tension between past and present because it decenters linear time and problematizes the border between democracy and impunity. The second image links the film's thematization of slave labor inside Olimpo and another site just around the corner from it, Automotores Orletti, a car dealership that housed another CDC.[21] The premises are private and were rented for use as a crucial CDC, the epicenter of the Condor Plan. Although Argentine prisoners did pass through it, most of the detainees in Automotores Orletti were foreign activists found in Argentina. The Condor Plan involved the planning, historicization, and justification of the elimination of subversion on an international level as part of the Cold War. It generated a joint narrative from the secret intelligence services of various countries (northern and southern Latin America and the United States), somewhat reminiscent of the composition of MERCOSUR.[22]

In 2002 it was discovered that Automotores Orletti was operating as a secret sweatshop for Bolivian immigrants who were forcibly housed on site. They worked all day and slept in the place, living with their children in what were once the cells of the disappeared. They were only allowed to leave the premises for one hour a week. The place looked the same as it had when it was a CDC. After the news broke about the sweatshop, the Bolivians were evicted. When journalists visited, they found marks (including blood) that recalled the past of the CDC in this new function. After arduous negotiations brokered by pro-memory groups between the owner of the premises and the government, Orletti was purchased by the state and is being converted into a memorial site. The narrativization of the history of the place will open up a new set of problems that other sites do not share, since Orletti was not an extermination site belonging to Argentina alone but was part of a secret operations network among various states in the Cold War dedicated to exterminating subversion on an international level. Thus the crucial question is how one creates the possibility of telling (hi)stories here. The site's survival as a sweatshop for Bolivian slave labor suggests new processes that situate the figure of theft and expropriation in zones that have yet to be examined, blindfolded by the same sites: race, class, labor.

This image of Orletti as sweatshop connects to the beginning of this book: the prison-mall is allied, in a discursive montage, with a CDC-sweatshop, as two modes of containment and forms of visibility-invisibility. In Orletti we find the site of production of merchandise (sold later in the mall) in a world that adjusted itself almost unchanged to the world of the CDC, pointing to a theme that remains neglected by postdictatorship studies: that of race and class. Where do we draw the line between the disappeared prisoners in Orletti and the Bolivian slave laborers, the *bolitas* and *cabecitas negras*? In this question, which evokes incommensurability instead of equivalence, lies a possible new way of seeing in postdictatorship studies. *Buenos Aires viceversa* and *Garage Olimpo* show a relationship between modes of disappearance and invisibility; in the former we see the emotional connection between Daniela, a daughter of the disappeared, and Bocha, who lives on the streets and never knew his mother, who was also a street worker. In *Garage Olimpo* we see the exploitation of the disappeared in the CDC as a slave labor force used to handle items stolen by the secret task forces. As the journalist and writer Samuel Blixen has documented, this practice also took place in Orletti, which processed money stolen from revolutionary groups. In the ESMA it was taken to the extreme of creating a zone dedicated to document forgery, money laundering, and a real estate agency to sell property expropriated from the disappeared.

By examining the figure of expropriation and the foreign (the *bolita* but also the common enemy of the Condor Plan that gave rise to this CDC), what emerges is a contrast between past and present in which each appears as multifarious (there is no one past nor one present but rather many), as an unexplored antagonism that needs to be theorized. What we see is the need to make invisible a series of antagonisms that mark the history of the nation and its narrativization. The images analyzed in this chapter open a dialogue with the invisibilization-indifference pair (beginning with the clear differentiation between people and nonpeople and what constitutes a legal person) and produce an effect of arrest that points to certain zones at which the dream of neoliberal freedom of the transitions never arrived. Here perhaps is where the power of this process of making invisibility visible without presuming a new essentialization lies; it may spur us to retheorize the constitutive splitting of people into those who do and do not count as people (visibly and legally), using the key reinvention of the articulation of class and racism that these two films activate as the very matrix of national regeneration.

Image, Dialectics, and Angle of Visibility

In a long passage in the "Convolut N" dedicated to the dialectical image, Benjamin writes of the need to rethink the "angle of vision" from which the excluded passes from dialectic to image:

> Modest methodological proposal for the cultural-historical dialectic. It is very easy to establish oppositions, according to determinate points of view, within the various "fields" of any epoch, such that on one side lies the "productive," "forward-looking," "lively," "positive" part of the epoch, and on the other side the abortive, retrograde, and obsolescent. The very contours of the positive element will appear distinctly only insofar as this element is *set off against* the negative. On the other hand, *every negation has its value solely as background for the delineation of the lively, the positive. It is therefore of decisive importance that a new partition be applied to this initially excluded, negative component so that, by a displacement of the angle of vision* (but not of the criteria!), a positive element emerges anew in it too—something different from that previously signified. And so on, ad infinitum, until the entire past is brought into the present in a historical apocatastasis.[23]

This is one of the few moments when Benjamin speaks directly of dialectic at play, and it helps us consider the type of turn the image retains when exposed in a relationship with vision, disposition of elements (constellation) and language as the site where the constellation occurs. The constitutive positivity of narratives of historical continuity (progress, regeneration of a nation, restoration of democracy) is constructed via parergon, an almost visual frame or framing of the constructive epistemology of history. Thus the positive does not exist as something that "displaces" the negative but instead, in order to constitute itself (this is the constitutive dialectic), it needs to contain that negativity. The task of the narrative of historical progress is to frame itself as "contrast" with that which becomes negativity; the condition of possibility of the positive is configured as the condition of impossibility of that which remains out of the picture. The border or frame that this visual, perceptual accommodation generates constitutes the narrativization (it marks what is and is not, what progresses and what interrupts progress). However, Benjamin writes at another point: "Overcoming the concept of 'progress' and overcoming the concept of 'period of decline' are two sides of one and the same thing."[24]

In this passage we see that progress and decline, success and defeat, are produced by the same frame that the dialectical image was attempting to interrupt by questioning what it leaves out—that is, what does not qualify as the sibling of this binarism of success and defeat, success and failure, dualities that presuppose historical processes that assume a "stage" and omit the possibility of survival that Benjamin wishes to "rescue" as image. This "overcoming" of binarism is premised in the quoted fragment as a work of the *gaze, of accommodating the framing* of which the binary, molar, oppositional (positive-negative) framing is an effect. The question is how to compose a frame that is not the effect of a binary frame, without creating images as a voluntarist gesture ex nihilo? This would presume the fantasy of an omnipotent angle beyond the finite, historical position from which we remember, a position that is itself the effect of a moment—each present generates the recognizable image of its past. Here we see a relation between dialectics and vision (perspective) that suggests treating the logic of oppositionality in a pictoral way, using the idea of foreground and background, in which the "contours of the positive element" of an era emerge as contrasting with the negative.

The value of the negative, reduced to the "background" of the positive (which makes the positive possible by contrast), is changed by Benjamin using a visual metaphor of the "displacement of the angle of vision" through which the excluded negative acquires another life (an afterlife) by making the positive visible in itself. This field of accommodation of the gaze is crucial to the notion of constellation, which does not depend on the specific elements that constitute it but on the gaze that configures it. In the same way that stars, without the gaze that configures them as part of a group or constellation, would remain simply stars, there can be a negativity that remains undifferentiated if the angle of vision does not configure that positive element (that) emerges anew in it too—something different from that previously signified. The act of displacement seems to use a language that takes the act of reading as a site of production, reproduction, and breakdown (transformation) of meaning—in this case, of the way of "seeing" dialectics, no less. Thus what the excerpt from Benjamin offers us is a view of novelty not as new information or new contents for the "cultural historical" dialectician but rather as a way for the gaze to produce a transformation in the way of approaching and signifying what has until now been mere negativity. It is perhaps this displacement of the angle of vision, this point at which the framing of an era as negative or positive blurs and needs to be rethought, that the films reveal in their way of making visible modes of invisibility.

NOTES

Introduction

Epigraph: Walter Benjamin, *The Arcades Project*, trans. Howard Eiland and Kevin McLaughlin (Cambridge: Harvard University Press, 1999), 460.

1. The decisions to grant impunity to the military vary from country to country (in the case of Argentina and Chile, by presidential and military decisions; in the case of Uruguay, by popular vote via plebiscite). In turn, decisions on revising impunity decades later, in the cases of Argentina and Uruguay, were again performed by presidential decision (by Néstor Kirschner, the president of Argentina) versus referendum and plebiscite (Uruguay). While in the Argentinean case the president showed a more committed attitude toward defending human rights issues, in Uruguay the results of the plebiscite in the 2009 national elections demonstrate a strange phenomenon. Although the majority of ballots went to the current president, José Mujica, who was one of the founders of the MLN-T (Tupamaros), the majority also voted in favor of impunity for the military, resulting in the reaffirmation of impunity for military crimes.

2. Andreas Huyssen, *Present Pasts: Urban Palimpsests and the Politics of Memory* (Stanford: Stanford University Press, 2003), 9–10; my emphasis.

3. Water Benjamin, "The Task of the Translator," in *Illuminations*, trans. Harry Zohn (New York: Schocken Books, 1969), 69–82.

4. Walter Benjamin, "One-Way Street," in *One-Way Street and Other Writings* (London: Verso, 1979).

5. Werner Hamacher, "'Now': Walter Benjamin on Historical Time," in *Walter Benjamin and History*, ed. Andrew Benjamin (New York: Continuum, 2005), 38, 42.

6. Besides her now-classic *State Repression and the Labors of Memory*, trans. Judy Rein and Marcial Godoy-Anativia (Minneapolis: University of Minnesota Press, 2003), Jelin has been organizing and editing a series titled *Memorias de la represión* since 2002 (Buenos Aires: Siglo Veintiuno Editores).

7. Michel Foucault, "The Eye of Power: A Conversation with Jean-Pierre Barou and Michelle Perrot," in *Power/Knowledge: Selected Interviews & Other Writings (1972–1977)*, ed. and trans. by Colin Gordon (New York: Pantheon Books, 1980), 149.

8. Alberto Moreiras, "Postdictadura y reforma del pensamiento," *Revista de crítica cultural* 7 (1993): 26–35, 29; my translation.

9. Moreiras, "Postdictadura y reforma del pensamiento," 27–28.

10. Idelber Avelar, *The Untimely Present: Postdictatorial Latin American Fiction and the Task of Mourning* (Durham: Duke University Press, 1999), published in Spanish the following year as *Alegorías de la derrota: La ficción postdictatorial y trabajo de duelo* (Santiago: Cuarto propio, 2000).

11. Avelar, *Untimely Present*, 3.

12. Ibid., 68.

13. During the transition that "end" became synonymous with the end of transformative imaginaries associated with liberationist, revolutionary, and Marxist histories, among others. Throughout the book I use the term "emancipatory" histories to refer to this heterogeneous horizon.

14. Deleuze has analyzed the diagrams of control societies in loose temporal terms in his classic essay "Postcript on Control Societies," in which he states that it was after World War II that discipline began to break down (in his *Negotiations,* translated Martin Joughin [New York: Columbia University Press, 1997], 178). Changes toward the control society can be analyzed in relation to the many modifications of power structures, labor, and time-space experience that encompassed life in the United States in the post–World War II era. However, following debates about the way in which to approach all these changes, we cannot think of the Cold War as a "premeditated" plan in which this shift would be concentrated. See, for instance, the collection ed. Lary May, *Recasting America: Culture and Politics in the Age of Cold War* (Chicago: University of Chicago Press, 1989). Foucault's description of the setting of the disciplinary diagram sheds light on how to approach the dynamics of diagrammatic changes: "The 'invention' of this new political anatomy must not be seen as a sudden discovery. It is rather a multiplicity of often minor processes, of different origin and scattered location, which overlap, repeat, or imitate one another, support one another, distinguish themselves from one another according to their domain of application, converge and gradually produce the blueprint of a general method" (Michel Foucault, *Discipline and Punish: The Birth of the Prison*, trans. Alan Sheridan [New York: Random House, 1995], 138). The crucial problem when we approach diagrams and intermediary diagrams (transitions) is how to take into account the multiple mechanisms that are invented and practiced without imposing a unifying causal sense on them.

15. Deleuze, "What Is the Creative Act?" in *Two Regimes of Madness: Texts and Interviews, 1975–1995,* ed. David Lapoujade, trans. Ames Hodges and Mike Taormina (New York: Semiotext(e), 2006), 322.

16. Because these transformations are ongoing, most of the sources of information for the new uses of the places are found on the Internet. The website of the Kresty Prison Museum (http://www.saint-petersburg.com/museums/kresty-prison-museum.asp) says: "Kresty has been infamous in recent years for chronic overcrowding, TB infection and corruption. Fortunately, plans are afoot to move prisoners to a larger modern facility outside the city in the near future. For now, if you are so inclined, you can join one of the guided tours organized by the prison's Preliminary Investigations Department. These take in the prison chapel and the in-house museum, which contains displays on some of the most famous past inmates, plus various artifacts crafted by unknown prisoners, and a pictorial explanation of the significance of Russian criminal tattoos. Much of this is fascinating, but

visitors' proximity to ongoing human misery is a little too keenly felt. Inmates can be seen and heard, and you may well see packages being passed through the shoddy fences that separate you from them by some of your fellow 'tourists.' All in all, this is probably best avoided." As another report explains: "The notorious Kresty building, the largest prison in Europe, may soon be transformed into an entertainment center, a shopping mall or a hotel, with a new prison facility being built to replace it on the outskirts of the city. . . . 'Kresty will be passed on to an investor, who will be able to develop it into a hotel, entertainment or office center—anything that comes to the investor's mind, *as long as the building is preserved*,' [my emphasis, here and below] Alexander Sidorov, head of [the] Federal Service for Punishment's public relations, said in a telephone interview. *The developers* will not be able to demolish the prison building, as the complex is *under state protection* and is considered to be one of the city's 'key architectural monuments,' as confirmed by the committee for the state control, usage and protection of cultural and historical monuments." See VB Excursions, "Kresty Prison Will Be a Hotel?" August 2, 2006, online at http://www.vb-excursions.com/news-18.html.

17. Travel guides promote the transformation of the prison into a mall as part of a whole new reconfiguration of the former "public" area that meets tourist requisites; also, part of it has been preserved as a museum: "The prison has been transformed into a mall with one block is [*sic*] preserved as a museum, a cell block where Soekarno, the first president of Indonesia, spent some time in there. The major transition is that now Alun-alun serves as an entertainment park, where shopping mall buildings are surrounding the square" (in "Bandung Activities: Outdoor activities," online at http://iguide.travel/Bandung/Activities/Outdoor_Activities). Regarding the Musheerabad Central Jail, the public announcement for open bidding stated: "The Musheerabad Central Jail premises is soon going to be transformed into a world class A.C. shopping centre within a couple of months. The state government is soon going to invite pre-qualified global tenders for the construction of the 200 core centrally Air-Conditioned international shopping center. This is going to be a joint venture between the Department of Tourism and private agencies." This information is from *Reachout Hyderabad*, online at http://www.reachouthyderabad.com/newsmaker/mall.htm.

18. Gayatri Chakravorty Spivak, "Subaltern Studies: Deconstructing Historiography," in *Subaltern Studies: Writings on South Asian History and Society*, vol. 4, ed. Ranajit Guha (Delhi: Oxford University Press, 1985), 4.

19. Pablo Oyarzún, *La dialéctica en suspenso: Fragmentos sobre historia* (Santiago: ARCIS-LOM, 1996).

20. Nelly Richard, "Introducción," in *Pensar en / la postdictadura*, ed. Nelly Richard and Alberto Moreiras (Santiago: Cuarto Propio, 2001), 9–20; my translation.

21. Besides Willy Thayer's "El golpe como consumación de la vanguardia" (*Revista Extremoccidente* 2, Dossier "La memoria perdida: A treinta años del golpe," 2002, 54–58); see also Tomás Moulian's classic *Chile actual: Anatomía de un mito* (Santiago: Arcis, 1997) for a more detailed analysis of the neoliberal experiment as a passive capitalist revolution. For a study of the neoliberal experiment in the Chilean dictatorial setting, see Juan G. Valdés, *Pinochet's Economists: The Chicago School of Economics in Chile* (Cambridge: Cambridge University Press, 1995), and David Harvey's "Neoliberalism and the Restoration of Class Power," in his book *Spaces of Global Capitalism: Toward a Theory of Uneven Geographical Development* (New York: Verso, 2006), 9–68.

22. I am referring to Marchesi's discussion of the term in the roundtable on "transition" at the Lost in Transition conference at Princeton University, Princeton, New Jersey, on March 5–6, 2010.

23. I am articulating the notion of coimplication described by the philosopher Judith Butler in *Bodies That Matter*: "the excluded and illegible domain that haunts the former domain as the specter of its own impossibility, the very limit to intelligibility, its constitutive outside" (in Butler, *Bodies That Matter: On the Discursive Limits of Sex* [New York: Routledge, 1993], xi).

24. For an in-depth analysis of the role of repetition in architecture, I refer to Andrew Benjamin's *Architectural Philosophy: Repetition, Function, Alterity* (New Brunswick: Athlone Press, 2000).

1. Prison-Malls: Architectures of Utopic Regeneration

1. See, for instance, Manuel Garretón, *Proceso político chileno* (Santiago: FLACSO, 1983).

2. Hugo Achugar, "Territorios y memorias *versus* lógica del mercado: A propósito de cartografías y shopping malls," in *Planetas sin boca: Escritos efímeros sobre arte, cultura y literatura* (Montevideo: Trilce, 2004), 217–28.

3. Brett Levinson, *The Ends of Literature: The Latin American "Boom" in the Neoliberal Marketplace* (Stanford: Stanford University Press, 2001), 45.

4. Jens Andermann, *The Optic of the State: Visuality and Power in Argentina and Brazil* (Pittsburgh: Pittsburgh University Press, 2007), 7.

5. Both *The Birth of the Penitentiary in Latin America* and *Crime and Punishment in Latin America* offer a spectrum of processes that highlight the specific forms achieved by penitentiary reform in different countries as well as the principles governing them: the ideal of spatial organization (into partitions) to improve hygiene and ideological regeneration, usually associated with the notion of whitewashing typically found in modernization as a disciplinary diagram. Ricardo D. Salvatore and Carlos Aguirre, *The Birth of the Penitentiary in Latin America: Essays on Criminology, Prison Reform, and Social Control, 1830–1940* (Austin: University of Texas Press, 1996); and Ricardo D. Salvatore, Carlos Aguirre, and G. M. Joseph, *Crime and Punishment in Latin America: Law and Society since Late Colonial Times* (Durham: Duke University Press, 2001).

6. Salvatore and Aguirre, *Birth of the Penitentiary in Latin America*, 25.

7. See Salvatore, Aguirre, and Joseph, *Crime and Punishment in Latin America*. In an attempt to offer a synthesis of a more complex process, I should like to note that the penitentiary project upholding the modernization of punishment revolves around the idea of regenerating or correcting the degenerate within the schematic of growing capitalist development (created simultaneously by a penal code that institutes this subject as the criminal-degenerate and, as such, establishes it as a norm). So too the schematic naturalizes the notion of productivity as the prison begins to acquire relevance as a space of converting souls. In relation to the development of the penitentiary system, see Carlos Aguirre, "Cárcel y sociedad en América Latina 1800–1940," in *Historia social urbana: Espacios y flujos*, ed. Eduardo Kingman Garcés (Quito: FLACSO, 2009), 209–52; also available online at http://www.flacsoandes.org/biblio/catalog/resGet.php?resId=25838.

8. Foucault notes that "there is an economico-moral self-evidence of a penalty that metes out punishments in days, months and years and draws up quantitative equivalences between offences and durations. Hence the expression, so frequently heard, so consistent with the functioning of punishments, though contrary to the strict theory of penal law, that

one is in prison in order to 'pay one's debt.' The prison is 'natural,' just as the use of time to measure exchanges is 'natural' in our society" (in Michel Foucault, *Discipline and Punish: The Birth of the Prison*, trans. Alan Sheridan [New York: Random House, 1995], 232–33).

9. As Aguirre and Salvatore have stated (in *Birth of the Penitentiary in Latin America*), the prison programs for a humanization of punishment, the primary goal of the modern penitentiary diagram, never worked in the ideal way it was supposed to. However, they functioned as powerful arenas in which a modern geography of power was staged. In this sense, approaching society from the transformations taking place in incarceration systems allows me to explore the ideals at stake in citizenship, justice, and freedom. The prison opens up to a stage from which to observe contentious ideals for what was defined as deviance and its materialization in specific geographies that produced breakdowns time and time again. The perpetual crisis of the prisons is reiterated by systems of social injustice presumably made invisible by them. For this reason, taking the figure of the prison as a space from which to observe political systems and imaginaries for progress (the geography, optics, and official discourse of the State) invites reflection on the limits it posits in order to imagine a different society.

10. The attorney Beatriz Scapusio has stated that 63 percent of the population imprisoned during the postdictatorship era in Uruguay were tried without sentence; a good number of women prisoners were housed in annexes to men's jails in the heart of the country given the lack of facilities. See Scapusio, "El sistema penal uruguayo y su repercusión carcelaria: La necesidad de su reforma," in *Reforma al sistema penal y carcelario en Uruguay*, ed. Raúl Ronzoni and Beatriz Scapusio (Montevideo: CADAL, 2008), 21–46, 35.

11. Víctor Espinoza Cuevas, ed., *Seminario internacional sobre la impunidad y sus efectos en los procesos democráticos* (Santiago de Chile: CODEPU, 1999).

12. Adolfo Pérez Esquivel, quoted in *Seminario internacional*, 22.

13. Even though clandestine detention centers (CDCs) function in different ways in each of the countries analyzed here, in all cases a key feature of the military regimes was to incite fear or panic in civilians. In Argentina the word *chupadero* (an underground military prison) proves crucial, because it gives the idea of disappearances as a black hole. Even though in Argentina the CDCs were central to the regime in a way not mirrored in Uruguay, where the prison was more widely used, both prisons and CDCs existed in these countries. The founding of the Caseros Jail in Buenos Aires, for example, interestingly refers to dictatorial panoptics created for military use, as was the case for Libertad Penitentiary in Uruguay, which I analyze in detail. Caseros has since closed, and its future is currently under debate; Libertad remains open.

14. For an excellent study of the relevance of orthopedics to the modernizing programs at the beginning of the twentieth century, see José Pedro Barrán, *Medicina y sociedad en el Uruguay del novecientos. Tomo 2: La ortopedia de los pobres* (Montevideo: Banda Oriental, 1993).

15. Some differences among countries should be noted here: in Chile, as a neoliberal laboratory, this process was central to the dictatorial process; in Argentina, privatization was introduced in the first round of Menemism in the "tough" economic program of austerity measures "without anesthesia." As the Argentine sociologist Alicia Iriarte has stated, the Law of State Reform and the Law of Economic Emergence "authorized the government to privatize partially or totally all state companies, to freeze subsidiaries in promoting industry as well as hiring state personnel, among other things" (in Alicia Iriarte, "La década del '90: Proyecto neoconservador, ajuste estructural y desigualdad social," in

La Argentina fragmentada: Aspectos de la nueva cuestión social [Buenos Aires: Proyecto Editorial, 2001], 18–19; my translation). In the case of Uruguay, privatization did not pass the plebiscite, and yet nevertheless it went ahead in a camouflaged way as a form of mixed services. In 1992, during Luis Alberto Lacalle's government, the law of public companies also went to a plebiscite, which lost in favor of not privatizing them. When Julio María Sanguinetti assumed power in 1995, his government program placed state reform in one of its clauses (to reduce the weight of the state) in a policy of privatization, de-monopolization, and deregulation of private enterprise.

16. Gruen came to America fleeing Nazi persecution. He considered the city as an ideal of democracy that America had to fulfill. Although he is considered to be the founder of the concept of the mall, he returned to Europe, disenchanted by the way his ideal had turned into consumerist enclaves and the corporate takeover of small-scale retail. For a detailed analysis of Gruen's invention, see Jeffrey Hardwick, *Mall Maker: Victor Gruen, Architect of an American Dream* (Philadelphia: University of Pennsylvania Press, 2003); for an analysis of Gruen's utopian ideas within the Cold War context, see Timothy Mennel's "Victor Gruen and the Construction of Cold War Utopias," *Journal of Planning History* 3 (2004): 116–50.

17. Quoted in Hardwick, *Mall Maker*, 72.

18. Mennel, "Victor Gruen," 123.

19. This persistent desire to configure the mall as the new ideal space for a protected and secured democracy that paradoxically followed the dream of protection was what characterized Gruen's failures in the United States time and time again (for example, during the civil rights uprisings) and then in Iran, where his project was again doomed to fail.

20. Mennel, "Victor Gruen," 116–17.

21. William Severini Kowinski, *The Malling of America: An Inside Look at the Great Consumer Paradise* (New York: W. Morrow, 1985).

22. Juan Carlos López has called attention to the importance of this idea as "spaces of social exchange" (see Juan Carlos López, "Entrevista: Juan Carlos López y asociados. Arquitecturas para la ciudad," *Arquitectura Sur* 1, no. 2 [1990]: 21–34).

23. An essential text to understand the concept of this imaginary is Victor Gruen's *The Heart of Our Cities: The Urban Crisis: Diagnosis and Cure* (New York: Simon and Schuster, 1964), in which the mall's inventor proposes a diagnosis and cure to the problem of urban planning. The author develops his notion of urban planning to counteract the lack of direction and growing segregation affecting U.S. cities at the time. Urban "evil" in this text refers to a lack of order and planning as well as an excessive planning of life in society, witnessed in some experiments in Los Angeles and Brazil as models for excessively planned, predictable places (Gruen, *Heart of Our Cities*, 135–36). Gruen viewed these plans as dehumanizers of the city, where urban planning was subsumed by political and economic interests, and as segregationist models for compartmentalized cities that likewise began to affect architectural practices.

24. Ira Zepp, *The New Religious Image of Urban America: The Shopping Mall as Ceremonial Center* (Colorado: University of Colorado Press, 1997).

25. Besides his work on housing plans, this ideal may have contributed to Rouse's receiving the Presidential Medal of Freedom from President Bill Clinton in 1995. Rouse also worked for the Eisenhower and Reagan administrations.

26. Juan Carlos López makes explicit this idea of exploiting the spectacular nature of the buildings to enhance their commercial value: "We started to realize the value of spectacle and the social stage these buildings could have, and the fact that acquiring this value could

be associated with the site's success as a commercial enterprise" ("Entrevista: Juan Carlos López y asociados," 22; my translation).

27. The transformation indicates that these new sites of encounter eradicate the political use of space from their terrain (prohibiting demonstrations, distributing pamphlets, and so on). As the architectural critic Witold Rybczynski has stated: "Are malls private property, as many mall owners have always maintained, or have they become, as the American Civil Liberties Union has argued, public places that should be obliged to observe the principles of free speech—to allow unlimited access to community groups, including petitioners and political demonstrators? Understandably, mall owners have not been keen on the idea of having abortion groups arguing their cases in the food court, or of hosting a violent altercation between the Ku Klux Klan and its opponents. . . . In a 1990 Gallup poll 73 percent of respondents said that malls shouldn't have to allow political gatherings" (in Witold Rybczynski, "The New Downtowns," *Atlantic Monthly* 271 [May 5, 1993]: 98–106, 101).

28. Ruben García Miranda, "Quisiera ser grande," *ElArqa, arquitectura & diseño* 3, no. 6 (1993): 4–5, 5; my translation.

29. Antonio Gervaz describes the malls as "Fukuyama's hypothesis incarnate" (in Antonio Gervaz, "Dimensiones de Hoy," *ElArqa, arquitectura & diseño* [Montevideo] 3, no. 6 [May 1993]: 20–32). Francis Fukuyama, *The End of History and the Last Man* (New York: Free Press, 1992).

30. The architect Julio Gatea has stated: "They are primarily shopping buildings that no longer only have commercial centers but also civic ones, the new forms of amusement" (Julio Gatea, "La ciudad transformada," *ElArqa arquitectura & diseño* [Montevideo] 4, no. 12 [December 1994]: n.p.; my translation). As a civic center, the mall emphasizes walking around; the mall's attraction is providing visitors with a closed city in which a self-contained world is posited in opposition to darkness and the dangers on the street (we will see this point in the literary texts). In the mall, "all the particularities of time and place lose their meaning. Once you step through the door, the sense is lost—and this is one of its attractions—of whether one is really in Punta Carretas, in Lagomar or in Los Angeles. And in reality, it doesn't matter, since all malls are basically the same" (in Raúl Velazquez, "Levantando centros," *ElArqa arquitectura & diseño* [Montevideo] 4, no. 12 [December 1994]: 8–9; my translation).

31. Adrián Gorelik, *Miradas sobre Buenos Aires: Historia cultural y crítica urbana* (Buenos Aires: Siglo Veintiuno Editores Argentina, 2004), 187; my translation; emphasis in the original.

32. López, "Entrevista: Juan Carlos López y asociados," 23; my translation.

33. Ibid., 34; my translation.

34. This was a crucial element in the 1990s a period of fatalism when, as Gorelik posits, "the social and urban fractures have been accepted by politics and society as an unchangeable fact; they have been introduced to everyday life organizing all cultural outlines in accordance with them. This is the definitive failure of politics as an instrument for change and for a society as its actor, which I believe should be seen at the base of these new representations of the city. And, in this sense, it could be said that for the first time in the tradition of urban culture in Buenos Aires, we are witnessing this lack of horizon" (in Gorelik, *Miradas sobre Buenos Aires*, 173–74; my translation).

35. Tomás Moulian, *Chile actual: Anatomía de un mito* (Santiago: Arcis, 1997), 113; my translation.

36. Security arises in López's speeches as one of the keys to improving pedestrian areas

within the new urban ideal, which involves imagining malling as a spatialized form of this progress from the streets that came before the mall: "At least from my own experience, there's a chance that the demands of commerce will serve to develop an architecture of more public uses, of more urban characteristics. On the other hand, what I'm saying is perfectly provable in contemporary cities, even in ours, where building complexes with commercial functions and their development, in some way superior to what the streets traditionally offered, today receive part of the vitality of urban life to control negative elements in this urban life, such as personal insecurity, variability and inclement weather, the diversity of social spaces, etc. That this situation is a consequence of commercial competence or of the necessities of consumerism's sophistication should not seem useless to us when trying to achieve results in urban architecture or when enriching the sites by endowing them with public uses" (in López, "Entrevista: Juan Carlos López y asociados," 22; my translation).

37. Gareth Williams, *The Other Side of the Popular: Neoliberalism and Subalternity in Latin America* (Durham: Duke University Press, 2002), 284.

38. Pablo Oyarzún, *La dialéctica en suspenso: Fragmentos sobre historia* (Santiago: ARCIS-LOM, 1996), 25; my translation and emphasis. The text is composed of an introductory essay by Oyarzún, some previously translated texts by Benjamin, and a section of the "Convolut N." The entire *Arcades Project* was subsequently published in 2006 in Spain.

39. On the notion of the end of history in postdictatorial narratives, and specifically in the predominant discourse on the right and left in the early 1990s, see the different approaches provided in Oyarzún's "Introduction" to *La dialéctica en suspenso*; José Luis Rebellato's *La encrucijada de la ética* (Montevideo: Nordan, 1995); Martín Hopenhayn's *Ni apocalípticos ni integrados: Aventuras de la modernidad en América* (México: Fondo de Cultura Económica, 1995); and José Aricó's *Entrevistas 1974–1981*, ed. Horacio Crespo (Córdoba: Centro de Estudios Avanzados, 1999).

40. Here it is relevant to note how architects saw superimposition as a form of cross-dressing postmodernization—a regionalist, neopopulist disguise for the market. "The central post-modern features, disguised in regionalism as seen fit—a new form of cultural crossdressing—seems to be one of the reuniversalizing models of investing in peripheral problematics" (in Roberto Fernández, "Crisis de la modernidad: Las fracturas regionalistas" *Arquitectura Sur* [Mar del plata, Argentina] 1, no. 2 [1990]: 38–42, 39; my translations).

41. Jane Rendell, *Art and Architecture: A Place Between* (London: I. B. Tauris, 2006), 116.

42. "Así será el Uruguay del 2000." Punta Carretas was the third mall to open in Uruguay, with more than sixty-five thousand square meters of space on its grounds and an investment of nearly forty-two million dollars. With its architectural recycling as an architectonic model for the state at the beginning of the century (it was a faithful copy of a French model), Punta Carretas was (and continues to be) the most visited mall in the country. The parties who bought the property, the Ministry of Interior and the Municipal Governor of Montevideo, came to an agreement to "conserve the largest percentage possible of its former prison structure" (in Daniel Erosa, "Punta Carretas: Del viejo penal a shopping," *Posdata* 30 set [1994]: 45–49; my translation).

43. Guía arquitectónica y urbanística de Montevideo (s/n). Despite having opened as a prison in 1910, the building's construction was already under way in 1905 and was completed in 1915.

44. Ruétalo traces a genealogy of building Punta Carretas as part of a continuity between systems of exclusion expressed by the penitentiary model in the constitution of the modern

State and the mall in the neoliberal State, contextualizing in detail the process of PC as a crucial instance in this shift to a correctional ideal. See Victoria Ruétalo, "From Penal Institution to Shopping Mecca: The Economics of Memory and the Case of Punta Carretas," *Cultural Critique* 68 (Winter 2008): 38–65, 48–49.

45. Ruétalo, "From Penal Institution to Shopping Mecca," 48.

46. I draw on information provided by Gonzalo Fernández in his *Historia de bandidos: Del "Cambio Messina" a la carbonería "El Buen Trato." Crónica del asalto y la fuga* (Montevideo: Fundación de Cultura Universitaria, 1993); Fernando O'Neill, *Anarquistas de acción en Montevideo, 1927–1937* (Montevideo: Recortes, 1993); and a recent documentary by director Virginia Martínez, *Acratas*, which investigates the story of Miguel Angel Rosigna, the most important anarchist figure in several Latin American countries, who planned the escape of anarchist prisoners in 1931 with a tunnel built from outside the prison walls to rescue his comrades.

47. The official name of Libertad Penitentiary is Establecimiento de Reclusión Número 1 (EMR N 1), although this name goes practically unused; "Libertad," dubbed so for the nearby town by the same name, is the word commonly used to refer to it (to be a prison in Libertad or "in freedom").

48. Quoted in Hugo Achugar, *Planetas sin boca: Escritos efímeros sobre arte, cultura y literatura* (Montevideo: Trilce, 2004), 222–23.

49. Quoted in Achugar, *Planetas sin boca,* 224.

50. Anthony Vidler, *The Architectural Uncanny: Essays in the Modern Unhomely* (Cambridge: MIT Press, 1994), 13–14.

51. The slogan "En Punta Carretas . . . ¡te vas a enamorar!" was publicized on billboards throughout the city as the date of the mall opening drew near. At the same time, a television spot used a bolero to depict the new space of "clean" history as the site in which all the contingencies and problems of life were to be resolved; interestingly enough, natural phenomena (that is, the weather) were primarily targeted: "Where do people go when it rains? To Punta Carretas mall!"

52. Former political prisoners state that torture was usual practice in the Punta Carretas prison, even though the place was not used exclusively for that purpose, unlike the CDCs in many military schools, private houses, or public offices, in which prisoners were temporarily held for "interrogation" purposes.

53. The transformation of Punta Carretas was carried out in different stages. First, the mall was officially opened in July 1994. Afterward, a Hotel Sheraton was built and a tunnel was created to connect the mall to the hotel. As part of its further expansion, a twelve-auditorium cineplex was added to the mall. The project as a whole received a Design Award from the International Council of Shopping Centers.

54. Moulian (*Chile actual*) distinguishes between the failure of the caracole (spiral) form, the preferred mall design in the late 1970s, and the absolute success of the malls endowed with "style" and kitsch. I read this difference in terms of the imminent role of fantasy and utopianism at the origins of the mall.

55. Fabián Giménez and Alejandro Villagrán, *Estética de la oscuridad: Posmodernidad, periferia y mass media en la cultura de los noventa* (Montevideo: Trazas, 1995), 121, 122, 123; my translation.

56. In tune with this idea, the cultural theorist Beatriz Sarlo has analyzed conversations on plastic surgery and the mall in her *Scenes from Postmodern Life.*

57. Quoted in Rendell, *Art and Architecture,* 69.

58. It seems relevant to note that in the 1997 documentary directed by Rainer Hoffmann and Heidi Spcogna, *Tupamaros*, two former political prisoners from the MLN walk through the mall, and this remaining doorway to the cellblock allows them to get their bearings, imagining what sections were the penitentiary and prison. After this point they are able to see where their cells were (replaced by shops today).

59. Gorelik, *Miradas sobre Buenos Aires*, 184.

60. López, "Entrevista: Juan Carlos López y asociados," 34.

2. Literary Afterlives of the Punta Carretas Prison: Tunneling Histories of Freedom

1. Antonio Bandera Lima, *El abuso* (Montevideo: Tae, 1986); Eleuterio Fernández Huidobro, *La fuga de Punta Carretas*, 2 vols. (Montevideo: Banda Oriental, 1998); and Samuel Blixen, *La comisión aspirina* (Montevideo: Trilce, 2007).

2. As a law student, Raúl Sendic traveled to the province of Artigas, in the northern part of the country, and started working with the sugarcane workers who had no rights and who were treated by landowners as slaves. The precarious working conditions, the lack of legal and constitutional protections for workers, and the feudal structure of work in that part of the country led to the foundation of the union UTAA. Workers started to press for decent working conditions (limitation of working hours, the right to health and housing, and so on). Negotiations proved fruitless, however, and the landowners refused to concede any right to the workers. Kidnappings and murders of union members began to take place. The MLN-Tupamaros was founded to fight for the rights of the oppressed. The experience of UTAA illustrated the enormous problems faced by the sugarcane workers, who were not even seen as a class of workers because they were in the northern part of the country, where the system of working-class rights that applied in the city did not pertain. For a detailed history of the conditions of the sugarcane workers, see Alberto Sendic, *Movimiento obrero y luchas populares en la historia uruguaya* (Montevideo: Edición del Movimiento de Independientes 26 de marzo, 1985). For the memories of a sugarcane worker, see María Esther Gilio, *El cholo González: Un cañero de Bella Unión* (Montevideo: Trilce, 2004). See also the recent documentary directed by Alejandro Figueroa in 2004, *Raul Sendic, Tupamaro*.

3. The first editions of *La fuga* were published by Tae (1990, 1991, 1993) and the last two by Ediciones de la Banda Oriental (1998 and 2005).

4. In 1970 and 1971 there were two consecutive escapes of political prisoners from the women's prison, code-named Plan Paloma and Plan Estrella. The ex-political prisoner Graciela Jorge narrates the escapes in Graciela Jorge and Eleuterio Fernández Huidobro, *Historia de 13 palomas y 38 estrellas: Fugas de la cárcel de mujeres* (Montevideo: Tae, 1994). After the prison breaks Punta de Rieles Penitentiary was turned into a detention center for female political prisoners, with the transfer of 175 political prisoners on January 16, 1971. The last female prisoners were freed in 1985. Some six hundred women passed through the center, cynically dubbed the Golden Cage by military personnel. Like Libertad Penitentiary, Punta de Rieles (which was formerly a Jesuit convent) was conceived exclusively for political prisoners. "Taller Vivencias," reprinted as the book *Memorias de Punta de Rieles en los tiempos del penal de mujeres: Memorias para la paz* (Montevideo: Editorial Vivencias, 2004), discusses the experience of women inmates together with the experience of women in the neighborhood, which changed with the arrival of the prison. Similarly, "Memorias para armar" (online at http://www.memoriapararmar.org.uy/) presents writings from the women prisoners and memories of the disappeared. The video documentary *Memorias de mujeres*, by Virginia Martínez, reconstructs the history of the site from the memories

of former inmates who lived together (Montevideo: Buen Cine Producciones, 2006). In contrast to Libertad prison, where prisoners have recalled the architecture as an integral component to torture tactics, Punta de Rieles is described as a space that maintained its aspect as a tranquil park that cynically contrasted the constant torture and abuse taking place inside. The cells (formerly the nuns' classrooms or bedrooms) had parquet floors.

5. In addition to Bandera Lima's *El abuso* (Montevideo: Tae, 1986), Fernández Huidobro's *La fuga de Punta Carretas*, and Blixen's *La comisión aspirina* (*La comisión aspirina* (Montevideo: Trilce 2007), references to the escapes are made in the *Actas Tupamaras* (Madrid: Revolución, 1982) and likewise in *Historia de los Tupamaros* (Montevideo: Tae, 1986). In recent years interest in the site has grown, demonstrated by the attempt to narrate other neglected stories, particularly on the anarchist prison break in 1931. In this regard, Gonzalo Fernández has written *Historia de Bandidos: Del "Cambio Messina" a la carbonería "El Buen Trato." Crónica del asalto y la fuga* (Montevideo: Fundación de cultura universitaria, 1993), and Fernando O'Neill, *Anarquistas de acción en Montevideo, 1927–1937* (Montevideo: Recortes, 1993). The 2006 documentary *Acratas* by Virginia Martínez covers the story of the anarchist leader Miguel Ángel Rosigna, who planned the escape of anarchist prisoners in 1931 with a tunnel excavated from outside the prison walls.

6. For excellent explorations of this transformation—from the figure of the epic militant to a victim within the framework of human rights—see Vania Markarian, *The Left in Transformation: Uruguayans Exiles and the Latin American Human Rights Network, 1967–1984* (New York: Routledge, 2005); and Emilio Crenzel, *La historia política del Nunca Más* (Buenos Aires: Siglo Veintiuno Editores, 2008).

7. On the process of transformation and legalization of the MLN-T into the MPP, see Adolfo Garcé, *Donde hubo fuego* (Montevideo: Fin de Siglo, 2006).

8. I refer to Jorge Zabalza's statements in his conversation with Clara Aldrighi (see Aldrighi's *La izquierda armada: Ideología, ética e identidad en el MLN-T* [Montevideo: Trilce, 2001]) and to Blixen's *La comisión aspirina*. The first detailed study of the role of the theory of "dual power" in the MLN-T is Pablo Harari's doctoral dissertation *Contribución a la historia del ideario del MLN-Tupamaros*, published in a limited edition in Paris in the mid-1970s and republished in Montevideo (by Editorial MZ) in 1986. According to Harari, the dual power strategy was at the very heart of the difference between the Tupamaros and the notion of the "foco" developed by Che Guevara and used by other liberationist movements. In his study of dual power, Bolivian philosopher René Zavaleta Mercado has written that it was one of the most common themes of discussion in Latin American Marxism in the late 1960s to early 1970s. However, he refers only secondarily to the peculiar case of dual power as used by the MLN-T. See René Zavaleta Mercado, *El poder dual en América Latina: Estudios de los casos de Bolivia y Chile* (Mexico City: Siglo XXI, 1974).

9. Jens Andermann, *The Optic of the State: Visuality and Power in Argentina and Brazil* (Pittsburgh: Pittsburgh University Press, 2007), 19, 22.

10. Fernández Huidobro, *La fuga de Punta Carretas,* vol. 1, 19; my translation.

11. Ibid., 23–24; my translation.

12. The architect Graciela Martínez has analyzed in detail the transformation of the surrounding area produced by the architectural conversion of Punta Carretas. Many people had to move to other neighborhoods because of the rising rents. In official discourse, however, it was argued that the transformation would "rescue" the area, as Martínez affirms: "It is Punta Carretas, once subtracted and now successfully rescued by and for them—the investors of the mall and the city they represent" (in Graciela Martínez, "El barrio, un ser

de otro planeta," *Bifurcaciones: Revista de estudios culturales urbanos* 3 [2004], online at http://www.bifurcaciones.cl/001/Martinez.htm; my translation).

13. In the most detailed study to date of this plan for Libertad, Gonzalo Fernández's *IV Seminario Sobre Cárceles: El fracaso del sistema penitenciario actual: Realidad y reformas urgentes,* República Federal de Alemania (Montevideo: Servicio Paz y Justicia and Konrad-Adenauer-Stiftung, 2003), Fernández states that overcrowding in urban prisons was overstated, emphasizing that this was rather a diagrammatic-ideological plan within the authoritarian framework in which it was conceived.

14. Fernández Huidobro, *La fuga de Punta Carretas,* vol. 1, 137; my translation.

15. Gonzalo Fernández, quoted in Alfredo Alzugarat, *Trincheras de Papel: Dictadura y literatura carcelaria en Uruguay* (Montevideo: Trilce, 2007), 20; my translation.

16. Quoted in Alfredo Alzugarat, *Trincheras de Papel: Dictadura y literatura carcelaria en Uruguay* (Montevideo: Trilce, 2007), 20; my translation.

17. Gonzalo Fernández, quoted in Alzugarat, *Trincheras de Papel,* 20; my translation.

18. Walter Phillipps-Treby and Jorge Tiscornia, *Vivir en Libertad* (Montevideo: Ediciones de la Banda Oriental, 2003), 24; all the quotations from this book are my translations.

19. Superimposed upon this plan, Libertad was repurposed as a military prison in the 1970s, in an attempt to improve on the failure of other prisons like Punta Carretas. This new power tactic was developed by the military dictatorship. This supports Foucault's argument that the prison was founded in response to a crisis whose solution was always, supposedly, the creation of better prisons.

20. Gonzalo Fernández, quoted in Alzugarat, *Trincheras de Papel,* 20.

21. Even though Libertad's original architecture was conceived two decades earlier and then abandoned by the state, it remains symptomatic that the prison was constructed on ninety-six columns raised above the ground "like an enormous centipede," as Phillipps-Treby and Tiscornia noted in their *Vivir en Libertad.* Undoubtedly, the prison's distance from the ground and its foundations is a clear message that the escape attempts in Libertad must find another route than those used in Punta Carretas.

22. Phillipps-Treby and Tiscornia, *Vivir en Libertad,* 21.

23. Liscano speaks of Libertad as "the negative reign of logos" in which "the most fundamental feature was the word, but not from absence or deformation, beginning with a name: Libertad Jail." See Carlos Liscano, "Una vida sin objeto(s)," in *La palabra en soledad* (Montevideo: Editorial Cal y Canto, 2003), 25–35; my translation.

24. As Liscano describes: "After years, when one thought he knew how something worked, he realized that he hadn't managed to get beneath the surface; that deep down, the organization had other complexities, nooks, dark indomitable areas for the most experienced administrator" (in Liscano, "Una vida sin objeto(s)," 26–27; my translation).

25. According to figures in Phillipps-Treby and Tiscornia's *Vivir en Libertad,* the penitentiary came to house approximately 2,873 political prisoners. For a country with a small population, this number of political prisoners is quite high. As Gonzalo Fernández states (quoted in Alzugarat, *Trincheras de Papel,* paraphrased from pages 142–43), in contrast to the high numbers of assassinations in Chile, or disappearances in Argentina, the military apparatus in Uruguay opted for another mode of extermination: not physical elimination but psychic destruction. Libertad was infamous for its intense psychological torture and induced suicide.

26. Fernández, *IV seminario sobre cárceles,* 143; my translation.

27. Ibid., 134; my translation.

28. The study carried out by the Instituto de Estudios Legales y Sociales del Uruguay states that, together with these neoliberal adjustments and measures, there was a growing naturalization of the view of the population as staying at the margins of working life: "Criminal policies have a close correspondence to adjustment policies, of 'criminalizing' social questions, constructing them as punitive questions." See Instituto de Estudios Legales y Sociales del Uruguay, *El Uruguay de los 90: Entre políticas sociales y políticas criminales* (Montevideo: Instituto de Estudios Legales y Sociales del Uruguay, 1997), 16; my translation.

29. Quoted in "El fracaso del sistema penitenciario actual: Realidad y reformas urgentes" (report produced by SERPAJ for the IV Seminar on prisons), in Instituto de Estudios Legales y Sociales del Uruguay, *El Uruguay de los 90.*

30. Liscano researches this experience in his work "Una vida sin objeto(s)," where space, the rigid architecture of the cell and prison, and language cannot be dissociated from each other, opening up a kind of materialism that characterizes prison writing. He notes that the gradual absence of objects, new material, or currents in everyday experience reiterates the problematics of naming, since a number substitutes the prisoner's name from the moment he is admitted to the site.

31. Antonio Gramsci best synthesized the influence of the prison experience on perception and language when he wrote: "The whole concatenation of cause and effect in prison life is fundamentally different from that of ordinary life, because all feelings, actions, and reactions *lack one basic element*—the freedom of originary existence, no matter how relative that freedom may be" (in Gramsci's *Letters from Prison,* ed. and trans. Lynne Lawner [New York: Noonday Press, 1989], 154–55; my emphasis). Automatism and the absence of new sensory material end up producing a notion of time wonderfully described by Gramsci and stressed by Antonio Blanqui in his work *L'Eternité par les astres.* That is, automatism invades every systematic repetition in the prisoner's life: "the routine, the privations and necessities, the enormous number of minute events that occur day after day, month after month, year after year, with the same mechanical rhythm of sand in an hourglass" (quoted in Gramsci, *Letters from Prison,* 125). The deprivation of a certain kind of freedom and the mechanical character of a time made repetitively eternal recur later in the creation of a writing style capable of expressing an outside world (that of free men) and an interior world in which the materiality of space (architecture), freedom, and words cannot be dissociated from each other.

32. Fernández Huidobro, *La fuga de Punta Carretas,* vol. 1, 22; my translation and emphasis.

33. "La fuga de 'El buen trato,'" *Búsqueda,* August 31, 1989, 52.

34. In a way the distinction between modes of criminality (ideological/common prisoner) reveals a search for legitimation at a moment in which the political past of the MLN was still seen, in the dominant language inherited from the military, as a zone of criminality. Introducing the quotation from the weekly publication *Búsqueda* that described the two escape attempts (by anarchists and Tupamaros) constitutes an unusual gesture, particularly because it was a right-wing publication. Nevertheless, when *La fuga* was written, the MLN continued to be perceived as a borderline criminal organization, just as anarchism was systematically excluded from national history and the prose of the political left itself. The legalization of the MLN-T began after the last prisoners were freed from Libertad in 1985, with the incorporation of Frente Amplio (FA) sought in 1986 (finally approved in 1989). The moment when the FA turned into the Encuentro Progresista likewise changed the redefini-

tions of the political left. For a series of speeches on the left's difficulties accepting the MLN during the transition, I refer to Raúl Sendic, *¿Por qué un frente grande?: Acto del MLN Tupamaros en el Estadio Franzini el 19/12/87* (Montevideo: MLN Tupamaros, 1988).

35. Fernández Huidobro, *La fuga de Punta Carretas,* vol. 2, 79–80; my translation.

36. Ibid., 82; my translation.

37. Ibid., 83–84; my translation and my emphasis.

38. Jacques Derrida, *Rogues: Two Essays on Reason,* trans. Pascale-Anne Brault and Michael Naas (Stanford: Stanford University Press, 2005), 167.

39. Nelly Richard, *Cultural Residues: Chile in Transition* (Minneapolis: University of Minnesota Press, 2004).

40. Gilles Deleuze and Felix Guattari, *Kafka: Toward a Minor Literature,* trans. Dana Polan (Minneapolis: University of Minnesota Press, 1986), 16.

41. Deleuze and Guattari, *Kafka,* 19.

42. In Peter Quint's *Epic and Empire: Politics and Generic Form from Virgil to Milton* (Princeton, N.J.: Princeton University Press, 1993), the author emphasizes the temporal mode of epic as the historical account of the victors. This implies an always unified measure of time that allows for a coherent teleological idea of a complete action. Diverging from this approach and seeking a modern sense of epic, Franco Moretti relies on N. Frye and E. Staiger's emphasis on the role of addition and accumulation as an encyclopedic drive. This drive implies a totality that is constituted by incommensurability (instead of a coherent whole). See Franco Moretti, *Modern Epic: The World-System from Goethe to García Márquez,* trans. Quintin Hoare (London: Verso, 1996), 96.

43. Walter Benjamin, *Understanding Brecht,* trans. Anna Bostock (London: Verso, 1983), 18; my emphasis.

44. Samuel Weber, *Benjamin's Abilities* (Cambridge: Harvard University Press, 2008), 101–2; my translation.

45. Antonio Gramsci, *Prison Notebooks,* vol. 2, ed. and trans. Joseph A. Buttigieg (New York: Columbia University Press, 2011), 21.

46. Gramsci, *Prison Notebooks,* vol. 2, 111.

47. Benjamin, *Understanding Brecht,* 18.

48. Deleuze and Guattari, *Kafka,* 17.

49. This is the characteristic element of writing in prison, where the very notion of individual, private space is denied to prisoners in the schematic of the prison itself, in which words and space are constantly coimplicated by a political circumstance of precariousness and deprivation.

50. Fernández Huidobro, *La fuga de Punta Carretas,* vol. 2, 83–84; my translation.

51. Gareth Williams, *The Other Side of the Popular: Neoliberalism and Subalternity in Latin America* (Durham: Duke University Press, 2002), 288.

52. Fernández Huidobro, *La fuga de Punta Carretas,* vol. 1, 22; my translation.

53. Note how *"venía"* in the original (meaning "came") appeals to a writing that continues to speak as if they were still in the prison—that is to say, the present of writing as the present of the prison pointing to a delay of (from) bodies (residue). I refer to this temporal dislocation (or de-spatialization) below, as it reemerges in the text at the end of the narrative.

54. Quoted in Fernández Huidobro, *La fuga de Punta Carretas,* vol. 2, 86; my translation and my emphasis.

55. Julia Kristeva, *Powers of Horror: An Essay on Abjection*, trans. Leon S. Roudiez (New York: Columbia University Press, 1982), 2.

56. Fernández Huidobro, *La fuga de Punta Carretas,* vol. 2, 146; my translation.

57. Ibid., 147; my translation and emphasis.

58. Ibid.

59. Walter Benjamin, *The Arcades Project*, trans. Howard Eiland and Kevin McLaughlin (Cambridge: Harvard University Press, 1999), 474.

3. The Workforce and the Open Prison: Awakening from the Dream of the Chilean Miracle in Diamela Eltit's *Mano de obra*

Epigraph: Diamela Eltit, *Emergencias: Escritos sobre literatura, arte y política*, ed. Leonidas Morales (Santiago: Planeta/Ariel, 2000), 25, 27; epigraph translations by Catherine Jagoe; my emphasis.

1. Eltit, *Emergencias*, 25.

2. Diamela Eltit, *Mano de obra*, in Eltit's *Tres novelas* (México: Fondo de Cultura Económica, 2004), 253–360; translations into English of this work throughout the chapter are my own.

3. The title "Las dos caras de la moneda" plays with *moneda* as coin and as the Palacio de la Moneda (the presidential palace that was bombarded on September 11, 1973). See "Las dos caras de la moneda," in Eltit, *Emergencias*.

4. Eltit, *Emergencias*, 18.

5. This literary turn is shown by an increasing interest in searching for key events of the recent past: the history of the working class and the repeated attempts to exterminate dissident bodies throughout the twentieth century (Eltit, *Mano de obra*); the founding assassinations of the coup besides the bombardment of La Moneda Palace that marked the role of the CIA in the destruction of the Unidad Popular, in Eltit's *De puño y letra* (Santiago: Seix Barral, 2005); and, finally, political militancy from the perspective of an insurgent woman and the play between the "cells" of the body and cells in a political movement in Eltit's *Jamás el fuego nunca* (Santiago: Seix Barral, 2007).

6. Jean Franco, "Malas palabras: Sobre *Mano de obra* de Diamela Eltit," in *Provisoriamente: Textos para Diamela Eltit*, ed. Antonio Gómez (Rosario: Beatriz Viterbo Editora, 2007), 143–53; 149; my translation.

7. Eltit, *Emergencias*, 29.

8. Eltit, *Los vigilantes* Spanish 98/English 67. In *Tres novelas* (Mexico City: Fondo de Cultura Económica, 2004), 33–139. The English translation, by Helen Lane and Ronald Christ, is *Custody of the Eyes* (New Mexico: Lumen, 2005).

9. "*Los vigilantes*, more than any other text of Eltit's, embraces the apocalyptic as its fundamental mode of relationship with time. The text cannot bear another return, because Eltit makes her protagonist the *last* survivor, the last carrier of the world" (in Idelber Avelar, *The Untimely Present: Postdictatorial Latin American Fiction and the Task of Mourning* [Durham: Duke University Press, 1999], 183).

10. Francine Masiello, *The Art of Transition: Latin American Culture and Neoliberal Crisis* (Durham: Duke University Press, 2001), 137.

11. Walter Benjamin, *The Arcades Project*, trans. Howard Eiland and Kevin McLaughlin (Cambridge: Harvard University Press, 1999), 458. For a study on Benjamin's connections and disconnections with surrealism, see Margaret Cohen's *Profane Illumination: Walter*

Benjamin and the Paris of Surrealist Revolution (Berkeley: University of California Press, 1995).

12. To listen to the echoes of the dictatorship's massacre, Eltit returns to the Iquique massacre as a parenthesis that titles half the work. Pointing to one of the most important resources both for the Chilean economy as a whole and for the coup—mining—she turns her literary inquiry in two directions: the lack of rights of mine workers, who are the basis of Chile's economy but whose lives are disregarded by the citizens of the metropolis (whom they sustain), and the theme of foreign monopolies that the "Chilean" nation massacred to protect. The text alludes to British capital (which monopolized Chilean mining at the turn of the century); U.S. capital (expropriated when the mines were nationalized by the Unidad Popular); and finally, the coordination of the coup by the United States and the economic and political program that Thatcher and Reagan decided to test in Chile using the dictatorship as a laboratory for their new freedom (of deregulation of the market and the reconfiguration of working conditions). It is curious how this theme—which was crucial at the beginning of the century in the organization of a white, Western Chilean imaginary and at the end of the century, when the Unidad Popular decided to nationalize the mines—enters literature in the peculiar configuration of a series of montages layering past and present. As in *La fuga*, this begs the question of how to read these intersections where times meet and separate, and where homogenizations or parallelisms confront us with a schizophrenic series of almost irresoluble historical imaginaries.

13. *Medidas preventivas: En el centenario de la huelga general de Iquique* (Santiago: Metales pesados, 2008) offers the first serious historicization of the Iquique massacre.

14. Alejandro Witker, *Los trabajos y los días de Recabarren* (Mexico City: Nuestro tiempo, 1977), 53.

15. Isabel Jara, "La huelga, el circo y la muerte: 1907 pese a todo," in *Medidas preventivas*, 23.

16. *El despertar de los trabajadores* was published weekly in Iquique from 1912 to 1927, with a total of 1,384 issues of four pages each (Witker, *Los trabajos*, 58). It was founded by the Cooperativa Tipográfica, organized by the nitrate workers, who donated it to the Workers' Party, becoming the latter's official publication (Osvaldo Arias Escobedo, *La prensa obrera en Chile* [Chillán: Universidad de Chile, 1970], 165). Although there were other Chilean publications in the first decades of the twentieth century with this name, the date and place in *Mano de obra*'s title show that Eltit is referring to this particular one.

17. Historians call Recabarren the father of the workers' press (Arias Escobedo, *La prensa obrera en Chile*, 194). Besides being the founder of approximately eleven proletarian periodicals, he was also the mentor of different projects for the creation of schools for the workers; see Ivan Ljubetic Vargas, *Historia de la asociación de pensionados de Chile: El primer cuarto de siglo (1938–1963)* (Santiago: Asociación chilena de pensionados y montepiadas, 1996), 10.

18. Ljubetic Vargas states that the founding of *El despertar* in 1912 was one of the steps taken toward "building the conditions to found the Revolutionary Party of Workers" (in Vargas, *Historia de la asociación de pensionados de Chile*, 10; my translation).

19. The creation of the publication and the consequent founding of the party were part of a typical enlightenment project since education played a central role (see Tomás Moulian and Isabel Torres's *Concepción de la política e ideal moral en la prensa obrera* [Santiago de Chile: Documento de Trabajo del Programa FLACSO–Santiago de Chile, 1987]). The Iquique massacre is usually seen as the endpoint of a movement in which the miners could make their voices heard only through the strike. The founding of *El despertar* began a dif-

ferent chapter in which the party became involved in the creation of an alternative education and culture. Although this is something that has yet to be analyzed in depth, Moulian and Torres attempt to delineate the role of the press in the rise of a Chilean working class (see Moulian and Torres, *Concepción de la política e ideal moral,* 2).

20. In this sense, *El despertar* implied a critique of the Sorelian visions dominant in workers' organizations, which not only led to the strike but also to a broader embrace of Leninism.

21. The scant bibliography on working-class history in Latin America (the majority of which has been written by historians) reproduces the register of an epic of the left, the fantasy of a unified and self-conscious (male) body of workers. Sergio Villalobos-Ruminott's related argument regarding issues that need to be addressed in postdictatorship theory would demand a rethinking of postdictatorship and subaltern studies (Villalobos-Ruminott, "Critical Thought in Postdictatorship," *Journal of Latin American Cultural Studies* 9, no. 3 [2000]: 229–34). All of the terms that I am using here ("consciousness," "proletarian culture," "Workers' Party") clearly require further critical analysis—more specifically, a subalternist critique.

22. The store in the novel is a hypermarket, typically referred to in the United States as a superstore, megastore, or big-box store—the site that Moulian refers to as the embodiment of the post-Pinochet utopia of the end of history.

23. Eltit's text is the first literary work to thematize post-Fordist working conditions in Chile and situate them within the larger history of working conditions at the beginning of the century; the creation of a working class; and the series of massacres of workers. All this concludes with a temporal doubling in the second section of the novel: "Puro Chile" (1970), which presents us with an empty evocation of Allende and the interruption of the work of the "Unidad Popular" by the military coup. The dialogue between the two sections can be read in the context of the role of foreign investors and their unconditional protection by the government until the nationalization of the mines (the first and last big act of redistribution by the Unidad Popular). This is a central issue in the background of the novel, since the massacre of nitrate miners (to protect the mine owners, mostly British investors) and the Allende government led to the second big massacre (with the mines again being at stake). This time, Pinochet's bombardment of the Palacio de la Moneda protected capital investors from possible "expropriation" and protected democracy and security from "deviations" and "subversion." On the so-called *democracia protegida* that still rules the Chilean Constitution, see Tomás Moulian's *Chile actual: Anatomía de un mito* (Santiago: Arcis, 1997).

24. Eltit, *Mano de obra,* 278; my emphasis.

25. Ibid., 277–78; my emphasis.

26. Walter Benjamin, "Theses on the Philosophy of History," in *Illuminations,* trans. Harry Zohn (New York: Schocken Books, 1969), 253–64, 255.

27. Jacques Derrida, "Différance," in *Margins of Philosophy,* trans. Alan Bass (Chicago: University of Chicago Press, 1985), 1–28, 22.

28. Benjamin, *Arcades Project,* 458; emphasis in the original.

29. Maintaining the play on the supermarket as the prison inherited from the dictatorship, the novel also evokes the extermination within the clandestine detention centers and the lists of the people who were going to be killed. The monologue of the second part repeatedly alludes to the threat of being added to the list of workers who were going to be fired. The imaginary presence of the list undermines solidarity. Losing competitiveness

increases the likelihood of being put on the list. The worker's loss of skills as his body deteriorates increases the possibility of being denounced as an unproductive, inefficient worker.

30. Eltit, *Mano de obra*, 267.

31. Ibid., 268–69.

32. Ibid., 216, 279, 286, 291; my emphasis.

33. David Harvey, *Spaces of Hope* (Berkeley: University of California Press, 2000), 168; my emphasis.

34. By using dates-places-publications that were central to the chaotic process of creating a counterculture able to resist to exploitation, Eltit's novel alludes to a whole range of cultural and political processes that were neglected and ignored in both postdictatorship critique and subaltern studies. Of course, there are some risks that we need to avoid: one is the mere archivization of those irrecuperable histories; another is the fetishization of the formation (*Bildung*) of a working class as if it constituted a transparent subject or an ideal "consciousness." Within the arena of Latin American subaltern studies, there has been either an essentialization of popular uprisings as local identities or an emphasis on the processes of capture of emancipatory movements by state language.

35. The historian Dipesh Chakrabarty has shown how education and enlightenment have so far been treated in the narration of working-class histories and failures as problematic supplements in *Rethinking Working Class History: Bengal 1890–1940* (Princeton, N.J.: Princeton University Press, 1989). I would add that these two concepts are still key to thinking about the past and also the present in which they become problematic as categories. Therefore the possibility of approaching formative (counter)culture(s) that have been subaltern within the constitution of leftist historicizations would open up other modes of approaching the formation of working-class experiences and captures, allowing the issue of political and cultural transformation to be problematized in more nuanced ways.

36. Eltit, *Mano de obra*, 280; my emphasis.

37. Ibid., 294; my emphasis.

38. Ibid., 295; my emphasis.

39. Jacques Derrida, "Force of Law: The Mystical Foundation of Authority," in *Acts of Religion*, ed. Gil Anidjar (New York: Routledge, 2002), 228–98, 272. I am making a slight change here regarding the English translation. In the French version, Derrida says "contamination *differantielle*," which I translate here as "*differantial* contamination" because by keeping the "*a*" of the French word *différance,* I maintain the idea of iterability that is crucial for my analysis. "*Differantielle*" keeps the idea of a delay that makes the fixation of a signified impossible. Thus the difference between "trace" and "mark" (seen in the multiple meanings of *retener* in the novel) is maintained.

40. It is interesting to note here Peter Bürger's analysis of how two opposite thinkers like Theodor Adorno and Georg Lukács could only agree on one issue: their dislike of the Brechtian idea of avant-gardism, a movement that Benjamin tried not only to understand in his "studies" on Brecht but also to theorize as a task of revolutionizing historical materialism. See Peter Bürger, *Theory of the Avant-Garde* (Minneapolis: University of Minnesota Press, 1984).

41. Dealing with the enlightenment differently implies a critical act that, as Foucault said, could transcend either being against or for it: "We have to move beyond the outside-inside alternative, we have . . . *to grasp the points* where change is possible and desirable . . . we know from experience that the claim to escape from the system of contemporary reality so as to produce the overall programs of another society, of another way of thinking,

another culture, another vision of the world, has led only to the return of the most danger-ous traditions." See Michel Foucault, "What Is Enlightenment?," in *Ethics, Subjectivity, and Truth*, ed. Paul Rabinow, vol. 1 (New York: The New Press, 1998), 303–20, 315–16.

42. Benjamin, *Arcades Project*, 458, 464; my emphasis.

43. Samuel Weber, *Benjamin's Abilities* (Cambridge: Harvard University Press, 2008), 171.

44. Benjamin, *Arcades Project*, 389.

45. I refer here to the following well-known passage: "There is a not-yet-conscious knowl-edge of what has been: its advancement has the structure of awakening" (in Benjamin, *Arcades Project*, 389).

46. Eduardo Cadava, *Words of Light: Theses on the Photography of History* (Princeton, N.J.: Princeton University Press, 1997), 69.

4. Freedom, Democracy, and the Literary Uncanny in Roberto Bolaño's *Nocturno de Chile*

Epigraph: Roberto Bolaño, "Una proposición modesta" [A modest proposal], in *Entre Paréntesis* (Barcelona: Anagrama, 2004), 95; my translation. I thank Catherine Jagoe for suggesting this title translation.

1. Bolaño, "Una proposición modesta," 64.

2. Ibid., 83–85; my translation and my emphasis.

3. This is mirrored by *Amuleto*, which was published in 1998, exactly three decades after the student movement massacres in 1968. It should also be pointed out that in another text, written during these same years, Bolaño states that his fiction should be read as a "love letter" to his generation, specifically to the political activists wiped out by the coup.

4. Tomás Moulian, *Chile actual: Anatomía de un mito* (Santiago: Arcis, 1997), 45–56.

5. For a concise study of the constitution of a protected democracy, see Fernando Durán-Palma, Adrian Wilkinson, and Marek Korczynski, "Labor Reform in a Neo-Liberal 'Protected Democracy': Chile 1990–2001," *International Journal of Human Resource Management* 16, no. 1 (2005): 65–89. The authors argue that, with the design of the 1980 constitution and the postauthoritarian "protected democracy" system (started in 1988), the Pinochet regime used a series of legal barriers that "prevented any attempt at significant labor reform" (in Durán-Palma, Wilkinson, and Korczynski, "Labor Reform in a Neo-Liberal 'Protected Democracy,'" 80).

6. Protected democracy represented the apex of the immunization paradigm (by protect-ing democracy in a nondemocratic way, the immunization is simultaneously immune to itself). Moulian has observed that "bombing the governmental palace from the air shows a wish for a clean slate, to create a new State on the ruins of the other" (Moulian, *Chile actual*, 30; my translation). Meanwhile, the role of the architectural fantasy of a "new" Chile immune to Marxism acquired a specific architecture when construction began on a new congress building in Valparaiso to replace the one in Santiago (see Simon Collier and William F. Sater, *A History of Chile, 1808–2002* [Cambridge: Cambridge University Press, 2004], 382).

7. Roberto Bolaño, *By Night in Chile*, trans. Chris Andrews (London: Harvill Press, 2003), 1–2, 1. This is a translation of Bolaño's *Nocturno de Chile* (Barcelona: Anagrama, 2000). Citations are given to the English edition first and the Spanish edition second. Refer-ences to the Spanish edition are taken from *Nocturno de Chile*.

8. Bolaño, *By Night in Chile*, 121; 141.

9. Sigmund Freud, *The Uncanny*, trans. David McLintock (New York: Penguin Classics, 2003), 132.

10. Alberto Moreiras, *The Exhaustion of Difference: The Politics of Latin American Cultural Studies* (Durham: Duke University Press, 2001), 206.

11. It should be mentioned that the novel's treatment of the uncanny falls within what the cultural theorist Diana Taylor has called "percepticide" in her *Disappearing Acts: Spectacles of Gender and Nationalism in Argentina's "Dirty War"* (Durham: Duke University Press, 1997). Taylor talks of the self-blinding of the population during the military regimes—the seeing without seeing, sensing without sensing, and so on, during military regimes.

12. Patrick Dove, "The Night of the Senses: Literary (Dis)orders in *Nocturno de Chile*," *Journal of Latin American Cultural Studies* 18, no. 2 (2009): 141–54.

13. Mark Wigley, *The Architecture of Deconstruction: Derrida's Haunt* (Cambridge: MIT Press, 1995), 117.

14. Wigley, *Architecture of Deconstruction*, 102.

15. Ibid.

16. Ibid., 120.

17. The character is based on one of Chile's most important literary critics, Hernán Díaz Arrieta, who wrote under the pseudonym "Alone."

18. Bolaño, *By Night in Chile*, 4; 14.

19. Ibid.

20. Ibid., 4; 15.

21. Ibid., 5; 15.

22. The literary house the priest imagines represents the ideal of Kantian aesthetic judgment in its disinterestedness, dramatizing the literary ideal that constituted Latin American elites (mocked and bedded by Farewell) with a desire of the literary city to be fixed and intemporal. This removes (makes invisible) the necessities and practical obligations that would soil the purity of the aesthetic ideal from the base up. For discussion of Urrutia Lacroix within the dominant imaginary of the Latin American literary city, I refer to the work of Ignacio López-Vicuña, "The Violence of Writing: Literature and Discontent in Roberto Bolaño's 'Chilean' Novels," *Journal of Latin American Cultural Studies* 18, no. 2 (2009): 155–66, 160.

23. Bolaño, *By Night in Chile*, 8; 19; my emphasis.

24. Ibid., 20–21; 32.

25. He remarks of another *campesino*: "The men who were walking away were ugly and their zigzag paths were incoherent. God have mercy on me and on them. Lost souls in the desert" (Bolaño, *By Night in Chile*, 21; 33). Here, the space outside the house is in some ways the place in which, instead of walking a path of roses, one runs into lost souls wandering in the desert. The contrast between a path and the nonarchitectural space of the desert makes it impossible to comprehend that time traced on skins that the poet can only contemplate with disgust, fear, and repugnance. This description of the lost souls opens up an interesting space in that it is the narrator who is lost in what, for lack of a clear path, looks to him like a desert.

26. Dove states that "patience, in other words, is precisely that which does not allow itself to be touched by the progressive spirit of world history, and which is therefore resistant to what the rest of the world acknowledges as the self-evident truths of modernization" (Dove, "Night of the Senses," 149).

27. Bolaño, *By Night in Chile*, 22–23; 34; my emphasis.

28. Ibid., 66; 80–81.

29. Ibid., 69; 84.

30. Ibid., 80; 96.

31. Ibid., 81–82; 96–99; my emphasis.

32. The chaos in the nation's grammar and geography (house-language) shows a split between types of democracy in its appeal to the logic of numbers, of what can be accounted for as the citizenship, where the invisible part, the part that functions as the non-Chilean part of Chile (what doesn't count in the structure of the great estates, their workforce) starts to make itself visible and countable in this democratic framework. Thus the reference to the census represents a threat for the priest, for in his paranoid logic that previously invisible part is in danger of becoming universalizable, or at least of being included (albeit disputedly) in the single-universal name of "Chilean" (which destabilizes the previous national framework and threatens to redraw the house).

33. There is a parallel here between Allende's "suicide" and Recabarren's death (also a suicide), which was indirectly evoked by Diamela Eltit in her *Mano de obra* (in *Tres novelas* [Mexico City: Fondo de Cultura Económica, 2004], 253–360) by making "The Awakening" a process without which the Popular Unity coalition could never have happened. However, Recabarren's death was caused by betrayal within the party he had played an active, paternal role in (like Allende). The double emerges with the duo Allende-Pinochet, the betrayal and the problematic relation between democracy and suicide with each process's way of defending itself (immunizing-autoimmunizing): Allende's last speech and Pinochet's letter mark the geography of two irreconcilable types of democracy. This is the split both texts perhaps urge us to contemplate. What also seems to be suggested here, if we connect the role of the Popular Unity at this moment of denarrativization with Bolaño's question about what would have happened if there had been no coup, is how the military dictatorship as a measure (like machine-gunning miners in Iquique) managed to exert control over the very concept of politics, using the specific policies that dramatized it. How, beginning with the policies that began, chaotically, under the Popular Unity (a schizophrenia we saw earlier in the awakening as [in]ability to sustain a coherent working-class subject), can one outline any possible meaning for structural transformability that threatens the notion of Chilean politics (architectural conservation)?

34. Bolaño, *By Night in Chile*, 83; 99; my emphasis.

35. The architectural theorist Anthony Vidler sees this point as a fundamental instance of the uncanny: "in its aesthetic dimension, a representation of a mental state of projection that precisely elides the boundaries of the real and the unreal in order to provoke a disturbing ambiguity, *a slippage between waking and dreaming*" (Anthony Vidler, *The Architectural Uncanny: Essays in the Modern Unhomely* [Cambridge: MIT Press, 1994], 11; my emphasis).

36. Bolaño, *Nocturno de Chile*, 142; my emphasis.

37. Bolaño, *By Night in Chile*, 122.

38. In the recent trial Callejas's sentence of twenty years was reduced to house arrest. She is already paying the sentence in the literary milieu, as no publishing house wants to publish her work anymore.

39. Bolaño, *By Night in Chile*, 119–20; 138–39; my emphasis.

40. Ibid., 120–21; 140–41.

41. Ibid., 126–27; 146–47.

42. Ibid., 127; 147.

43. Ibid., 128; 148; my emphasis.

44. Sergio Villalobos-Ruminott, "A Kind of Hell: Roberto Bolaño and the Return of World Literature," *Journal of Latin American Cultural Studies* 18, no. 2 (2009): 193–205, 195.

45. Jacques Derrida, *Rogues: Two Essays on Reason,* trans. Pascale-Anne Brault and Michael Naas (Stanford: Stanford University Press, 2005), 152.

46. In Bolaño, *Entre paréntesis,* 158; my emphasis and translation.

47. Ibid., 157–58; my translation.

48. Samuel Weber, "The Sideshow, or: Remarks on a Canny Moment," *Modern Language Notes* 88, no. 6 (December 1973): 1102–33.

49. Freud, *Uncanny,* 155; my emphasis.

50. Ibid.

51. Ibid., 157.

52. Weber, "Sideshow," 1112, 1113.

53. Ibid., 1129.

54. At the same time, by becoming more attractive sites for global tourism than for national (hi)stories, the issue becomes the following: if the installation of global spaces is based on an assumed normalization of horror that seeks to repaint what is otherwise abject, the relevance of secrecy in contemporary art suggests another type of articulation of space and history that refers to the problem of the public and the way in which, so far, the public is one of the greatest dramas of the state. On the tourist spectrum it would be a public scene *for export* but still complex in national narrativization since it appeals to the limitation of the national in drawing its geography.

55. The novel *Una casa vacía* by Carlos Cerdá is another narrative retelling of these houses of the legacy of the postdictatorship period: the cohabitation of horror and aesthetic work. See Cerdá's *Una casa vacía* (Santiago: Aguilar Chilena de Ediciones, 1996).

5. Memorialistic Architectonics and Memory Marketing

1. A first meeting of Southern Cone memory museums took place in Montevideo in April 2008.

2. Daniel Moya, "De cárcel a espacio abierto para la cultura," *Clarín* (May 13, 2008), online at http://www.clarin.com/suplementos/arquitectura/2008/05/13/a-01670562.htm.

3. "Córdoba-Argentina-Mujeres-y-Represión: Cárcel del Buen Pastor," *Palanca digital* (March 24, 2008), online at http://palancadigital.blogspot.com/2008/03/cordoba-argentina-paseo-del-bumujeres-y.html.

4. Mariana Tello Weiss, "La cárcel del Buen Pastor en Córdoba: Un territorio de memorias en disputa," *Revista Iberoamericana del Instituto Iberoamericano de Berlín* 10, no. 40 (2010): 145–65.

5. An *escrache* is a type of political action invented by the Argentine organization HIJOS (Hijos e Hijas por la Identidad y la Justicia contra el Olvido y el Silencio), founded in 1995. It involves drawing attention to the presence of ex-torturers or ex-CDCs in public life. Thus it exhibits the continued invisibilization of authoritarian forms of the past in the realm of everyday, contemporary life. Colectivo Situaciones, *Conversación con HIJOS* (Buenos Aires: Colectivo Situaciones, 2000), provides a history of this topic. I am following Mariana Tello Weiss's idea of reading the intervention of prisoners in the day of inauguration as a form of *escrache* (personal conversation).

6. Lucía Torres and Matías Herrera, directors, *Buen Pastor: Una fuga de mujeres* (Córdoba: El Calefón, 2010).

7. Francine Masiello, *The Art of Transition: Latin American Culture and Neoliberal Crisis* (Durham: Duke University Press, 2001), 7.

8. Masiello, *Art of Transition,* 7.

9. For an excellent analysis of the two logics (the global and the national) permeating this process, see Silvia Tandeciarz, "Citizens of Memory: Refiguring the Past in Postdictatorship Argentina," *Publication of the Modern Languages Association (PMLA)* 122, no. 1 (2007): 151–69. For an analysis of trauma tourism, see Laurie Beth Clark and Leigh Payne, "Trauma Tourism in Latin America," in *Accounting for Violence: The Memory Market in Latin America,* ed. Ksenija Bilbija and Leigh Payne (Durham: Duke University Press, 2011), 99–126, which traces the term back to its first uses (to refer to Rwanda and Cambodia) and examines how these tourism targets were developed and promoted. For a detailed analysis of different memory products, see Susana Kaiser, "Memory Inventory: The Production and Consumption of Memory Products in Argentina," in *Accounting for Violence: The Memory Market in Latin America,* ed. Ksenija Bilbija and Leigh Payne (Durham: Duke University Press, 2011), 313–38.

10. For the groups fighting to appropriate the sites, the participation of the state has been the most delicate and controversial topic. The guided tour of "Olimpo" states that many groups originally involved in the struggle over the appropriation-transformation of the premises withdrew when Olimpo was acquired by the state, believing that since it was the state that had carried out the extermination, it was cynical for it to finance and support the defense of human rights there. The key point here is the notion of capture or control by the state and the rejection of institutionalization.

11. The IEM, created by Law No 961/02, defines as its goal "the protection and transmission of memory and history of the facts that took place during the State Terrorism of the 1970s and early 1980s until the recovery of the rule of law, as well as the antecedents, later stages and consequences, with the aim of promoting the reinforcement of the democratic system, the consolidation of human rights and the prevalence of solidarity values in life, freedom and human dignity" (see http://www.institutomemoria.org.ar).

12. Elizabeth Jelin and Victoria Langland, eds., "Introducción: Las marcas territoriales como nexo entre pasado y presente," in *Monumentos, memoriales y marcas territoriales* (Buenos Aires: Siglo XXI, 2003), 1–18.

13. The sites are reminiscent of the negative-form monument practiced by Horst Hoheisel in Germany, in the sense that the void of disappearance starts to embody a core element in some of them (the ESMA, for instance). See Robert Young, *At Memory's Edge: After Images of the Holocaust in Contemporary Art and Architecture* (New Haven, Conn.: Yale University Press, 2002).

14. Jens Andermann, Philip Derbyshire, and John Kraniauskas, "No Matarás ('Thou Shalt Not Kill'): An Introduction," *Journal of Latin American Cultural Studies* 16, no. 2 (2007): 111–13.

15. Information on these disappeared persons can now be found at "El Proyecto Desaparecidos: Por la memoria, la verdad y la justicia," online at http://www.desaparecidos .org.

16. As Clark and Payne have argued in their "Trauma Tourism in Latin America," the ex-CDC Villa Grimaldi exemplifies one of the most sophisticated advances in memory marketing in Latin America. By following the demands of a global market for horror tourism, Villa Grimaldi has become a problematic center of reconciliation. Its marketing and architectural work of recycling and reconstruction seems close to the kind of conversion strategy (and pseudo-reconciliation) seen in Punta Carretas. Given the context of its transformation and the way in which it functioned as part of an attempt at reconciliation, Villa Grimaldi helped create a series of prejudices about the proliferation of memory sites.

As the cultural critic Michael Lazzara has explained, Villa Grimaldi embodies a key space for the negotiation of an idea of reconciliation that remains under suspicion. See Michael Lazzara, *Chile in Transition: The Poetics and Politics of Memory* (Gainesville: University of Florida Press, 2006).

17. I am paraphrasing the information provided in the brochure handed out during the tour of the premises.

18. Marcelo Brodsky, *Memoria en construcción: El debate sobre la ESMA* (Buenos Aires: La Marca, 2005).

19. Jens Andermann, *The Optic of the State: Visuality and Power in Argentina and Brazil* (Pittsburgh: Pittsburgh University Press, 2007).

20. Didier Maleuvre, *Museum Memories: History, Technology, Art* (Stanford: Stanford University Press, 1999), 11.

21. Maleuvre, *Museum Memories*, 9.

22. Ibid., 11.

23. For an excellent treatment of this topic, see Horacio González, "Las sombras del edificio," in Brodsky, *Memoria en construcción*, 76.

24. Hugo Vezzetti, *Pasado y presente: Guerra, dictadura y sociedad en la Argentina* (Buenos Aires: Siglo XXI), 2003.

25. The dual operation of prisons and CDCs is illustrated by the opening of the Caseros prison in Argentina in 1979. This implied an architectonic investment in a panoptic at a time in which disciplinary power was completely broken. However, it points to a return to the prison as project, repeating the architectonic gesture of the early twentieth century but with no process or ideal of regeneration. Caseros was more a façade than a prison—a legalized and monumentalized CDC that concealed the dynamics of a new imprisonment system which would privilege the clandestine. Like Uruguay's Libertad prison, which recycled the fascist penitentiary model of the 1930s, Caseros poses a question about the panoptic regime during the dictatorship and about the monumentality of the state that built this central prison in the middle of a hyperpopulated area to demonstrate the reconstruction of the penal apparatus at the height of the dictatorship. The closing of Caseros in 2001, and the debate about what to do with it, have shown how the dynamics of the CDC became a core element of the penal system that supposedly opposed it. The documentary *Caseros, en la cárcel*, directed by Julio Raffo in 2005, reconstructs life within the facility.

26. As Calveiro has emphasized, disappearance had been used previously, but it was not until 1974 that it became a semiofficial extermination practice following the Operativo Independencia in Tucumán. This ushered in "an institutional policy of disappearance of persons, with the silence and consent of the Peronist government, the Radical opposition and broad sectors of society. Some people, as usual, knew nothing about it; and others chose not to know. It was then that the first institutions indissolubly linked to this repressive modality appeared: the concentration-extermination camps. So, the figure of the disappearance, as a technology of the established power, with its institutional correlative, the concentration-extermination camp appeared when the so-called democratic institutions were still in force. . . . The 1976 coup represented a major change: disappearance and concentration-extermination camps ceased to be one of the repressive modalities to become *the* ruling repressive modality, directly executed by military institutions" (in Calveiro, *Poder y desaparición*, 26–27; my translation). CDCs and society became part of a network of coimplication in which the camps were part of, and affected, daily life but citizens had to make all knowledge about their operation disappear to go on living as if the

CDCs were not there. This is the key to disappearance, the "as if." Calveiro says: "The camp and society are part of the same milieu" (147; my translation).

27. Diana Taylor, *Disappearing Acts: Spectacles of Gender and Nationalism in Argentina's "Dirty War"* (Durham: Duke University Press, 1997).

28. The historian Aldo Marchesi has proposed that rather than being an exceptional situation that subsequently disappears, dictatorship in fact configures an ideal of citizenship that fails to disappear when the authoritarian period comes to a close. See Aldo Marchesi, "Una parte del pueblo uruguayo 'feliz, contento, alegre': Los caminos culturales del consenso autoritario durante la dictadura," in *La dictadura cívico-militar: Uruguay 1973–1985*, ed. Carlos Demasi, Aldo Marchesi, Vania Markarian, Alvaro Rico, and Jaime Yaffé (Montevideo: Banda Oriental, 2009), 323–98.

29. In the case of Punta Carretas, the prison reopens as a mall that does not refer to its own past as a prison but does include a plaque commemorating the Holocaust victims. The use of Holocaust language functions in dictatorial forms of commemoration as a way of avoiding questions about the politics implied in the processes of refunctionalization. Thus whenever sites are appropriated by the state or by the global marketing of trauma tourism, it is crucial for the politics of memory to problematize the victimization and depoliticization that can occur, without repoliticizing the sites as an epic of heroes that ends up reducing politics to the language of dictatorship as division between friends and enemies. The sites force us to maintain a critical outlook on the language of global museification and of national narrative.

30. As the ESMA web page indicates, information from an ex-detainee confirms that the site was already used as a detention center before the military coup. See Instituto Espacio para la memoria, online at http://www.institutomemoria.org.ar/exccd/esma.html.

31. See Munu Actis, Cristina Aldini, and Miriam Lewin, *Ese infierno: Conversaciones de cinco mujeres sobrevivientes de la ESMA* (Buenos Aires: Editorial Sudamericana, 2001), 302.

32. "Se descubrieron dos inscripciones de un desaparecido de la ESMA," *Página 12*, July 22, 2008, online at http://www.pagina12.com.ar/diario/ultimas/20-108286-2008-07-22 .html.

33. The site is surrounded by the following streets: Ramón Falcón, Lacarra, Fernandez, Rafaela, and Olivera.

34. This information has been deduced from survivors' testimonies. See "Mesa de trabajo y Consenso del Ex-Centro Clandestino de Detención, Tortura y Exterminio Olimpo," online at http://exccdolimpo.org/.

35. A visit to the former CDC begins outside, by reading the graffiti on the walls that signals the territorial and symbolic struggles occurring around the place—the struggle to force the police to abandon this site, the internal struggle among those who maintain that the site should be run by the state, and the struggle of those who withdrew because they believe the site should remain autonomous (the graffiti reads "the Government of Buenos Aires," and below it, "the people"). There is also a reference to the current struggle among political parties in the form of a poster demanding that Jorge Julio López reappear alive and well. López is a key witness in the case against Miguel Echecolatz, the chief police commissioner of Buenos Aires, responsible for several CDCs.

36. Both differ from memory museums, such as the one found in Montevideo at former dictator Máximo Santos's cottage. It follows a traditional museum approach, with collections of objects corresponding to the moment of the coup, exile, the prisons, and the transition. See Horacio González, "Las sombras del edificio," 71–78, 76.

37. Silvia Tandeciarz, "Citizens of Memory: Refiguring the Past in Postdictatorship Argentina," *PMLA* 122, no. 1 (2007): 151–69; 153.

38. Vania Markarian, *The Left in Transformation: Uruguayans Exiles and the Latin American Human Rights Network, 1967–1984* (New York: Routledge, 2005).

39. Etienne Balibar, "'Rights of Man' and 'Rights of the Citizen': The Modern Dialectic of Equality and Freedom," in *Masses, Classes, Ideas: Studies on Politics and Philosophy before and after Marx*, trans. James Swenson (New York: Routledge, 1994), 39–60, 39–40; my emphasis.

40. Balibar, "'Rights of Man' and 'Rights of the Citizen,'" 41.

41. Ibid., 44.

42. Ibid., 45; my emphasis.

43. Ibid., 46; my emphasis.

44. Ibid., 47.

45. Ibid., 49; my emphasis. Balibar suggests the need to establish two differences. The first difference is that the identification of man and citizen implied in his reading of the *Declaration* must not be read as an update of the Greek *zoon politikon*, in which equality depends on freedom as status: "equality within the limits of freedom, considered as a social *status*" (45); "equality here is only a consequence, an attribute of freedom" (45–46). The second difference refers to liberalism's separation of the social and the political (considered as a unit by Greeks) in the *Declaration*. It is on this separation that the split between a public and a private sphere is based. Balibar emphasizes here that "the materiality of the text" does not allow this reading because the "man in the *Declaration* is not a private individual" in opposition to the citizen who would be the member of the state. He is precisely the citizen, and recognizing this fact should lead us to question how the notion of the state could be so problematic in a revolutionary text whose purpose—at least in the eyes of its drafters—was to establish a new state. This question can only be answered by examining the subversive effects of a radically new idea about the relation between equality and freedom that is called "universal" (46).

46. Silvia Tandeciarz, "Citizens of Memory: Refiguring the Past in Postdictatorship Argentina," *PMLA* 122, no. 1 (2007): 151–69.

47. Emilio Crenzel, *La historia política del Nunca Más* (Buenos Aires: Siglo Veintiuno Editores, 2008), 182.

6. It Goes without Seeing: Framing the Future Past of Violence in Postdictatorship Film

1. Elizabeth Jelin and Victoria Langland, "Introducción: Las marcas territoriales como nexo entre pasado y presente," in *Monumentos, memoriales y marcas territoriales*, ed. Elizabeth Jelin and Victoria Langland (Buenos Aires: Siglo XXI, 2003), 3.

2. *Escrache* is a type of political action invented by the Argentine organization HIJOS (Hijos e Hijas por la Identidad y la Justicia contra el Olvido y el Silencio), founded in 1995. It involves drawing attention to the presence of ex-torturers or ex-CDCs in public life. Thus it exhibits the continued invisibilization of authoritarian forms of the past in the realm of everyday, contemporary life.

3. Alejandro Agresti, director, *Buenos Aires Viceversa* (Buenos Aires: SBP, 1996), available in English as *Buenos Aires Vice Versa*. Marco Bechis, director, *Garage Olimpo* (Ayacucho: SBP, 1999).

4. The 1990s were characterized by abuse of the executive power over the other branches—a phenomenon that was called presidentialism. For a detailed analysis of this

process, see Alberto Bonnet, *La hegemonía menemista: El neoconservadurismo en Argentina, 1989–2001* (Buenos Aires: Prometeo, 2007).

5. I do not have space to devote here to Martín Kohan's *Dos veces junio* (Buenos Aires: Sudamericana, 2002), but it is interesting that, although published a decade later, it is also about the border, the play of gaze-language and how to write about the CDCs through fiction.

6. The cultural critic Christian Gunermann traces the connection to the 1970s in the production style of protagonist Daniela's first video in "Filmar como la gente," in *Lazos de familia: Herencias, cuerpos, ficciones*, ed. Ana Amado and Nora Domínguez (Buenos Aires: Paidos, 2004), 85–59. Valeria Manzano, "*Garage Olimpo* o cómo proyectar el pasado sobre el presente (y viceversa)," in *El pasado que miramos: Memoria e imagen ante la historia reciente*, ed. Claudia Feld and Jessica Stites-Mor (Buenos Aires: Paidós, 2009), 154–80.

7. The stories all involve screens: the television screen that transmits the news, dysfunctional screens being repaired by the technicians, security camera screens in the Motel and the Mall, the camera Daniela borrows from her boyfriend to film the city, the TV screen on which the two old people watch their videos—a screen on which we only catch odd glimpses of images as we listen to the commentaries (the two videos are off-limits to us in their complete form).

8. Martín Sorbille, "Argentine Military Terrorism: Insatiable Desire, Disappearances, and Eruption of the Traumatic Gaze-Real in Alejandro Agresti's Film *Buenos Aires viceversa*," *Cultural Critique* 68 (2008): 106.

9. The house is eventually expropriated by a squad member who, after promising María's mother she can have her daughter back in return for the house, murders María and keeps the property.

10. Manzano, "*Garage Olimpo* o cómo proyectar el pasado sobre el presente (y viceversa)," 159. Manzano says that, symptomatic of the 1990s, both characters appear unmoored from historical time, as if they had just begun to exist the moment the camera started rolling. Both the torturer and the victim are presented as largely depoliticized subjects. Even though María is first shown teaching literacy to elderly people in the slums and then with a "contact" to show that she is a Peronist political activist, Manzano stresses that politics is not dramatized in the movie, which focuses more on the stripping of the characters' identities. The three elements Manzano points to as typical of the 1990s (the vacuum of history, the vacuum of politics, and reversed character development) operate as limitations that frame the film as the prisoner of its historical moment (Manzano, "*Garage Olimpo* o cómo proyectar el pasado sobre el presente (y viceversa)," 173–74).

11. Although I agree with Beatriz Sarlo that the category of postmemory film uses a rather problematic notion of memory, assuming a kind of immediacy in the notion of witnesses that differentiates it from later generations' more fleshed-out work, I do not share her response to the (subjectivist) memorial boom as a division between hyperintellectualized work and the emotions. This way of framing the practice of remembering, in which only the "academic intellectualization" of Pilar Calveiro's *Poder y desaparición* and Emlio de Ipola's *Bemba: Acerca del rumor carcelario* (Buenos Aires: Siglo XXI, 2002) are interesting, fails to problematize a crucial nexus between intellectualization and affect in connection to other divisions by class, episteme, and so on. The collection "Militancias" is attempting to construct this in the production of histories in the crossroads of class, memory, and affect. See Beatriz Sarlo, *Tiempo pasado: Cultura de la memoria y giro subjetivo* (Buenos Aires: Paidos, 2006).

12. Gilles Deleuze, *Cinema 2: The Time-Image,* trans. Hugh Tomlinson and Robert Galeta (Minneapolis: University of Minnesota Press, 1989).

13. Deleuze, *Cinema 2: The Time-Image,* 81.

14. Ronald Bogue, *Deleuze on Cinema* (New York: Routledge, 2003), 126.

15. Walter Benjamin, *The Arcades Project,* trans. Howard Eiland and Kevin McLaughlin (Cambridge: Harvard University Press, 1999), 462; my emphasis.

16. Benjamin, *Arcades Project,* 462; emphasis in the original.

17. The problems of race and class are fundamental and yet are shown as dearticulated from the possibility of a discourse. In the film *Pizza, birra, faso* [Pizza, beer, and cigarettes], by Adrián Caetano and Bruno Stagnaro (Instituto nacional de artes audiovisuales, 1998), the characters—all of whom are dispossessed—hang out at the foot of the Obelisk. In *Los rubios* [The blonds], by Albertina Carri (Buenos Aires: SBP S.A., 2005), the crucial moment that gives rise to the title is the visit to the neighborhood where the director's disappeared parents once lived. One of their neighbors, a woman of different class and race, remembers them as alien to the logic of the barrio (that is, blonds).

18. Godliness played a fundamental role within the CDCs, not only because of the importance of the Catholic Church in Argentina but also because once detainees were admitted to the center, they surrendered their will to live or, potentially, to die. The artworks produced on the walls of the centers, as well as many survivors' testimonies, emphasize the fact that entrance there involved entering a state of limbo. The detainee's power over his or her life and death was usurped. This was part of the dehumanizing process, where death/disappearance (and, equally, depriving prisoners of death) was the final feature. For examples, see the detailed study on godliness as the deprivation of death in Pilar Calveiro's work on concentration camps in Argentina (in *Poder desaparición: Los campos de concentración en Argentina* [Buenos Aires: Colihue, 2006], 53–60).

19. The program covers two things: the weather and the economy. I don't wish to overinterpret the connection between the two films, but it is curious that in *Buenos Aires viceversa* the weather forecast for the entire nation is also discussed in the first TV image and followed at the end by the twisted narrative of events in the mall. There is possibly an interesting sequence here in which weather and malls emerge as the beginning and end of a series, linking to the originating concept of malls as shopping spaces that were roofed in because of the climate.

20. In a visit to the memorial site Olimpo, one of the activists working on the transformation of the place told me that when they took possession of the former CDC, they asked neighbors what they would like to have there if the place were to be refunctionalized. It seems that some people answered that they would like to have a hypermarket.

21. Samuel Blixen says that in the codes of Tactical Operation 18, the garage on Calle Venancio Flores, numbers 3519–21, on the corner of Emilio Lamarca, was designated the "cave" or the "garden"; but the sign on the entrance said "Automotores Orletti" (in Samuel Blixen, "Memorias de Orletti: En nombre de la patria y con ánimo de lucro," *Semanario Becha* [Uruguay], September 16, 2001).

22. Here we see the problems of a "MERCOSUR-Memory" on the level of capturing a market (tourism). What international memory can be generated from these sites?

23. Benjamin, *Arcades Project,* 459; my emphasis.

24. Ibid., 460.

BIBLIOGRAPHY

Achugar, Hugo. "Territorios y memorias *versus* lógica del mercado: A propósito de cartografías y shopping malls." In *Planetas sin boca: Escritos efímeros sobre arte, cultura y literatura*, 217–28. Montevideo: Trilce, 2004.

Actis, Munu, Cristina Aldini, and Miriam Lewin. *Ese infierno: Conversaciones de cinco mujeres sobrevivientes de la ESMA*. Buenos Aires: Editorial Sudamericana, 2001.

Agresti, Alejandro. *Buenos Aires Viceversa*. Buenos Aires: SBP, 1996.

Aguirre, Carlos. "Cárcel y sociedad en América Latina 1800–1940." In *Historia social urbana: Espacios y flujos*. Edited by Eduardo Kingman Garcés, 209–52. Quito: FLACSO, 2009.

Aldrighi, Clara. *La izquierda armada: Ideología, ética e identidad en el MLN-T*. Montevideo: Trilce, 2001.

Alzugarat, Alfredo. *Trincheras de Papel: Dictadura y literatura carcelaria en Uruguay*. Montevideo: Trilce, 2007.

Andermann, Jens. *The Optic of the State: Visuality and Power in Argentina and Brazil*. Pittsburgh: Pittsburgh University Press, 2007.

———, Philip Derbyshire, and John Kraniauskas. "No Matarás ('Thou Shalt Not Kill'): An Introduction." *Journal of Latin American Cultural Studies* 16, no. 2 (2007): 111–13.

Arias Escobedo, Osvaldo. *La prensa obrera en Chile*. Chillán: Universidad de Chile, 1970.

Aricó, José. *Entrevistas 1974–1981*. Edited by Horacio Crespo. Córdoba: Centro de Estudios Avanzados, 1999.

Avelar, Idelber. *The Untimely Present: Postdictatorial Latin American Fiction and the Task of Mourning*. Durham, N.C.: Duke University Press, 1999.

Balibar, Etienne. "'Rights of Man' and 'Rights of the Citizen': The Modern Dialectic of Equality and Freedom." In *Masses, Classes, Ideas: Studies on Politics and Philosophy before and after Marx*, 39–60. Translated by James Swenson. New York: Routledge, 1994.

Bandera Lima, Antonio. *El abuso*. Montevideo: Tae, 1986.

Barrán, José Pedro. *Medicina y sociedad en el Uruguay del novecientos. Tomo 2: La ortopedia de los pobres*. Montevideo: Banda Oriental, 1993.

Bechis, Marco. *Garage Olimpo*. Ayacucho: SBP, 1999.

Benjamin, Andrew. *Architectural Philosophy: Repetition, Function, Alterity.* New Brunswick: Athlone Press, 2000.

Benjamin, Walter. *The Arcades Project.* Translated by Howard Eiland and Kevin McLaughlin. Cambridge: Harvard University Press, 1999.

———. "One-Way Street." In *One-Way Street and Other Writings.* London: Verso, 1979.

———. "The Task of the Translator." In *Illuminations,* 69–82. Translated by Harry Zohn. New York: Schocken Books, 1969.

———. "Theses on the Philosophy of History." In *Illuminations,* 253–64. Translated by Harry Zohn. New York: Schocken Books, 1969.

———. *Understanding Brecht.* Translated by Anna Bostock. London: Verso, 1983.

Bertino, Magdalena, Reto Bertoni, Héctor Tajam, and Jaime Yaffé. "La larga marcha hacia un frágil resultado, 1900–1955." In *El Uruguay del siglo XX: La economía,* 9–63. Montevideo: Banda Oriental-Instituto de Economía, 2001.

Blixen, Samuel. *La comisión aspirina.* Montevideo: Trilce 2007.

———. "Memorias de Orletti: En nombre de la patria y con ánimo de lucro." *Semanario Becha* (Uruguay), September 16, 2001.

Bogue, Ronald. *Deleuze on Cinema.* New York: Routledge, 2003.

Bolaño, Roberto. *Entre paréntesis.* Barcelona: Anagrama, 2004.

———. *By Night in Chile.* Translated by Chris Andrews. London: Harvill Press, 2003.

———. *Nocturno de Chile.* Barcelona: Anagrama, 2000.

Bonnet, Alberto. *La hegemonía menemista: El neoconservadurismo en Argentina 1989–2001.* Buenos Aires: Prometeo, 2007.

Brodsky, Marcelo. *Memoria en construcción: El debate sobre la ESMA.* Buenos Aires: La Marca, 2005.

Bürger, Peter. *Theory of the Avant-Garde.* Minneapolis: University of Minnesota Press, 1984.

Butler, Judith. *Bodies That Matter: On the Discursive Limits of Sex.* New York: Routledge, 1993.

Cadava, Eduardo. *Words of Light: Theses on the Photography of History.* Princeton, N.J.: Princeton University Press, 1997.

Calveiro, Pilar. *Poder y desaparición: Los campos de concentración en Argentina.* Buenos Aires: Colihue, 2006.

Cerda, Carlos. *Una casa vacía.* Santiago: Aguilar Chilena de Ediciones, 1996.

Chakrabarty, Dipesh. *Rethinking Working Class History: Bengal 1890–1940.* Princeton, N.J.: Princeton University Press, 1989.

Clark, Laurie Beth, and Leigh Payne. "Trauma Tourism in Latin America." In *Accounting for Violence: The Memory Market in Latin America.* Edited by Ksenija Bilbija and Leigh Payne, 99–126. Durham, N.C.: Duke University Press, 2011.

Cohen, Margaret. *Profane Illumination: Walter Benjamin and the Paris of Surrealist Revolution.* Berkeley: University of California Press, 1995.

Colectivo Situaciones. *Conversación con HIJOS.* Buenos Aires: Colectivo Situaciones, 2000.

Collier, Simon, and William F. Sater. *A History of Chile, 1808–2002.* Cambridge: Cambridge University Press, 2004.

Crenzel, Emilio. *La historia política del Nunca Más.* Buenos Aires: Siglo Veintiuno Editores, 2008.

De Ipola, Emilio. *Bemba. Acerca del rumor carcelario.* Buenos Aires: Siglo XXI, 2002.

Deleuze, Gilles. *Cinema 2: The Time-Image.* Translated by Hugh Tomlinson and Robert Galeta. Minneapolis: University of Minnesota Press, 1989.

————. "Postcript on Control Societies." In *Negotiations*, 177–82. Translated by Martin Joughin. New York: Columbia University Press, 1997.

————. "What Is the Creative Act?" In *Two Regimes of Madness: Texts and Interviews, 1975–1995*. Edited by David Lapoujade, 312–24. Translated by Ames Hodges and Mike Taormina. New York: Semiotext(e), 2006.

————, and Félix Guattari. *Kafka: Toward a Minor Literature*. Translated by Dana Polan. Minneapolis: University of Minnesota Press, 1986.

————. *A Thousand Plateaus: Capitalism and Schizophrenia*. Minneapolis: University of Minnesota Press, 1987.

Derrida, Jacques. "Différance." In *Margins of Philosophy*, 1–28. Translated by Alan Bass. Chicago: University of Chicago Press, 1985.

————. "Force of Law: The Mystical Foundation of Authority." In *Acts of Religion*. Edited by Gil Anidjar, 228–98. New York: Routledge, 2002.

————. *Rogues: Two Essays on Reason*. Translated by Pascale-Anne Brault and Michael Naas. Stanford, Calif.: Stanford University Press, 2005.

Dove, Patrick. "The Night of the Senses: Literary (Dis)orders in *Nocturno de Chile*." *Journal of Latin American Cultural Studies* 18, no. 2 (2009): 141–54.

Durán-Palma, Fernando, Adrian Wilkinson, and Marek Korczynski. "Labor Reform in a Neo-Liberal 'Protected Democracy': Chile 1990–2001." *International Journal of Human Resource Management* 16, no. 1 (2005): 65–89.

Eltit, Diamela. *Custody of the Eyes*. Translated by Helen Lane and Ronald Christ. New Mexico: Lumen, 2005.

————. *Emergencias: Escritos sobre literatura, arte y política*. Edited by Leonidas Morales. Santiago: Planeta/Ariel, 2000.

————. *Los vigilantes*. In *Tres novelas*, 33–139. Mexico City : Fondo de Cultura Económica, 2004.

————. *Mano de obra*. In *Tres novelas*, 253–360. Mexico City : Fondo de Cultura Económica, 2004.

Erosa, Daniel. "Punta Carretas: Del viejo penal a shopping." *Posdata* 30 set (1994): 45–49.

Espinoza Cuevas, Víctor, ed. *Seminario internacional sobre la impunidad y sus efectos en los procesos democráticos*. Santiago de Chile: CODEPU, 1999.

Fernández, Gonzalo. *Historia de bandidos: Del "Cambio Messina" a la carbonería "El Buen Trato." Crónica del asalto y la fuga*. Montevideo: Fundación de cultura universitaria, 1993.

————. *IV Seminario Sobre Cárceles: El fracaso del sistema penitenciario actual: Realidad y reformas urgentes*. República Federal de Alemania. Montevideo: Servicio Paz y Justicia and Konrad-Adenauer-Stiftung, 2003.

Fernández, Roberto. "Crisis de la modernidad: Las fracturas regionalistas." *Arquitectura Sur* 1, no. 2 (1990): 38–42.

Fernández Huidobro, Eleuterio. *La fuga de Punta Carretas*. 2 vols. Montevideo: Banda Oriental, 1998.

————. *La historia de los tupamaros*. 3 vols. Montevideo: Tae, 1986.

Foucault, Michel. *Discipline and Punish: The Birth of the Prison*. Translated by Alan Sheridan. New York: Random House, 1995.

————. "The Eye of Power: A Conversation with Jean-Pierre Barou and Michelle Perrot." *Power/Knowledge: Selected Interviews & Other Writings (1972–1977)*. Edited and translated by Colin Gordon, 146–65. New York: Pantheon Books, 1980.

———. "What Is Enlightenment?" In *Ethics, Subjectivity, and Truth*. Vol. 1. Edited by Paul Rabinow, 303–20. New York: The New Press, 1998.

Franco, Jean. "Malas palabras: Sobre *Mano de obra* de Diamela Eltit." *Provisoria-mente: Textos para Diamela Eltit*. Edited by Antonio Gómez, 143–53. Rosario: Beatriz Viterbo Editora, 2007.

Fraser, Valerie. *Building the New World: Studies in the Modern Architecture of Latin America, 1930–1960*. London: Verso, 2001.

Freud, Sigmund. *The Uncanny*. Translated by David McLintock. New York: Penguin Classics, 2003.

Fukuyama, Francis. *The End of History and the Last Man*. New York: Free Press, 1992.

Garcé, Adolfo. *Donde hubo fuego*. Montevideo: Fin de Siglo, 2006.

García Miranda, Ruben. "Quisiera ser grande." *El Arqa, arquitectura & diseño* (Montevideo) 3, no. 6 (1993): 4–5.

Garretón, Manuel. *Proceso político chileno*. Santiago: FLACSO, 1983.

Gatea, Julio, "La ciudad transformada." *ElArqa, arquitectura & diseño* (Montevideo) 4, no. 12 (Deccember 1994): n.p.

Gervaz, Antonio. "Dimensiones de Hoy." *ElArqa, arquitectura & diseño* (Montevideo) 3, no. 6 (May 1993): 20–32

Gilio, María Esther. *El cholo González: Un cañero de Bella Unión*. Montevideo: Trilce, 2004.

Giménez, Fabián, and Alejandro Villagrán. *Estética de la oscuridad: Posmodernidad, periferia y mass media en la cultura de los noventa*. Montevideo: Trazas, 1995.

González, Horacio. "Las sombras del edificio." In *Memoria en construcción: El debate sobre la ESMA*. Edited by Marcelo Brodsky, 71–79. Buenos Aires: La marca, 2005.

Gorelik, Adrián. *Miradas sobre Buenos Aires: Historia cultural y crítica urbana*. Buenos Aires: Siglo Veintiuno Editores Argentina, 2004.

Gramsci, Antonio. *Letters from Prison*. Edited and translated by Lynne Lawner. New York: The Noonday Press, 1989.

———. *Prison Notebooks*. Vol. 2. Edited and translated by Joseph A. Buttigieg. New York: Columbia University Press, 2011.

Gruen, Victor. *The Heart of Our Cities: The Urban Crisis: Diagnosis and Cure*. New York: Simon and Schuster, 1964.

Gunermann, Christian. "Filmar como la gente." In *Lazos de familia: Herencias, cuerpos, ficciones*. Edited by Ana Amado and Nora Domínguez, 85–59. Buenos Aires: Paidos, 2004.

Hamacher, Werner. "'Now': Walter Benjamin on Historical Time." In *Walter Benjamin and History*. Edited by Andrew Benjamin, 38–68. New York: Continuum, 2005.

Harari, Pablo. *Contribución a la historia del ideario del MLN-Tupamaros*. Montevideo: Editorial MZ, 1986.

Hardwick, Jeffrey. *Mall Maker: Victor Gruen, Architect of an American Dream*. Philadelphia: University of Pennsylvania Press, 2003.

Harvey, David. *Spaces of Global Capitalism: Toward a Theory of Uneven Geographical Development*. London: New York: Verso, 2006.

———. *Spaces of Hope*. Berkeley: University of California Press, 2000.

Hoffmann, Rainer, and Heidi Spcogna, directors. *Tupamaros*. Berlin: Spcogna Filmproduktion, 1997.

Hopenhayn, Martín. *Ni apocalípticos ni integrados: Aventuras de la modernidad en América*. Mexico City: Fondo de Cultura Económica, 1995.

Huyssen, Andreas. *Present Pasts: Urban Palimpsests and the Politics of Memory*. Stanford, Calif.: Stanford University Press, 2003.

Instituto de Estudios Legales y Sociales del Uruguay. *El Uruguay de los 90: Entre políticas sociales y políticas criminales*. Montevideo: Instituto de Estudios Legales y Sociales del Uruguay, 1997.

Iriarte, Alicia. "La década del '90. Proyecto neoconservador, ajuste estructural y desigualdad social." In *La Argentina fragmentada: Aspectos de la nueva cuestión social*, 11–41. Buenos Aires: Proyecto Editorial, 2001.

Jara, Isabel. "La huelga, el circo y la muerte: 1907 pese a todo." In *Medidas preventivas: En el centenario de la huelga general de Iquique*, 11–25. Santiago: Metales Pesados, 2008.

Jelin, Elizabeth. *State Repression and the Labors of Memory*. Translated by Judy Rein and Marcial Godoy-Anativia. Minneapolis: University of Minnesota Press, 2003.

———, and Victoria Langland. "Introducción: Las marcas territoriales como nexo entre pasado y presente." In *Monumentos, memoriales y marcas territoriales*. Edited by Elizabeth Jelin and Victoria Langland, 1–18. Buenos Aires: Siglo XXI, 2003.

Jorge, Graciela, and Eleuterio Fernández Huidobro. *Historia de 13 palomas y 38 estrellas: Fugas de la cárcel de mujeres*. Montevideo: Tae, 1994.

Kaiser, Susana. "Memory Inventory: The Production and Consumption of Memory Goods in Argentina." In *Accounting for Violence: The Memory Market in Latin America*. Edited by Ksenija Bilbija and Leigh Payne, 313–38. Durham, N.C.: Duke University Press, 2011.

Kohan, Martín. *Dos veces junio*. Buenos Aires: Sudamericana, 2002.

Kowinski, William Severini. *The Malling of America: An Inside Look at the Great Consumer Paradise*. New York: W. Morrow, 1985.

Kristeva, Julia. *Powers of Horror: An Essay on Abjection*. Translated by Leon S. Roudiez. New York: Columbia University Press, 1982.

Lazzara, Michael. *Chile in Transition: The Poetics and Politics of Memory*. Gainesville: University of Florida Press, 2006.

Levinson, Brett. *The Ends of Literature: The Latin American "Boom" in the Neoliberal Marketplace*. Stanford, Calif.: Stanford University Press, 2001.

Liscano, Carlos. "Una vida sin objeto(s)." In *La palabra en soledad*. Montevideo: Editorial Cal y Canto, 2003.

López, Juan Carlos. "Entrevista: Juan Carlos López y asociados. Arquitecturas para la ciudad." *Arquitectura Sur* 1, no. 2 (1990): 21–34.

López-Vicuña, Ignacio. "The Violence of Writing: Literature and Discontent in Roberto Bolaño's 'Chilean' Novels." *Journal of Latin American Cultural Studies* 18, no. 2 (2009): 155–66.

Maleuvre, Didier. *Museum Memories: History, Technology, Art*. Stanford, Calif.: Stanford University Press, 1999.

Manzano, Valeria. "*Garage Olimpo* o cómo proyectar el pasado sobre el presente (y viceversa)." In *El pasado que miramos: Memoria e imagen ante la historia reciente*. Edited by Claudia Feld and Jessica Stites-Mor, 154–80. Buenos Aires: Paidós, 2009.

Marchesi, Aldo. "Una parte del pueblo uruguayo 'feliz, contento, alegre.' Los caminos culturales del consenso autoritario durante la dictadura." In *La dictadura Cívico-Militar: Uruguay 1973–1985*. Edited by Carlos Demasi, Aldo Marchesi, Vania Markarian, Alvaro Rico, and Jaime Yaffé, 323–98. Montevideo: Banda Oriental, 2009.

Markarian, Vania. *The Left in Transformation: Uruguayans Exiles and the Latin American Human Rights Network, 1967–1984*. New York: Routledge, 2005.

Martínez, Graciela. "El barrio, un ser de otro planeta." *Bifurcaciones: Revista de estudios culturales urbanos* 3 (2004). Online at http://www.bifurcaciones.cl/001/Martinez.htm.

Martínez, Virginia. *Acratas.* Montevideo: Buen Cine Producciones, 2006.

———. *Memorias de mujeres.* Montevideo: Buen Cine Producciones, 2006.

Masiello, Francine. *The Art of Transition: Latin American Culture and Neoliberal Crisis* Durham, N.C.: Duke University Press, 2001.

May, Lary, ed. *Recasting America: Culture and Politics in the Age of Cold War.* Chicago: University of Chicago Press, 1989.

Mennel, Timothy. "Victor Gruen and the Construction of Cold War Utopias." *Journal of Planning History* 3 (2004): 116–50.

Moreiras, Alberto. *The Exhaustion of Difference: The Politics of Latin American Cultural Studies.* Durham, N.C.: Duke University Press, 2001.

———. "Postdictadura y reforma del pensamiento." *Revista de crítica cultural* 7 (1993): 26–35.

Moretti, Franco. *Modern Epic: The World-System from Goethe to García Márquez.* Translated by Quintin Hoare. London: Verso, 1996.

Moulian, Tomás. *Chile actual: Anatomía de un mito.* Santiago: Arcis, 1997.

———, and Isabel Torres. *Concepción de la política e ideal moral en la prensa obrera.* Documento de Trabajo del Programa FLACSO. Santiago de Chile: FLASCO, 1987.

Movimiento de Liberación Nacional–Tupamaros. *Actas Tupamaras.* Madrid: Revolución, 1982.

Moya, Daniel. "De cárcel a espacio abierto para la cultura." *Clarín,* May 13, 2008. Online at http://www.clarin.com/suplementos/arquitectura/2008/05/13/a-01670562.htm.

O'Neill, Fernando. *Anarquistas de acción en Montevideo, 1927–1937.* Montevideo: Recortes, 1993.

Oyarzún, Pablo. *La dialéctica en suspenso: Fragmentos sobre historia.* Santiago: ARCIS-LOM, 1996.

Palanca Digital. "Córdoba-Argentina-Mujeres-y-Represión: Cárcel del Buen Pastor." March 24, 2008. Online at http://palancadigital.blogspot.com/2008/03/cordoba-argentina-paseo-del-bumujeres-y.html.

Phillipps-Treby, Walter, and Jorge Tiscornia. *Vivir en libertad.* Montevideo: Ediciones de la Banda Oriental, 2003.

Quint, Peter. *Epic and Empire: Politics and Generic Form from Virgil to Milton.* Princeton, N.J.: Princeton University Press, 1993.

Rebellato, José Luis. *La encrucijada de la ética.* Montevideo: Nordan, 1995.

Rendell, Jane. *Art and Architecture: A Place Between.* London: I. B. Tauris, 2006.

Richard, Nelly. *Cultural Residues: Chile in Transition.* Translated by Alan West-Durán and Theodore Quester. Minneapolis: University of Minnesota Press, 2004.

———. "Introducción." In *Pensar en / la postdictadura.* Edited by Nelly Richard and Alberto Moreiras, 9–20. Santiago: Cuarto Propio, 2001.

Ruétalo, Victoria. "From Penal Institution to Shopping Mecca: The Economics of Memory and the Case of Punta Carretas." *Cultural Critique* 68 (Winter 2008): 38–65.

Rybczynski, Witold. "The New Downtowns." *Atlantic Monthly* 271 (May 5, 1993): 98–106.

Salvatore, Ricardo, and Carlos Aguirre. *The Birth of the Penitentiary in Latin America: Essays on Criminology, Prison Reform, and Social Control, 1830–1940.* Austin: University of Texas Press, 1996.

Salvatore, Ricardo D., Carlos Aguirre, and G. M. Joseph. *Crime and Punishment in Latin*

America: Law and Society since Late Colonial Times. Durham, N.C.: Duke University Press, 2001.

Sarlo, Beatriz. *Scenes from Postmodern Life*. Translated by Jon Beasley-Murray. Minneapolis: University of Minnesota Press, 2001.

———. *Tiempo pasado: Cultura de la memoria y giro subjetivo*. Buenos Aires: Paidos, 2006.

Scapusio, Beatriz. "El sistema penal uruguayo y su repercusión carcelaria: La necesidad de su reforma." In *Reforma al sistema penal y carcelario en Uruguay*. Edited by Raúl Ronzoni and Beatriz Scapusio, 21–46. Montevideo: CADAL, 2008.

Sendic, Alberto. *Movimiento obrero y luchas populares en la historia uruguaya*. Montevideo: Edición del Movimiento de Independientes 26 de marzo, 1985.

Sendic, Raúl. *¿Por qué un frente grande?: Acto del MLN Tupamaros en el Estadio Franzini el 19/12/87*. Montevideo: MLN Tupamaros, 1988.

Sorbille, Martín. "Argentine Military Terrorism: Insatiable Desire, Disappearances, and Eruption of the Traumatic Gaze-Real in Alejandro Agresti's Film *Buenos Aires Viceversa*." *Cultural Critique* 68 (2008): 86–128.

Spivak, Gayatri Chakravorty. "Subaltern Studies: Deconstructing Historiography." In *Subaltern Studies: Writings on South Asian History and Society*. Vol. 4. Edited by Ranajit Guha, 3–34. Delhi: Oxford University Press, 1985.

Taller Vivencias. *Memorias de Punta de Rieles en los tiempos del penal de mujeres: Memorias para la paz*. Montevideo: Editorial Vivencias, 2004.

Tandeciarz, Silvia. "Citizens of Memory: Refiguring the Past in Postdictatorship Argentina." *Publication of the Modern Language Association (PMLA)* 122, no. 1 (2007): 151–69.

Taylor, Diana. *Disappearing Acts: Spectacles of Gender and Nationalism in Argentina's "Dirty War."* Durham, N.C.: Duke University Press, 1997.

Tello Weiss, Mariana. "La cárcel del Buen Pastor en Córdoba: Un territorio de memorias en disputa." *Revista Iberoamericana del instituto Iberoamericano de Berlín* 10, no. 40 (2010): 145–65.

Thayer, Willy. "El golpe como consumación de la vanguardia." *Revista Extremoccidente* 2, Dossier "La memoria perdida: A treinta años del golpe" (2002): 54–58.

Torres, Lucía, and Matías Herrera. *Buen Pastor: Una fuga de mujeres*. Córdoba: El Calefón, 2010.

Valdés, Juan G. *Pinochet's Economists: The Chicago School of Economics in Chile*. Cambridge: Cambridge University Press, 1995.

Vargas, Ivan Ljubetic. *Historia de la asociación de pensionados de Chile: El primer cuarto de siglo (1938–1963)*. Santiago: Asociación chilena de pensionados y montepiadas, 1996.

Vezzetti, Hugo. *Pasado y presente: Guerra, dictadura y sociedad en la Argentina*. Buenos Aires: Siglo XXI, 2003.

Vidler, Anthony. *The Architectural Uncanny: Essays in the Modern Unhomely*. Cambridge: MIT Press, 1994.

Villalobos-Ruminott, Sergio. "Critical Thought in Postdictatorship." *Journal of Latin American Cultural Studies* 9, no. 3 (2000): 229–34.

———. "A Kind of Hell: Roberto Bolaño and the Return of World Literature." *Journal of Latin American Cultural Studies* 18, no. 2 (2009): 193–205.

Weber, Samuel. *Benjamin's Abilities*. Cambridge: Harvard University Press, 2008.

———. "The Sideshow, or: Remarks on a Canny Moment." *Modern Language Notes* 88, no. 6 (December 1973): 1102–33.

Wigley, Mark. *The Architecture of Deconstruction: Derrida's Haunt*. Cambridge: MIT Press, 1995.

Williams, Gareth. *The Other Side of the Popular: Neoliberalism and Subalternity in Latin America*. Durham, N.C.: Duke University Press, 2002.

Witker, Alejandro. *Los trabajos y los días de Recabarren*. Mexico City: Nuestro tiempo, 1977.

Young, Robert. *At Memory's Edge: After Images of the Holocaust in Contemporary Art and Architecture*. New Haven, Conn.: Yale University Press, 2002.

Zavaleta Mercado, René. *El poder dual en América Latina: Estudios de los casos de Bolivia y Chile*. Mexico City: Siglo XXI, 1974.

Zepp, Ira. *The New Religious Image of Urban America: The Shopping Mall as Ceremonial Center*. Colorado: University of Colorado Press, 1997.

INDEX

Punta Carretas prison-mall, 2–3, 6, 9, 15, 20, 23, 29, 36–40, 44–55

Richard, Nelly, 18–19, 82

Sarlo, Beatriz, 42
Spivak, Gayatri Chakravorty, 18, 92, 101
subalternity: affect, 89–90, 134; alternative calendars, 82, 96–98, 108–11; historicity, 84

Tandeciarz, Silvia, 171, 174
Taylor, Diana, 167
transition: architectonics, 12, 14–15, 22–24; critique, 18–20

Villalobos-Ruminott, Sergio, 144–46

Weber, Samuel, 84, 146
Wigley, Mark, 80, 131